The Films, of Ginger Rogers

HOMER DICKENS

The Films of

Ginger Rogers

The Citadel Press   Secaucus, N.J.

Also by Homer Dickens

The Films of Marlene Dietrich
The Films of Gary Cooper
The Films of Katharine Hepburn
The Films of James Cagney

First paperbound printing, 1980

Copyright © 1975 by Homer Dickens   All rights reserved
Published by Citadel Press   A division of Lyle Stuart, Inc.
120 Enterprise Avenue, Secaucus, N.J. 07094
In Canada: George J. McLeod Limited   73 Bathurst St., Toronto, Ont.
Manufactured in the United States of American by Halliday Lithograph Corp., West Hanover, Mass.

Book design by Peretz Kaminsky

Library of Congress Cataloging in Publication Data

Dickens, Homer.
    The films of Ginger Rogers.

    Filmography: p.
    1. Rogers, Ginger, 1911-   I.   Title.
PN2287.R72D5   791.43'028'0924   75-25577

Dedicated with love
To the memory of
PEG AND R. C. MOSELEY
together again

ACKNOWLEDGMENTS: A work of this kind inevitably owes a great deal to many people—friends and buffs and experts—who have given freely of their advice, time, and help. It could not have been accomplished without them.

Marjorie Aronson, Bob Board, DeWitt Bodeen, Val Boily, Carlos Clarens, John Cocchi, Chuck Eicherly, George Geltzer, Alex Gordon, Herbert Graff, Philip Kendal, William Kenly, Al Kilgore, Jerry Kropkiewicz, Miles Kreuger, Cliff McCarty, Dion McGregor, Norman Miller, Gunnard Nelson, Arthur Nicholson, John W. M. Phillips, Mark Ricci, Gene Ringgold, Charles Smith, Alexander Soma, Michael Sparks, Eric Spilker, Lou Valentino, Jerry Vermilye, Sheila Whitaker, Douglas Whitney, Christopher Young, Fred Zentner, and the capable staff of the Theater and Film Collection, New York Public Library at Lincoln Center of the Performing Arts; The Academy of Motion Picture Arts and Sciences; United Press International (Los Angeles and New York City); The British Film Institute (London); The Memory Shop (New York City); and The Cinema Book Shop (London).

CONTENTS

Ginger
Rogers

**The
American
Girl**

Few motion-picture stars have projected what could be termed an "American image," as well as Ginger Rogers. Ginger's evolution as a screen actress grew out of a native humor and an instinctual sense of what was right. Her straightforwardness, honesty, and naturalness of playing made her a favorite with moviegoers over four decades. Despite her years in vaudeville and on the stage, Ginger is a product of the motion picture, where she nurtured, and eventually perfected, a style all her own. Her humor was never forced, her emotional scenes were believable, and her singing and dancing, while not spectacular, were good. Her teaming with Fred Astaire in 1933 proved to be a lucky break for them both. Ginger's career had reached a virtual standstill while Astaire, a brilliant stage dancer, knew nothing about screen technique or the projection of a screen personality. It has been said that she gave him sex appeal and he gave her class; whatever it was, they clicked!

Life magazine described Ginger this way:

Ginger has become an American favorite—as American as apple pie—because Americans can identify themselves with her. She could easily be the girl who lives across the street. She is not uncomfortably beautiful. She is just beautiful enough. She is not an affront to other women. She gives them hope that they can be like her. She can wisecrack from the side of her mouth, but she is clearly an idealist. Her green eyes shine with self-reliance. She believes in God and love and a hard day's work. She is a living affirmation of the holiest American legend: the success story.

In an article written in 1966 for *Films in Review*, she was quoted as saying, "My first picture was *Kitty Foyle*. It was my mother who made all those pictures with Fred Astaire." Ginger never said that line; it was pure fiction. But the fact that she *might* have said it is of more importance. This is the kind of humor that Ginger Rogers has been delighting audiences with since she was fourteen.

Making comparisons, *Time* magazine once wrote: "Less eccentric than Carole Lombard, less worldly-wise than Myrna Loy, less impudent than Joan Blondell, she has a careless self-sufficiency which they lack."

Ginger was born Virginia Katherine McMath on July 16, 1911, in a little house at 100 Moore Street in Independence, Missouri, to Eddins and Lela Emogene (Owens) McMath. Eddins, an electrical engineer in Kansas City, first met dynamic Lela Owens at a dancing school and, by the time Lela accompanied her father—a contracting engineer—to Utah, the young couple was engaged. They were wed on Lela's eighteenth birthday (Christmas Day) in Salt Lake City.

The young couple found the first few years of their marriage tough. Their first child died in infancy (a third was stillborn) but after Virginia's birth, Eddins accepted a position in Ennis, Texas, with Hetty Green's railroad and took his family along. After many months of enduring a humdrum existence, Lela left Eddins and moved into a local hotel with Virginia.

With her father Eddins McMath

Hoping to persuade Lela to return, Eddins resorted to "kidnapping" his own daughter. Divorce proceedings followed, and the court ruling left him only Sundays to visit with his daughter "because of his reckless behavior."

Determined to get his daughter back, her father kidnapped Virginia for a second—and much longer—time, but Lela and her parents hired detectives who located father and daughter in St. Louis after an exhausting search. The court then ruled out Sundays altogether. He was only to see his daughter a few more times before his death, when Virginia was eleven.

At 2½

Mother and daughter lived with Lela's parents and an aunt and uncle, while Virginia attended public school in the old Sixth Ward of Kansas City. She was described by teachers as "a freckle-faced, gangling child." Meanwhile, Lela got nine dollars a week as a Montgomery Ward typist.

Virginia was five when Lela went to California hoping to get a writing job with one of the studios. They were separated for almost a year. Fox bought one of Lela's stories, *Honor System*, but used only the title; the finished product was unrecognizable. Eventually, however, she wrote scripts at the old Balboa Studio, for such Fox stars as Theda Bara, Gladys Brockwell and Baby Marie Osborne (who was to be Ginger's stand-in during the mid-thirties and for Betty Hutton in the early forties). Working on scripts for Baby Marie (one of the first big silent child stars) took Lela to New York City, where she was joined by Virginia at the Hotel Bristol.

Virginia was enrolled at the Forty-sixth Street Public School, which was near the Fox Film Corporation entrance. Lela once told an interviewer, "One afternoon I came home from work to find a note from our maid. It said, 'Mr. Burton George has taken us all to the Fort Lee Studio. He is putting Virginia in George Walsh's new picture.' I was determined they were never going to put my growing child in pictures. I had spent two years working with youngsters in pictures, writing their stories on the set while they worked, and I knew I wanted no such life for my child." Indeed, few child actors ever met with success in their adult years, and Lela Rogers was taking no chances on stunting Virginia's growth. The year was 1917.

Lela refused to let her daughter return for the two additional days' shooting required for the part, and Mr. George got another little girl. Years later Ginger commented, "Look, no one knows this, but I could have been a child star at six. I was offered a contract but Mom said no, I was too young."

With World War I raging in Europe, Lela joined the publicity staff of the Marine Corps (using her professional name, Lela Leibrand) and served as a clerk in Washington helping edit *The Leatherneck*, the Corps' official journal. Virginia was sent back to Kansas City.

After the armistice, Lela returned to Kansas City and, in 1922, just after the death of her first husband, became the wife of Kansas City insurance broker John Logan Rogers—a former childhood sweetheart—who later legally adopted Virginia. The marriage was to last seven years. Eventually, Mr. Rogers' business was to take him to Fort Worth, where Lela was reporter and theater critic on the *Fort Worth Record* (she had held a similar position earlier on the *Kansas City Post*), while she also managed a symphony orchestra.

Besides this active career, in her spare time Lela managed to write little playlets based on Texas history and, in one of these PTA-sponsored plays performed at Fort Worth Central High School, Virginia appeared in *The Death of St. Denis*.

Virginia's earliest ambition was to be a pianist. At

Ginger's first magazine cover (1926)

Ginger and her mother circa 1929

A Broadway star at 19 in Gershwin's *Girl Crazy*

Attending early Oscar dinner with Bette Davis

With early mentor Mervyn LeRoy. At right is Una O'Connor

eleven, she played MacDowell's *To a Wild Rose* in a local auditorium and was considered quite promising; however, her interests changed. Besides being musical, Virginia won the title of "best all-around athlete" of her class. She then expressed a desire to become a schoolteacher, probably admiring one of her teachers, who roomed with the family. Yet she was never to finish her formal schooling.

At home, the name Virginia was already being replaced by "Ginga" because her baby cousin Phyllis (Fraser)—later Mrs. Bennett Cerf—was having trouble saying her name. Soon everyone was calling her *Ginger*—and the name stuck.

In 1925, vaudevillian Eddie Foy was playing Fort Worth, and found himself in need of a substitute dancer in his company. Against her will, Lela agreed to help Foy out, but vowed that her daughter was still "too young." However, just a few months later, vaudevillians Henry Santry and Ann Seymour staged an amateur Charleston contest for the kids of Oklahoma and Texas and got Interstate Theaters to sponsor the event. The first prize was a four-week engagement with the Interstate circuit at $100 per week. Despite her mother's objections, Ginger finally got her way. After all, the Charleston was the rage of the mid-twenties and Ginger had already won local medals and cups.

With second husband Lew Ayres, Fay Wray, and Claudette Colbert

Dating Howard Hughes

She won the local competition held at Fort Worth's Majestic Theater against 120 contestants and qualified for the finals at the Baker Hotel's Peacock Terrace in Dallas. This was November 1925, and, at fourteen, Ginger was wide-eyed, enthusiastic, and confident that this was to be her night. It was. She won, and her act

(composed of the two runners-up) toured the circuits as "Ginger and Her Redheads" with as many as five shows a day for an additional twenty weeks.

By spring, Ginger had made her first magazine cover—the March 19, 1926, issue of *The Vaudeville News*—but, once this particular engagement had terminated, it was back to Fort Worth and school. This was short-lived, though, for the summer found Ginger singing and dancing in a Galveston cafe, an engagement which led to a road tour ending in St. Louis, where her billing was "The Original John Held, Jr. Girl."

Then came three years of vaudeville in the Midwest and Southwest, with mother as manager (20 percent of her daughter's income), chaperone, and writer of material for the act. Ginger went into the Paramount-Publix circuit, appearing in short musical revues in first-class movie houses, and her weekly salary climbed to $350. These acts played stage shows in the larger Paramount theaters throughout the country.

The acts ranged from Ginger's singing and dancing to giving baby-talk "recaltations about the amunals, including the Mama Nyceroserous and Papa Hip-popapumis," which proved popular with audiences. In fact, Ginger still uses this baby-talk with friends, and this "technique" has also been worked into many of her screenplays.

While in New Orleans in 1928 on a three-week layoff, young Ginger married Jack Edward Culpepper (known to vaudeville audiences as Jack Pepper) a young hoofer

With close friend Nancy Carroll at Warner Bros.

Actually, Ginger was not new to films. She had made two short subjects before *Top Speed* opened. While appearing at the Brooklyn Paramount, she had made a short called *Campus Sweethearts* (1929), in which she sang with Rudy Vallee's orchestra. This film was made by NBC using the split lens invented by George Spoor at RCA Victor's recording studios on East 25th Street. Mr. Vallee told me some years ago that it "was not very good, as sound and its use was hardly understood and the direction was very bad."

whom she knew as a kid in Texas. After a brief honeymoon, they went on the road as the two spices, "Ginger and Pepper," but this traveling marriage was doomed from the start. It lasted only ten months; their divorce became final in Dallas on July 15, 1931.

After her original vaudeville booking, Ginger had received an offer from Paul Ash for a New York engagement, but Lela did not think she was ready and the offer was refused. Instead, Helen Kane was given the opportunity. Scoring a big hit in Memphis, St. Louis (32 weeks) and Chicago's Oriental Theater (18 weeks), Ginger headlined a show with Eddie Lowry, and this time did not refuse Paul Ash's offer to appear at the Brooklyn Paramount.

Comedian Eddie Cantor saw her act and hoped to use Ginger in his show *Whoopee*, but arrangements could not be made. Then Charlie Morrison, owner of the famous Mocambo nightclub in Hollywood, introduced Ginger to Guy Bolton, Bert Kalmar, and Harry Ruby, who were just preparing their musical, *Top Speed*, for Broadway. Playing the lissome hoyden, Babs Green, in this show, Ginger was a hit, even in the pre-Broadway tryout at the Chestnut Street Opera House in Philadelphia. The show opened at the 46th Street Theatre on December 25, 1929, with Ginger delighting all with her number, "Hot and Bothered."

Writing in *The New York Times*, Brooks Atkinson noted, "an impudent young thing, Ginger Rogers, . . . carries youth and humor to the point where they are completely charming," while William Boehnel, in the *Tribune* said, "*Top Speed* is one of those musical comedies that just misses being an excellent and diverting show. . . . It is rather ordinary stuff, except when Mr. Allen and Miss Rogers are present to make it lively and entertaining." Alison Smith, in the *New York World*, quipped, ". . . a new and lively young comedienne who didn't seem at all depressed by her name of Ginger Rogers."

Hermes Pan, who later became dance director of some of the Astaire-Rogers pictures, was in the chorus of this show. Laura Lee played Babs Green in the film version. On opening night, Paramount producer Walter Wanger arranged a screen test for Ginger and, later (after another test), she was signed to a contract. Thus, her mornings and afternoons, when no matinees were scheduled, were spent at Paramount's Astoria Studios.

Escorted to a premiere by Fredric March

Ginger's test for role of Elizabeth I in John Ford's *Mary of Scotland*

With George Gershwin

A self-portrait in charcoal

Because of her vaudeville tie-up with Paramount-Publix, Ginger had also appeared in the Melody Comedy short *A Night In A Dormitory* (1929), singing two songs. Material used in this short had been lifted from some of her vaudeville routines, which consisted mainly of songs, sketches and dances.

During this period Ginger also appeared many times on Mr. Vallee's radio program.

Zoung Man of Manhattan was Ginger's first feature-length motion picture; it starred Claudette Colbert and Norman Foster. Ginger was partnered with Charles Ruggles in this newspaper story, which utilized her comic gifts as a wisecracking flapper named Puff, who could not stop running after Norman Foster. She coined a popular expression—"Cigarette me, Big Boy!"—which was used throughout the film. She also sang "I Got IT But IT Don't Do Me No Good." After seeing herself on the screen in *Young Man of Manhattan*, she said, "My stomach did a flip-flop—I so much wanted to do it all over again."

Her second feature was *Queen High* (1930), which had been especially geared to the talents of Charles Ruggles and Frank Morgan; Ginger was almost lost in the background. She sang a few songs, none very notable, but Ruggles' rendition of "I Love the Ladies in My Own Peculiar Way" was funny.

Ginger was then added to the cast of Claudette Colbert's *Secrets of a Secretary*, only to be replaced by Betty Garde as the comedy relief. Ginger then reported for work in Jack Oakie's *The Sap from Syracuse* (1930). In this, her third film, Ginger spent most of her time being chased by Oakie. She gave a charming and amusing performance.

After *Sap* was completed, Ginger was starred in *Office Blues* (1930), a one-reeler directed by Mort Blumenstock and featuring Clayborne Bryson and E.R. Rogers. Ginger played a young stenographer in love with her boss, while a co-worker was in love with her. Johnny Green composed the songs: "We Can't Get Along" and "Dear Sir."

When *Top Speed* closed, Ginger was about to leave for Hollywood on loan-out to United Artists for Douglas Fairbanks' *Reaching for the Moon*, but she remained in New York instead to star in George Gershwin's *Girl Crazy*. She was replaced in the film by June MacCloy.

Girl Crazy was a once-in-a-lifetime opportunity, and her decision proved to be right. She had one of the best songs, "But Not for Me," but, soon after rehearsals started, it became apparent to Gershwin that she needed another song. He wrote "Embraceable You," one of his most enduring melodies.

During the rehearsals, Fred Astaire (then rehearsing *Smiles* with his sister Adele) was called in "because the producers were in a pinch," to help choreograph the dance number which accompanied "Embraceable You." The only available place for Mr. Astaire to rehearse Ginger and Allen Kearns was in the lobby of the Alvin Theatre. Thus, the first meeting of Astaire and Rogers.

The show opened October 14, 1930, and played for forty-five weeks. Ginger's salary was $1,000 a week, plus an additional $500 for her film work and radio appearances. She was nineteen years old, and it was the first year of the Depression. During the run of the play, Ginger avoided being late by hiring an ambulance to rush through thick New York traffic.

Ginger's fourth film appearance was in a comedy with the working title *Manhattan Mary* (1930), which starred Ed Wynn and relied too much on his "Perfect Fool" characterization and not enough on good dialogue and situations. A boring film, it was further hampered by the obnoxious antics of Lou Holtz. Ginger was not particularly good, nor was she well photographed. However, in interviews, she always recalls this venture, although one would think it would be best forgotten. When released, this nonsense was called *Follow the Leader*.

Another undistinguished picture, despite its first-string cast, followed: *Honor among Lovers* (1931) starring Claudette Colbert and Fredric March. The one interesting bit came when March did a cigarette bit with Colbert; it went totally unnoticed in 1931. When Paul Henreid performed a similar piece of business for Bette Davis in Warners' *Now, Voyager*, in 1942, rockets went up! That is the difference a good picture can make—the little nuances are remembered by audiences. Ginger was again Charles Ruggles's zany friend in *Honor*, but most of the action revolved around Colbert and March.

After the run of *Girl Crazy*, Ginger asked for a release from her Paramount contract because she was finding her schedule taxing. Her wish was granted, but Jesse Lasky is reported to have muttered when signing it, "I'm afraid the day will come when I shall regret this."

At this time, a Pathe contract was dangled in front of Ginger, and she readily accepted. She and mother departed for Hollywood at once. The mainstay of Pathe was, of course, action and plenty of it, and Ginger was immediately put into *Eddie Cuts In* (1931), with Eddie Quillan and Robert Armstrong. It was not a bad little picture and, as Baby Face, Ginger was deliciously sassy as a prizefighter's girl who innocently becomes involved with a repairman. The following film, *Suicide Fleet* , was about rough-and-ready navy men who become involved with a mystery ship. Ginger was the girl on shore.

Her next Pathe film, *Carnival Boat* (1932), again teamed her with her *Suicide Fleet* co-star, William Boyd. This time, the action moved to the land of the large lumber camps and Ginger, along with Marie Prevost, traveled up the river as an entertainer. She had one good song, which she delivered with verve: "How I Could Go for You."

A youthful Ginger was quoted during this juncture: "I don't know which I like best. I love the applause on the stage. But pictures are so fascinating—you reach so many millions through them. And you make more money, too."

Just before going to Hollywood, Ginger had briefly returned to vaudeville in A.S. Beck's *Brevities* and, once her three Pathe pictures were concluded, she returned to the circuit. As one of a trio (with Eddie Dowling and Ray

A highly publicized project which never materialized

Signing the cement in front of Grauman's Chinese Theater

With Alfred Lunt, Lynn Fontanne, and James Stewart the night she won the Oscar for Kitty Foyle

Dooley), she performed at B.S. Moss's Broadway Theatre revue. It was the second edition of *Varieties*, and the trio was supported by the twenty-four Albertina Rasch Girls. Ginger impersonated various members of the cast of *Girl Crazy*, as well as Maurice Chevalier and Al Jolson. She then appeared in a sketch with Dowling, Bill Longen, and Maxine Carson; the quartet sang "Underneath the Moon." Said the *Motion Picture Herald*: "Miss Rogers has beauty, youth, appeal and showmanship, four things that will go a long way in making her a great star."

Ginger appeared in two more Paramount short subjects, imaginatively entitled *Hollywood on Parade No. 1* (1932) and *Hollywood on Parade No. 9* (1933), which were used as program fillers. In the former, Fredric March was the master of ceremonies and Ginger and Jack Oakie burlesqued "The Girl Who Used to Be You." In the latter, Ginger appeared with the other Wampus Baby Stars of 1932 in a dreary sketch featuring artist Willy Pogany and Johnny Mack Brown.

Ginger free-lanced in 1932. At First National, she was a pert stenographer to Joe E. Brown's daffy Texas cowboy in *The Tenderfoot* (1932). Then she moved on to Monogram for *The Thirteenth Guest* (1932), a thriller in which she played a nosy relative who is almost electrocuted.

At Fox, she was Sally Eilers's witty chum who sells bootlegged liquor under the counter in *Hat Check Girl* (1932). Returning to First National, she was again opposite Joe E. Brown in *You Said a Mouthful* (1932), which was better-than-average Brown fare.

All of this was, of course, good experience, but no one took the trouble to exploit her as star material until Ginger met director Mervyn LeRoy. They were soon seeing each other constantly, and he urged her to take a small, but distinctive, part in Warner's *Forty-Second Street* (1933), which he felt would boost her career. It was good advice.

Forty-Second Street was then, and is today, one of the all-time great film musicals. Ginger, as Anytime Annie, was pure bliss with phony accent and monocle as the chorine who goes classy. Nothing was spared on the production, and the cast was perfection: Warner Baxter, Bebe Daniels, George Brent, Ruby Keeler (in her movie debut), Dick Powell, Guy Kibbee, and Una Merkel.

Lloyd Bacon directed the actors in the scenes, but it was Busby Berkeley's elaborate production numbers (stories in themselves) that truly made the film. *Shuffle Off to Buffalo* was sung by Keeler and Powell, with a stanza given to Rogers and Merkel to help things along. Keeler also stood out with her rendition of the title song. Bebe Daniels sang *You're Getting to Be a Habit With Me*.

Joan Blondell went to Fox to star in *Broadway Bad* (1933), and Ginger went along to support her. It was well directed by Sidney Lanfield and photographed by Blondell's husband, George Barnes. It was, without doubt, Joan's picture, but Ginger had some good moments.

LeRoy then signed Ginger for his film *Gold Diggers of 1933* (1933), and had her open the film singing the enticing version of the Gold Digger's Song (*We're in the Money*) in a dress of glittering coins. The second verse was sung in pig latin, to capitalize on that current craze, and done so in full close-up. Another number had been originally staged—but later deleted from the film—with Ginger in black singing before a white piano in the nightclub sequence. She probably reprised *I've Got to Sing a Torch Song*, which Dick Powell had sung earlier. A fleeting glance of her on stage can still be spotted in existing prints as the camera passes a mirrored pillar.

The three production numbers by Busby Berkeley were standouts: Joan Blondell's moving *Remember My Forgotten Man*, Keeler and Powell's *Pettin' in the Park*, and the wonderfully wild *Shadow Waltz*.

At this time LeRoy dropped Ginger and married the boss's daughter, Doris Warner, but his influence on Ginger's career had left its mark—she went up like a skyrocket.

She reported to RKO Radio Pictures for an amusing satire on radio personalities, *Purity Girl of the Air*, later retitled *Professional Sweetheart* (1933). This was, indeed, her entree to stardom, for it was here that she first appeared with Fred Astaire. As a temperamental radio star, Ginger selects as her husband a humble backwoodsman (Norman Foster), who eventually teaches her the joys of outdoor living. The only song, *My Imaginary Sweetheart*, was pleasant enough, but Ginger's voice, for some reason, was dubbed. *The New York Times* stated, "Miss Rogers has rarely been more entertaining."

A Shriek in the Night (1933) for an independent company, Allied, followed. It was shot on the RKO lot; she and her co-star, Lyle Talbot, played reporters trying to outscoop one another on a murder case. *Don't Bet on Love* (1933) at Universal was a cute little comedy-drama of no particular consequence, except for the fact that Ginger met Lew Ayres and fell in love with him while making this film.

She went back to Paramount for Harry Joe Brown's *Sitting Pretty* (1933). In this better-than-average musical comedy, her co-stars were Jack Oakie and Jack Haley as a songwriting team Ginger joins on the road to fame and fortune. The Gordon and Revel songs were among their best. Ginger sang *Good Morning Glory, There's a Bluebird at My Window* and did a fan dance in the sassy seminude production number, *Did You Ever See a Dream Walking?*

By Hollywood standards, her progress up to this time was not bad, nor was it spectacular. Then she made the picture that made her a star—*Flying Down to Rio* (1933).

The film was to star Dolores Del Rio and Joel McCrea after their sensational appearance in King Vidor's *Bird of Paradise*, but McCrea was tied up with another film, so Gene Raymond replaced him. Arline Judge was given the part of Honey Hale until it was learned that RKO had signed Fred Astaire, who had just finished making his movie bow in Joan Crawford's *Dancing Lady* at M-G-M. That film was still in the cutting stage when RKO got Astaire.

This meant that a suitable partner had to be found for Astaire. Exit Arline, enter Ginger! RKO executives remembered her from *Forty-Second Street* and *Gold Diggers of 1933*, and thought she would make the perfect partner for Fred; they were right. What started out as a romantic picture for sleek and soignee Dolores Del Rio turned out to be the first Astaire-Rogers picture. Although studio brass were leery about large production numbers, they gambled heavily on *The Carioca*, which became an instant hit. Soon, exhibitors and the public (and the press) were clamoring for more of this lyric duo.

The other numbers in *Flying Down to Rio* were also lovely: *Orchids in the Moonlight* which Astaire sang to, and danced with, Dolores; Ginger's delightful *Music Makes Me* and the catchy title song, sung while gold-suited girls strapped to airplanes—led by Ginger—flew over a South American resort hotel. This film, expertly directed by Thornton Freeland and choreographed by Dave Gould, remains a classic musical.

Once *Rio* was finished, Astaire (who had a prior commitment in New York and London for Cole Porter's *The Gay Divorce*) left the Coast. Ginger made six more films.

Chance at Heaven (1933) paired her with Joel McCrea in a little programmer which greatly benefited from Ginger's naturalness of playing. It was the usual Ben Hecht triangle, but direction and acting gave the script a better shake than it deserved. *Rafter Romance* (1934) was a little comedy-drama with Ginger appearing for the third time with Norman Foster. It did not fare well with critics and the public alike; in fact, it bore a strange flat-footed resemblance to *The More the Merrier*.

At Warners, she helped Dick Powell get over mike fright in *Twenty Million Sweethearts* (1934) and gave a sprightly delivery to the song *Out for No Good*. Warners later remade this as *My Dream Is Yours*, with Doris Day. Ginger than replaced Sally Eilers at Fox for Gaynor and Farrell's *In Love With Life*, which was also called *The*

With Jean Gabin

World Is Ours. She was extremely good in a "bad girl" role (unusual for her). The release title was called *Change of Heart* (1934).

Warners got her back for the very fine *Upperworld* (1934) (also referred to in a two-word version *Upper World*), which Roy Del Ruth directed from a Ben Marckson screenplay based on a story by Ben Hecht. Again, the naturalness of Ginger's playing uplifted a love-triangle. As a chorus girl who falls in love with a neglected millionaire, Ginger was delightful on the runway singing *Shake Your Powder Puff*. Later, she packed her emotional scenes with honesty before being shot by J. Carrol Naish as she protects Warren William. This was the only time Ginger died on the screen.

Ginger was mentioned for many projects during the months after *Flying Down to Rio* was completed. Warners wanted her for a remake of *The Patent Leather Kid* with James Cagney; she and William Gargan were to do *Blarney Smith*, but the idea was shelved and they were then announced for *The Great American Harem*. This was finally called *Bachelor Bait*, with Rochelle Hudson and Stuart Erwin. Ginger was also up for *Young Bride*, but, this time, Arline Judge replaced *her*. In May 1933, *The Death Watch* was announced for Ginger and Betty Furness, to be directed by Irving Pichel. Ginger was ultimately replaced by Dorothy Wilson, and the title was changed to *Before Dawn*. She was also named for *Hips, Hips Hooray*.

Astaire was now available for the film version of his stage success *The Gay Divorce* (1934), which the new Production Code insisted be changed to *The Gay Divorcee* (only in England did the original title prevail).

Thus the Astaire-Rogers formula came into being. The plots were to be as relatively simple as possible. Usually, Astaire was a hoofer who knew no bounds in chasing his lady-love—the self-possessed Ginger—and getting her, no matter how many songs had to be sung or dances danced. The productions were glossy: pure white

With third husband Jack Briggs

With Alice Faye, Hy Gardner and Frank Sinatra during a radio broadcast.

settings, fixtures, and furniture. The musical numbers were all to be an integral part of the story line, and Astaire was to have at least one specialty, while Ginger was to have one solo. The supporting cast would contain an Edward Everett Horton, a Helen Broderick, an Eric Blore, or a Franklin Pangborn, or all four.

In *Flying Down to Rio*, they had supported Dolores Del Rio, but with *The Gay Divorcee*, Fred and Ginger were elevated to movie stardom. The only song taken from the original play was Cole Porter's haunting *Night and Day*, which provided the pair with a sensually beautiful waltz, one of their finest dances. Ginger sang *Don't Let It Bother You*, Astaire sang and danced to *Looking for a Needle in a Haystack*, and Betty Grable and Edward Everett Horton clowned to the jazzy *Let's K-Nock K-Nees*.

The production number, by Herb Magidson and Con Conrad was the hit of the film. The interminable length of *The Continental* seemed to employ everybody at the RKO lot. The number originally ran 35 minutes, but was eventually cut to about 20 minutes. This number was sung and danced to by so many people in various rhythms that musical director Max Steiner wisely relieved the sameness of the tempos by changing the pace of the orchestration from foxtrot to various Latin, waltz, and broken rhythms. Ginger's stand-in on this film was (Baby) Marie Osborne.

At this time Ginger won a suit on May 12, 1934, filed against NBC, Radio Station KFI, Health Bread Company and Madame Sylvia, on charges that she had been impersonated on the air—in a health interview—without her consent. Part of the settlement was a public apology.

Ever since *Don't Bet on Love*, Ginger had been seen everywhere with Lew Ayres. Finally, on November 14, 1934, they were married. The fan magazines, in keeping with the general publicity surrounding Ginger's growing onscreen image, immediately labeled this union "a high school girl's dream." Janet Gaynor was maid of honor and Ben Alexander best man. The wedding party included Mary Brian, Andy Devine, Phyllis Fraser, and Bob Burns. Lois Wilson caught the bridal bouquet.

The next Astaire-Rogers film was announced as *Radio City Revels*, but it then became *Ringstrasse*, a German play by Adler Laszlo. Finally, RKO bought *Roberta* instead and began getting it ready for production.

Meanwhile, Ginger appeared in a romantic comedy-drama called *Romance in Manhattan* (1934), directed by Stephen Roberts and co-starring Francis Lederer as a Czech immigrant in New York who is befriended by chorus-girl Rogers. Andre Sennwald in *The New York Times* noted that: "Miss Rogers continues to be among the most pleasing of the young Hollywood actresses."

Jerome Kern's Broadway musical *Roberta* (1935) was now ready, and Irene Dunne co-starred with Astaire and Rogers. Scripters Jane Murfin and Sam Mintz turned the film version into a lavish picture and, because of the added dances, some of the original songs had to be cut. The fashion sequence, in which all three stars appeared, was shot in color. Fred and Ginger danced to *I Won't*

Dance, *I'll Be Hard to Handle*, and *Lovely to Look At*, while Miss Dunne sang a Russian folk song, *Yesterdays* and *Smoke Gets in Your Eyes*, and *Lovely to Look At*.

While it was found necessary to relegate *The Touch of Your Hand* to instrumental background music, Kern, with Jimmy McHugh, composed *Lovely to Look At* expressly for the film version. M-G-M bought the right to refilm *Roberta* in 1951 and called its version *Lovely to Look At*. Since that time, the original *Roberta* has had only a few random screenings in Los Angeles and New York and has never been viewed on television, where the other Astaire-Rogers pictures always prove popular. *Roberta* offered Ginger her first chance at acting in a picture with Fred. Her sassy French accent was good; she even sang with it.

Ginger kept insisting to the studio heads that she must continue her straight dramatic and/or comic career, as well as her musical films. The result was *Star of Midnight* (1935), a pale mystery drama, which should have been one of the best of the sophisticated comedy-mysteries, although it was not. Co-star William Powell and Ginger labored with a trite script about a missing actress, a star kidnapped at midnight, that the audience never sees.

Top Hat (1935) the fourth Astaire-Rogers film, is, in many ways, their best. Mark Sandrich directed this witty and engaging Irving Berlin show. The production number *The Piccolino* was fantastically realized in a Venice Lido set, complete with canals, bridges, and gondolas; the lyric pair danced the number to perfection. Near the end of the film, when the plot line had been neatly tied, Fred and Ginger continued the number and danced right off the screen as the final title credits appeared: a fine piece of direction.

The romantic adagio *Cheek to Cheek* (inspired by Chopin's A Flat Major Polonaise) provided another graceful look at this nimble pair as they glided to and fro with Ginger in white feathers—a dress that caused havoc on the RKO sound stage when the feathers began to fly everywhere during a dress rehearsal. Fred's solos were *No Strings—I'm Fancy Free* and the machine-gun-like *Top Hat, White Tie, and Tails* number. The pair also displayed their educated feet to full advantage during the *Isn't This a Lovely Day (to Be Caught in the Rain)* routine in a Hyde Park setting.

Their international appeal is best summed up by the French review in *L'Intransigeant*: "Astaire and Rogers are pure rhythm and make the most natural couple in the world. Delightful spectacle of musical charm and movement."

In Person (1935), from a story by Samuel Hopkins Adams, was originally offered to Fred Astaire right after *Roberta*, but was eventually given to Ginger instead. It was her first solo starring vehicle. The premise was a novel one: a movie star who suffers from agoraphobia disguises herself in an effort to avoid her clamoring public. Her disguises in a dark wig, horn-rimmed glasses and false teeth were a hoot. George Brent co-starred. This was RKO's way of pacifying her desire to star in films other than those with Fred Astaire.

With Gary Cooper and director Bill Lawrence on Screen Guild Players' *Good Sam* in 1949

After two years of marriage, the typical marriage of stars collapsed. They separated in 1936 and got the final divorce in 1941. Later, Ginger told Hedda Hopper about Lew Ayres: "He is a brilliant fellow. But, like so many who are introverted, he doesn't show his true brilliance. He's written books and plays and all kinds of music, including symphonic." Once separated from Ayres, Ginger was often seen in the company of multimillionaire Alfred Gwynne Vanderbilt, actor James Stewart and, much earlier, billionaire Howard Hughes. Reportedly, she is the only person who ever made Hughes cry.

Ginger, like other fellow actors in Hollywood, became increasingly aware of the box-office receipts of her pictures and she soon demanded more money, equal billing and publicity, and a $10,000 bonus. RKO tried to bluff her by threatening to replace her with Jessie Matthews, but, after two days of heated discussions, Ginger's demands were met.

Her next picture was *Follow the Fleet* (1936), from Herbert Osborne's 1922 success *Shore Leave*. By this time, the studio felt that more emphasis should be placed on a subplot. Thus, the parts played by Harriet Hilliard and Randolph Scott were built up, causing the excessive length (it is their longest picture—110 minutes) and causing audiences to yawn.

Ginger was charming singing *Let Yourself Go* in the radio-station sequence. Earlier, she and Fred gave it a jazzy treatment at the dance hall. Fred had two solos which were not particularly newsworthy: *We Saw the Sea* and *I'd Rather Lead a Band*. However, together, the spirited pair were fantastically limber in a camp-rehearsal number called *I'm Putting All My Eggs in One Basket* and the divine dance they did to Berlin's *Let's Face the Music and Dance*. The latter was sheer poetry of motion and, without doubt, the highlight of this picture. For the number, Ginger wore a twenty-five-pound beaded dress which seems all the more incredible when one considers how effortlessly she moved.

All in all, *Follow the Fleet* was grand fun but could have done without the constant "chewing" Fred was forced to emulate in order to appear a "common" sailor. Being in a sailor suit was enough of a jolt to Fred, whom

Bond Street had just voted one of the world's ten best-dressed men. This was also the perfect time for Governor Allred of Texas to make Ginger an honorary admiral in the Texas Navy!

During this period, Lela Rogers was constantly at her daughter's side (as adviser) on the sets of her pictures. The studio wisely created a new position for her and she became "head of new talent." Two actors who reaped the harvest of Lela's energies and zeal in this new job, were Lucille Ball and Jack Carson. They not only appeared in several of Ginger's pictures, but were also brought to the attention of other directors through Lela's persistence.

Ginger's ambition to develop her own reputation as a dramatic actress came into sharper focus when RKO announced plans to film Maxwell Anderson's *Mary of Scotland*, under John Ford's direction. Katharine Hepburn was signed to play Mary Stuart and Fredric March was cast as the Earl of Bothwell. Ginger had her eye on the brief, but effective, part of Elizabeth I, which was still uncast. When RKO's head of production, Pandro S. Berman, turned her down, she enlisted the help of Katharine Hepburn, a makeup man, and director John Ford to help her masquerade as Lady Ainsley, a visiting English beauty. Hepburn agreed to say she was a dear "old friend," while Ford agreed to push the idea of a test with Berman.

Once Berman met "Lady Ainsley," he was most impressed and ordered a short test made. The test pleased him, but, for a final decision, a more elaborate test was in order. Since this would have been expensive, Ginger broke down and confessed the plot. Needless to say, she did not get the part. Ford finally selected March's wife, Florence Eldridge, who gave a distinguished portrayal.

In 1936 Ginger bought some property in Coldwater Canyon above Beverly Hills and began construction on a "fun house," which six RKO set decorators and designers helped to create from ideas supplied by Ginger and Lela. The team was headed by Van Nest Polglase, who designed all of the Astaire-Rogers films. There was the main house, garage, pool, dressing rooms, tennis court, projection room, private study and studio, and even a soda fountain. It may not have been in the "grand Hollywood tradition," but it came pretty close to it.

Swing Time (1936), directed by George Stevens, was the next Astaire-Rogers picture. Howard Lindsay and Allan Scott supplied the witty script, while Jerome Kern and Dorothy Fields provided some of their most memorable songs. Each of their three numbers defied description, and all were unforgettable: *Pick Yourself Up*, *Never Gonna Dance*, and *Waltz in Swing Time*.

Together, they sang the cute *A Fine Romance*, and Fred sang to Ginger *The Way You Look Tonight*, which won the Academy Award for Best Song of 1936. Fred's solo was one of the outstanding moments of his dancing career—the sensational *Bojangles of Harlem*.

The spirited pair spent a total of 350 hours of rehearsal for the "effortless" routines in *Swing Time*. Said Ginger, "The first hundred hours are the most difficult, because they are the kindergarten course for the new routines. With the new steps learned, it becomes more fascinating to fit them together and perfect the execution of the routines."

Astaire and Rogers were on the Top Ten Money Making Stars list for three consecutive years: 1935 (fourth); 1936 (third); and 1937 (seventh). In 1938, Ginger alone was listed as eighteenth.

In late 1936, Ginger was given police protection for two weeks after receiving extortion notes threatening her life. The following year, in a gayer frame of mind, Ginger sold a kiss for $400. The purchaser was Harold Lloyd, who had outbid Cary Grant, during a special benefit in Los Angeles for victims of the 1937 Ohio River flood.

Shall We Dance (1937), their seventh picture, had them searching for more variety in their routines, which accounts for the novel dance on roller skates to *Let's Call the Whole Thing Off*. Ginger sang *They All Laughed*, after which she and Astaire danced to it. Fred sang *I've Got Beginner's Luck*, and together they captivated the audience with the big production number, *Shall We*

On Bob Hope Buick Show's *Potomac Madness* with Hope and Perry Como (1960)

21

Television debut in *Three by Coward* with Gloria Vanderbilt and director Otto Preminger

Dance. Fred sang and danced the hit song *They Can't Take That Away from Me* with Harriet Hoctor. And Ginger danced a brief rhumba with a new partner, Pete Theodore, while Miss Hoctor did some classical steps with Fred. Mark Sandrich, who had directed three of their previous hits, did an equally fine job here. The Ira and George Gershwin songs put everything into high gear.

Producer David O. Selznick tried to make a deal with RKO for Ginger's services for *Prom Girl*, a college musical in Technicolor, with songs by Rodgers and Hart. At the same time, Warners was hoping to get her for *Hollywood Hotel*, with Dick Powell. RKO had other plans.

Ginger finally got her chance to break the musical-mold when she was cast in Gregory LaCava's version of the George S. Kaufman-Edna Ferber play, *Stage Door* (1937). It was quite a challenge for Ginger, and she met it head on. LaCava was inspired in casting RKO's two leading females opposite each other. Katharine Hepburn proved, once again, that she was the best actress in Hollywood. Rogers proved, finally, that she possessed a rich storehouse of talent which had never been properly tapped. Together, under LaCava's improvisional direction, they were terrific. Morrie Ryskind and Anthony Veiller wrote such a brilliant adaptation that George S. Kaufman himself was moved to quip, "Why didn't he [LaCava] call it *Screen Door?*" *Stage Door* remains one of the finest films on theatrical life ever made.

Said the *National Board of Review* magazine in November, 1937: "Ginger Rogers, triumphantly making use of a full-fledged opportunity to show what she has often indicated before, that she is much more than the lucky team-mate of Fred Astaire, a brilliant and individual comedian, with a capacity for feeling of no small order."

As early as 1936, Ginger was slated to appear in the film version of *Mother Carey's Chickens*, by Kate

Douglas Wiggin. She had even gone so far as to dye her hair, but unsatisfactory scripts and/or other commitments never brought star and property together. It was just as well. Shortly after, RKO tried to force it on Katharine Hepburn, who had just completed her brilliantly comic *Bringing Up Baby*, and Miss Hepburn used this "insult" to pry herself out of her RKO contract. That done, she rushed to Columbia, where George Cukor was filming Philip Barry's *Holiday*.

As a matter of fact, on February 5, 1938, Ginger was signed by Columbia on loan-out to play opposite Hepburn and Cary Grant in *Holiday*, with Robert Cummings as Ned. As things turned out, RKO canceled the loan contract and Doris Nolan replaced her, while Lew Ayres (Ginger's estranged husband) won the role of Ned. It was like musical chairs. Finally, Ruby Keeler ended up with the dreadful *Mother Carey's Chickens*, and RKO announced that Ginger would co-star with Charles Boyer in *Perfect Harmony*, a romantic drama which Edward Kaufman was to produce and Rouben Mamoulian to direct. The studio also bought *Irene* for Ginger, but alas, nothing came of either of these projects. British actress Anna Neagle later made *Irene*.

Almost any script would have been better for Ginger than the one she had to play next. Arthur Kober's delightfully Jewish play *Having Wonderful Time* (1938), was whitewashed and reduced to pointless Gentile nonsense. One of the studio's lesser directors, Alfred Santell, was given the chore of whipping everything into some sort of shape—a task he did not meet with enthusiasm. It was Ginger's only sour note in an otherwise exciting three-year period.

Alfred Santell was next assigned to direct Ginger in *Vivacious Lady* (1938), but happily was replaced after a few days by George Stevens. Although Stevens directed this script in a leisurely fashion, it was fun from start to finish. Ginger could not have been more charming as a swinging nightclub entertainer who marries a bashful botany professor visiting New York. James Stewart's particular brand of wholesome, small-town humor was a perfect foil for Ginger's flip style. She sang one song at the beginning—*You'll Be Reminded of Me*, but thereafter, relied on her comic skill, especially on the train with Stewart, Maude Eburne, and Spencer Charters, and later, when she punches Frances Mercer in the mouth at the country club. My favorite scene, however, was the wild *Big Apple* number with sedate Beulah Bondi and James Ellison, later joined by Charles Coburn. Now *there* was a vivacious lady!

It was enormously popular at the box office, and when Ginger and Jimmy Stewart both won Oscars in early 1941, it was re-released.

About the time *Vivacious Lady* was being entered into the sixth Venice Film Festival, Ginger's studio was announcing her for Thelma Strabel's original script *You Can't Escape Forever*, which Hal Wallis was to produce at Warners. Had this project taken shape, she would have co-starred with Errol Flynn. RKO, however, had Stanley Rauh writing a story especially for her, *She*

With fourth husband Jacques Bergerac

Married for Money, which George Haight was to produce. RKO also purchased screen rights to Sir Arthur Pinero's *The Enchanted Cottage*. Ginger was to make none of these.

Instead, she made *Carefree* (1938), with Fred Astaire. After seeing Ginger in *Stage Door* and *Vivacious Lady*, it was decided that more comedy would be added to her next film. In fact, as a general rule, more concentration on the script was in full evidence here. Ginger has a great deal of fun as a radio singer who can't make up her mind about marriage. Eventually she falls for psychiatrist Astaire (switching motivations), but not before they have danced, in slow motion, to *I Used to Be Color Blind*, and the country-club number *The Yam*, which is a composite of all of their best movements. The highlight is the beautifully staged *Change Partners*, in which Ginger dances trancelike with Astaire on a flagstone terrace.

Ginger later recorded some of Irving Berlin's numbers from *Carefree* with Hal Borne's orchestra for Bluebird (Victor's 35¢ label) Records.

Fred and Ginger's last film together for RKO was the memorable *The Story of Vernon and Irene Castle* (1939), which had initially been called simply, *The Castles*. This marked their first period piece and their first script to end tragically. H. C. Potter directed this elaborate musical biography with taste and accuracy. The accuracy was abetted by Irene Castle, who was hired as a technical adviser, since the screenplay was based on her two books, *My Husband* and *My Memories of Vernon Castle*.

Since it dealt with the famous husband-and-wife team that popularized ballroom dancing during the years 1913–1918, Astaire and Rogers were given the opportunity to re-create the Castle Walk, the one-step, the fox-trot, the maxixe, and others. Their routines were less spectacular in this film, and therefore more in keeping with the period. Songs like *Pretty Baby*, *Darktown Strutters' Ball*, *When You Wore a Tulip* and *Waiting for the Robert E. Lee* were used throughout. Only one new song was especially written for the film—*Only When You're in My Arms*, by Con Conrad, Bert Kalmar, and Harry Ruby.

The pilot for *The Ginger Rogers Show* in which she played twins. Co-star was Charles Ruggles. (1961)

With fifth husband William Marshall

In *Terror Island* on the Bob Hope Chrysler Theater (1965).

Irene Castle never seemed to be pleased with Ginger. Either it was her hair (she wanted it dark), or her costumes (Irene personally supervised their design and execution). However, by the time it was previewed, she had to admit that she liked the film.

Creating, rehearsing, and filming dances in the Astaire-Rogers pictures consumed about 500 hours per film (or 4,000 hours for their eight *starring* pictures).

Robert deGrasse, photographer on *The Castles*, said at that time:

Mr. Astaire and Miss Rogers first walk through the figures of the dance in minute detail. Then camera lines are marked on the stage floor, foregrounds designated, and all the mechanics of the scene rehearsed. The cameraman watches the complete "take" through the camera so that the dancers never will be "lost" at any time during the shot.

With the completion of *The Story of Vernon and Irene Castle*, 125,000 feet of dancing film had been recorded on their pictures. Of this, approximately 75,000 feet were printed, but only 25,000 feet were included into the final release prints.

Warner Bros. bid for Ginger to co-star with James Cagney in a planned film version of the Rodgers and Hart musical *On Your Toes*, but their offer was refused because RKO was just about to start shooting *Little Mother*, with Douglas Fairbanks, Jr. By the time Ginger started filming this engaging comedy, David Niven had replaced Fairbanks, and Garson Kanin had been selected as director.

Finally called *Bachelor Mother*, this became one of Ginger's all-time best movies and one of 1939's best comedies. Ginger portrays a jobless salesgirl who finds an abandoned baby and immediately gets assistance from the man who fired her. Besides a heated dance

number with Frank Albertson, Ginger delivered, with stinging accuracy, some beautiful wisecracks. Needless to say, the 1956 remake, *Bundle of Joy*, lacked the charm and wit of the original.

Fifth Avenue Girl (1939) once again gave her the opportunity to work with director Gregory LaCava. It was a revamped version of his earlier success, *My Man Godfrey*. When negotiations to borrow Franchot Tone from M-G-M failed, LaCava decided to showcase Ginger in what was originally the William Powell role and back her up with a strong supporting cast. It all was a grand idea, and one can sense that Ginger was having a fine time, but, at best, it is minor LaCava. Her very next film, however, was far superior, and this time the director did his star justice.

Primrose Path (1940), from the play by Robert Buckner and Walter Hart and the novel *February Hill* by Victoria Lincoln, gave Ginger a part she could sink her teeth into. To get fully into her characterization of a seventeen-year-old girl from the wrong side of the tracks who is striving to uplift herself by shedding the evil influences of her tawdry background, Ginger insisted on wearing no makeup. She appeared with a scrubbed face and an understanding of this role that was uncanny. She was, in a word, superb.

She was believable, straightforward and honest—how many actresses wish they could convey the elements of a woman's character so faithfully? Ginger did just that. The play had been toned down for the screen, but a sterling cast created the proper atmosphere with the down-to-earth dialogue. Notable were Marjorie Rambeau, who won an Academy Award nomination for her supporting performance, Joel McCrea, Henry Travers, Queenie Vassar, Vivienne Osborne and Miles Mander.

Despite the watered-down script, *Primrose Path* ran into censor problems, but on a local level. Detroit, for example, banned it, along with the excellent Crawford-Gable *Strange Cargo*, on the grounds that it "*might be obscene.*" Interestingly, New York's posh Radio City Music Hall booked *Primrose Path* into its hallowed halls on Ginger's name alone, until the management learned what the picture was about.

Ginger's next film is best forgotten. It was called *Good Luck* when Garson Kanin refused to direct it, and had been changed to *Change Your Luck* when Rouben Mamoulian indicated his displeasure with the script. When it was offered to Ginger, Lewis Milestone had assumed the directorial seat, and Ronald Colman had been picked as co-star. Based on Sacha Guitry's *Bonne Chance*, the title was finally changed to *Lucky Partners* (1940). No matter what title was selected, it was not worth the talent acquired to play it; both Ginger and Colman struggled bravely to make it play, but need not have bothered.

RKO producer David Hempstead was responsible for Ginger's next film and nothing could have been more apropos. He had sent her a copy of Christopher Morley's novel *Kitty Foyle* when it was hot off the press, and the property was soon purchased for her. Ginger gave this white-collar-girl's life the poignancy it needed.

The film (1940) was well-mounted and a fine cast was selected to support Ginger, but the direction by Sam Wood was not always on target. His stream-of-consciousness effects were muddled and unrealistic. However, despite the unevenness of the direction, she delivered a totally honest portrayal in this saga of the modern working girl.

For this deft piece of acting, Ginger received a nomination (her first) for the Best Actress "Oscar," and the competition was extremely heavy. Joan Fontaine was the favorite, for her vital portrait of *Rebecca*, while Katharine Hepburn had just won the New York Film Critics' prize for her stunning re-creation of Tracy Lord in *The Philadelphia Story*. Bette Davis was up for one of her finest acting chores, in *The Letter*, and newcomer Martha Scott was nominated for *Our Town*.

Alfred Lunt and Lynn Fontanne were on hand to present the Best Acting awards on February 27, 1941—the first time the Academy of Motion Picture Arts and Sciences used sealed envelopes to divulge the winner. Nobody was more surprised to find that she was the winner than Ginger. The excitement of the occasion caused her to forget her prepared speech, but she did manage to thank her mother, and utter, "This is the happiest moment of my life." Twenty-five years later, Ginger returned the favor when she presented the Lunts with an Emmy for their television performances in *The Magnificent Yankee*.

After *Kitty Foyle*, Ginger left for New York, where *Time* magazine reported: "Ginger, with her shoulder-length tresses, her trim figure, her full lips, her prancing feet and honest-to-goodness manner, is the flesh-and-blood symbol of the U.S. working girl."

At this time, RKO and Warner Bros. were trying to trade John Garfield for *They Knew What They Wanted*, while Ginger was to appear with James Cagney in *City for Conquest*, but terms were never reached. RKO also bought Elmer Rice's *Two on an Island* for her, but did not make it.

Returning to Hollywood, Ginger gave one of her finest portrayals in Garson Kanin's *Tom, Dick and Harry* (1941). She was perfectly cast as Jane, the dizzy working girl whose life is complicated by three attentive suitors. Paul Jarrico wrote a highly amusing story that was so good that the musical remake, *The Girl Most Likely* with Jane Powell, also met with success.

Bosley Crowther noted in *The New York Times*: "She plays the girl as no other actress we know could, with a perfect combination of skepticism and daffiness." Her suitors, Burgess Meredith, George Murphy, and Alan Marshal, were all good in their respective roles, with Meredith taking the lead.

Next on the Rogers agenda was *Roxie Hart* (1942), William A. Wellman's outrageous satire of a sassy, gum-chewing broad who takes a murder rap for her no-good husband for publicity purposes. Ginger attacked this part with great gusto and an odd kind of relish. Many felt that Barbara Stanwyck would have made a more ideal Roxie, but Wellman later used Barbara in his marvelous *Lady of Burlesque*, a role—and milieu—not unlike that of *Roxie Hart*.

The script was a rich burlesque supercharged with high (camp) farce and slapstick. The cast, which had a field day, included Adolphe Menjou, Lynne Overman, Iris Adrian, Spring Byington, Phil Silvers, and George Montgomery, who not only wins Roxie but narrates the saga. Wellman knew how to utilize his players, regardless of the situation, and his touches filled the air as the action flew by.

Ginger stayed at 20th Century-Fox to appear, briefly, in the episodic, all-star *Tales of Manhattan* (1942), directed by Julien Duvivier. The (originally) six episodes were linked together by a gentleman's dress suit, passed from one person to another, but each story was otherwise separate from the others. Edward G. Robinson appeared in the best, while Ginger and Henry Fonda were stuck in the weakest. The segment which starred W. C. Fields was cut after completion because the film was too long.

Paramount then offered her *The Major and the Minor* (1942), which Billy Wilder was given as his first directorial film. Ray Milland co-starred, and the two of them had a delightful time. Ginger once again had the opportunity to play a young girl (as she had done so beautifully in *Kitty Foyle*), but this time it was done as a gag and audiences loved her kidding ways. Her balloon-squeezing scene on the train, to the continual annoyance of certain gentlemen travelers, was a high point of the film.

Lela Rogers played Ginger's mother in the film, in which Ginger masqueraded as her "mother" in order to fool Milland. The supporting cast was especially good, particularly Diana Lynn as a knowledgeable teen-ager and Rita Johnson as a peeved fiancee.

At her home studio, Ginger began working for director Leo McCarey in a seriocomic melodrama, *Once upon a Honeymoon.* Despite sharp-edged playing by Ginger and Cary Grant, the humor was grim. By the time it was released (1942), America was deeply involved in World War II, and the sight of newspaperman Grant chasing ex-chorus-girl Rogers through Hitler-infested areas trying to convince her that she married a Nazi (Walter Slezak), did not seem very funny.

Ginger bought a large ranch at Eagle Point, Oregon, right in the heart of the Rogue River country. One thousand acres with two and a half miles of lakefront gave her a place to which she could retreat from the pressures of picture making. She married marine Jack Briggs on January 16, 1943, in San Diego, while on one of her USO tours. They had met in 1941, when he had a small part in *Tom, Dick and Harry.* After the war, the Briggses spent much time on the Rogue River ranch. Mario Lanza reportedly used to work off his excess weight on her ranch during the early 1950s while he was working for M-G-M.

In 1942, Dalton Trumbo, who wrote the screenplay for *Kitty Foyle,* finished *Tender Comrade* (1943), a script which Edward Dmytryk was to direct. Ginger struggled to make this oversentimentalized slush viable, but was defeated by trite direction and soapy dialogue. The cast was a formidable one, but wasted on this nonsense: Robert Ryan, Patricia Collinge, Ruth Hussey, Mady Christians, and Kim Hunter.

From October 1936 until May 1943, Ginger appeared eleven times on Cecil B. DeMille's renowned "Lux Radio Theater." She acted in the following: *Curtain Rises,* with Warren William, Alan Mowbray and Verree Teasdale (Said *Variety*: "The Rogers-William combo tackled the job with gusto."); *A Free Soul,* with Don Ameche; *Brief Moment,* with Douglas Fairbanks, Jr.; *Stage Door,* with Rosalind Russell and Adolphe Menjou; *She Married Her Boss,* with George Brent and Edith Fellows; *Bachelor Mother,* with Fred MacMurray; *Fifth Avenue Girl,* with Edward Arnold and John Howard; *Kitty Foyle,* with Dennis Morgan and James Craig; *Tom, Dick and Harry,* with Burgess Meredith, George Murphy, and Alan Marshal; and *The Major and the Minor,* with Ray Milland and her mother, Mrs. Lela Rogers.

Between her USO camp shows, Ginger made a U.S. training film, *Safeguarding Military Information* with Walter Huston. It ran 10 minutes and was released in 1943. Later, she and James Cagney narrated *Battle Stations* (1943), a short for 20th Century-Fox. Directed by Garson Kanin, it stressed the shore jobs that Coast Guard SPARS took over from men who had gone to battle.

With Walter Pidgeon in the remake of Rodgers and Hammerstein's television production of *Cinderella* (1965).

Hello, Dolly!—taking over the role of Dolly Gallagher Levi from Carol Channing

She then made *Ginger Rogers Finds a Bargain* (N.D.), a trailer (5 minutes) for the Fourth War Loan Drive. Although Ginger had cut many records during the thirties, they were usually songs from her films. However, in 1944, Ginger cut a record of *Alice in Wonderland*. Victor Young composed and conducted the music, and George Wells directed his adaptation of the children's classic. The songs were provided by "Lewis Carroll" and Frank Luther. The cast included Bea Benaderet, Martha Wentworth, Lou Merrill, and Ferdinand Munier.

Paramount then scheduled the elaborate screen adaptation of Moss Hart's *Lady in the Dark* (1944) for her. Frances Goodrich and Albert Hackett wrote the script, and Mitchell Leisen was assigned to direct. Many of the Kurt Weill-Ira Gershwin songs were filmed as part of the original screenplay, but only a few were retained in the final release prints.

Other than the fashion finale of *Roberta* and (possibly) the dream sequences of *Carefree*, *Lady in the Dark* was Ginger's first color film. Paramount gave this enterprise a massive budget, which was most unusual at that time, due to the mandatory wartime restrictions on film productions. The cast was an impressive one and it did a landslide business at the box office, but Ginger was just not Liza Elliott. She seemed to be trying too hard to act the lady and missed the essence of the character. To state merely that she was miscast does not excuse the fact that Ginger was just not fun; it was not the Ginger audiences had come to love.

Her next film was David O. Selznick's production of *Double Furlough* (1944), which George Cukor began directing. After a short lapse of time and many arguments with the front office, he walked out and was replaced by William Dieterle. The tale of a shell-shocked soldier meeting a parolee from a woman's prison at Christmas was an interesting one, and Ginger and Joseph Cotten were both touching in their roles. Shirley Temple, who had previously appeared in a bit part in *Change of Heart* (1934) with Ginger, did a fine job as a snide teen-ager. When released, the title was changed to *I'll Be Seeing You*.

Ginger then reported to Metro-Goldwyn-Mayer for the first time, to star in the studio's glossy rehash of Vicki Baum's *Grand Hotel*. This modernization was entitled *Week-End at the Waldorf* (1945) and boasted a slick screenplay by Sam and Bella Spewack. Ginger's co-stars were Lana Turner, Walter Pidgeon, and Van Johnson. Like all female stars on the M-G-M lot, she was given first-class treatment: twelve Irene gowns, with a Sidney Guilaroff coiffure to match each of them.

Lana Turner portrayed a stenographer who dreams of the glamorous life of Park Avenue, but settles for soldier Van Johnson. Ginger was the opposite: a glamorous actress yearning for the simple things of life she had given up for success, who discovers a thief (Walter Pidgeon) in her room and sets out to reform him. Ginger's scenes with Pidgeon, who is actually a war correspondent, sparkle with good humor. Perhaps Ginger and Lana should have reversed roles.

Ginger returned to RKO for Morrie Ryskind's adaptation of the French film *Battement de Coeur*, which was called *Heartbeat* (1946). Sam Wood directed an expert cast, including Jean Pierre Aumont, Adolphe Menjou, Basil Rathbone, and Mona Maris. All in all, it should have been better than it was.

Universal-International's *Magnificent Doll* (1946) was Ginger's first venture into historical drama, from which she should have been warned. Irving Stone provided a screenplay that resembled soap opera set against a historical background. It was clearly undistinguished, as was the direction of the once-perceptive Frank Borzage.

The searing conflict between Dolly Payne Madison, Aaron Burr and James Madison should have produced sparks, if not fire, on the screen. However, *Magnificent Doll* produced only smoke. Burgess Meredith and David Niven, both previous Rogers co-stars, were also trapped by the ineptness of it all. The critics tore it apart.

Columbia beckoned next and Ginger made a harmless little comedy with Cornel Wilde called *It Had to Be You* (1947). There were some good moments in it, but most of it was silly, despite its two directors.

Ginger continued her radio work and was most effective with Paul Douglas in Kenyon Nicholson's *The Barker* on NBC's "Theatre Guild on the Air." With Gary Cooper, she appeared on NBC's "Screen Guild Players" in a script based on Cooper's film *Good Sam*.

When Judy Garland and Fred Astaire became a socko combination at the box office in *Easter Parade*, M-G-M immediately hired Betty Comden and Adolph Green to create another vehicle. Thus, *The Barkleys of Broadway* (1949) was born. However, soon after the production had begun, Judy became too ill to continue and M-G-M managed to get Ginger to replace her. Said Ginger, "I didn't want to do any musicals, I was satisfied to keep on with the straight ones. But I guess it'll turn out all right. Anyway, we'll have some fun."

The Barkleys certainly did "turn out all right." It was a lighthearted, cheerful combination of songs, dances, and comedy, which was imbued with something audiences had not seen in nearly ten years—Astaire and Rogers. Their old magic had not diminished. They were as spirited as ever, and their educated feet glided through such numbers as *They Can't Take That Away from Me*, which had been a big hit in *Shall We Dance*; *Manhattan Downbeat, The Swing Trot*, and their kilt number, *My One and Only Highland Fling*.

In June 1949, Ginger asked Universal-International to release her from a contract she had signed for Crane Wilbur's story, *Tehachapi: The Story of Molly X*; they agreed if a replacement star could be found before the August shooting date. Luckily, June Havoc was available.

On September 7, 1949, Ginger divorced Jack Briggs.

Ben Hecht and Charles MacArthur's old play, *Ladies and Gentlemen*, provided Ginger with her next property. At Warners, the name was changed to *Perfect Strangers* (1950), and her co-star was Dennis Morgan (their first appearance together since *Kitty Foyle*).

On the Ed Sullivan Show

Ginger was appealing as a divorcee who falls for an unhappily married man during the course of a murder trial. The supporting cast, headed by Margalo Gillmore, Thelma Ritter, and Anthony Ross, helped immeasurably. The direction of Bretaigne Windust was better than average.

Storm Warning (1950), which followed, provided her with a part into which she could sink her teeth. As a traveling dress model who witnesses a Ku Klux Klan murder in a small Southern town, Ginger gave one of her best performances of her later career. The Daniel Fuchs-Richard Brooks scenario was reminiscent of the hard-hitting Warners films of the 1930s. Stuart Heisler directed with a deft hand, and Doris Day, excellent as Ginger's sister, and Steve Cochran, as her brother-in-law, were also first-rate.

Jack Carson, mentioned earlier, had benefited from the interest Lela Rogers had shown in him during the mid-thirties at RKO and had progressed, over the years, from an extra in her films to bit parts to supporting roles. At this juncture, he was Ginger's co-star in an independently produced mess, *The Groom Wore Spurs* (1951). Filmed on the Universal-International lot (and released theatrically by the studio), the picture was directed by Richard Whorf. It was low comedy, beneath the talent of this pair, to say nothing of Joan Davis.

During this period, Paramount was trying to get Ginger to co-star with Betty Hutton in a biography of the famous Duncan Sisters called *Topsy and Eva*, with Ginger as Vivian Duncan (the "Eva" of the title) and Hutton as Rosetta. Billing, salaries, and other preferences became major issues and the project was soon dropped.

Ginger then decided to return to Broadway—after twenty-one years—in Louis Verneuil's *Love and Let Love*, in 1951. She looked lovely in an assortment of Jean Louis gowns, but the vehicle was old hat and tiresome. Brooks Atkinson noticed, "She is beautiful and alive and has a sunny sense of humor . . . no one that gorgeous can be entirely overwhelmed by a playwright's dullness!"

Back in Hollywood, Ginger went to 20th Century-Fox for a segment in the all-star *We're Not Married* (1952). Her section, with Fred Allen, was one of the very best; sharp, brittle dialogue and clever situations gave her a fine part indeed. Edmund Goulding directed with a fine sense of humor. The others in the cast were Marilyn Monroe, David Wayne, Eve Arden, Paul Douglas, Eddie Bracken, Mitzi Gaynor, and Victor Moore.

Fox then offered her Howard Hawks's *Monkey Business* (1952), with Cary Grant, which she joyfully accepted. The original Harry Segall story was adapted by Ben Hecht, Charles Lederer, and I. A. L. Diamond. Grant was amusing, as were some of the scenes, but Ginger had a case of the "cutes" whenever she reverted to being a little girl. Too much of an even good thing is boring.

Dreamboat (1952), on the other hand, gave Ginger a perfect chance to be funny in an interesting way and to look extremely glamorous in gowns by Travilla. As a former silent-film star getting a new lease on life by appearing for a perfume company on a television program showing her old films, she and co-star Clifton Webb were excellent, especially in their silent-movie scenes. This was one of the first, and certainly best, satires on television's use of motion pictures as part of its daily programming.

During an extensive trip to France in 1952, Ginger met Jacques Bergerac, a young lawyer. He was entranced by her and followed her everywhere. Before anyone knew it, Ginger—now back in Hollywood—announced that they would marry. She was then forty-two; he twenty-six. The gossip-mongers began to waggle their tongues, but not before Ginger said, "When you're happy, you don't count the years." They were married on February 7, 1953. Ginger was influential in getting Jacques a job in one of the studios where he could learn about acting.

Meanwhile, Ginger returned to Paramount to do a script based on James M. Barrie's short play *Rosalind* (which turned out to be a watered-down *All About Eve*) called *Forever Female* (1953). Irving Rapper directed a good cast that included William Holden, Paul Douglas, and newcomer Patricia Crowley. The *Saturday Review* observed; "As the aging grande dame, Ginger Rogers is taut, mannered, efficient. . . . . One of the most capable actresses on the American screen."

In November 1953, Paramount tried out its coin-in-the-slot Telemeter system of premiering new films on a closed-circuit television audience on the inhabitants of Palm Springs, California, and later in other locales. The premiere price was $1.35. *Forever Female* was the first new feature film to get this treatment. The novelty did not catch on and it soon died.

Next, at 20th Century-Fox, Ginger joined Van Heflin, Gene Tierney, George Raft, Reginald Gardiner, and Peggy Ann Garner in Nunnally Johnson's *Black Widow* (1954). Johnson based his screenplay on a novel by Patrick Quentin which concerned a young theater hopeful (Garner) who gets involved with an older man (Gardiner) and is later slain. Again, Ginger was an actress and wore many gowns in this Technicolor melodrama in CinemaScope.

In 1954 she went abroad with husband Jacques Bergerac to film *Lifeline* in England. This was a turgid melodrama which did not do anything for her career, but she was well photographed. Herbert Lom and Stanley Baker were her co-stars, along with Bergerac, and it was released under the title *Beautiful Stranger* (1954). In the United States, it became *Twist of Fate*. It was her first foreign-made picture.

Columbia next acquired her talents for a film based on Lenard Kantor's play *Dead Pigeon*, which Phil Karlson directed with verve. Released as *Tight Spot* (1955), it concerned a brassy, beat-up blonde, snatched from a four-year stay in prison to help District Attorney Edward G. Robinson get the goods on a big-time gangster (Lorne Greene) while a young cop is assigned to guard her in her hotel room (Brian Keith).

It was one of her best roles. Said John L. Scott in the *Los Angeles Times*, "Miss Rogers gets her teeth into this offbeat characterization and enjoys an actor's field day."

On October 18, 1954, Ginger made her television debut on the premiere of "Producer's Showcase" in *Three by Coward*, directed by Otto Preminger. Ilka Chase, Gloria Vanderbilt, Martyn Green, Gig Young, Estelle Winwood, Margaret Hayes and Trevor Howard rounded out an excellent cast. The three Noel Coward plays, originally collected as *Tonight at 8:30* were *Red Peppers*, *Still Life*, and *Shadow Play*. The reviews were mixed.

RKO-Radio, in its last bid for quality stars and projects, proposed a script to Mae West entitled *The First Traveling Saleslady* (1956), but Miss West could not see making a comeback in this particular vehicle. Ginger accepted the assignment—for a reason known only to her—and looked becoming in the period clothes as a corset saleslady in the Old West. That is all that was good about this tedious, obvious and hackneyed film. The cast included Carol Channing, Barry Nelson, and two of television's brightest young Western heroes: James Arness and Clint Eastwood.

Ginger then reported to 20th Century-Fox for Edmund Goulding's *Teenage Rebel* (1956), which had been adapted from Edith Sommer's play *A Roomful of Roses*. Neither title made much sense, but the film was beautifully directed and superbly acted by Ginger, Michael Rennie, and a fine supporting cast.

Nunnally Johnson then cast her in his adaptation of Edward Chodorov's successful Broadway play *Oh, Men! Oh, Women!* (1957). It was given a lavish production and a big-name cast, but somehow the fun of the play was not there. This was to be her last released film for eight years.

In 1957 Kay Thompson helped Ginger whip up a nightclub act, ably assisted by The Toppers, which opened at the Havana Riviera, in Cuba. More than one customer took note that the act contained more Thompson than Rogers. Despite this, however, Ginger's act took her to the Hotel Sahara in Las Vegas. The customers seemed to love her 40-minute stint. It was also rumored that Ginger would sign for a year's run in the National Company of *The Bells Are Ringing*, but this venture never materialized.

Jacques Bergerac and Ginger were divorced on July 7, 1957 (he later married actress Dorothy Malone), and Ginger began getting involved with the straw-hat circuit around the country. In 1958, she successfully toured the summer circuits in John Van Druten's *Bell, Book and Candle*, thus providing the hinterlands with "star" glamour and quality. Her co-star was long-time friend William Marshall.

Meanwhile, Ginger busied herself with various television assignments. She did her own television spectacular and in 1958 did *The Ginger Rogers Show* for the Pontiac Parade of Stars. With her were Ray Bolger, the Ritz Brothers, and Nelson Riddle and his orchestra. The show was produced and directed by Bob Banner. Said Jack Gould in *The New York Times*:

> Miss Rogers always will be remembered for the motion pictures in which she danced with Fred Astaire . . . . Last night, in the company of Dante di Paolo, she re-created that mood of floating romance with great effectiveness. Her "Night and Day" dance was really delightful in its crisp delicacy. Moreover, Miss Rogers also manages to put over a song, perhaps not with the same melodic lilt as some others, but with a warm sincerity that is winning.

The following year she did a taped audition at NBC for a proposed half-hour weekly musical-variety show but the finished product, with Ricardo Montalban, did not pan out. Ginger then became one of television's busiest "guest stars" appearing innumerable times with Bob Hope, Dinah Shore, Perry Como, Steve Allen, Jack Benny and Pat Boone. Ginger even went "Western" on a *Zane Grey Theater* story.

Ginger returned to the stage in Leslie Stevens's Broadway-bound musical-comedy *The Pink Jungle* in 1959. An extensive tour began on the West Coast with Agnes Moorehead, Leif Erickson and Maggie Hayes in the cast. Vernon Duke wrote the music and lyrics, while Joseph Anthony directed. Jean Louis designed her gowns. The play had many holes that never seemed to get plugged, and never reached Broadway.

Ginger and William Marshall were married on March 17, 1961, and shortly thereafter they reactivated their tour of *Bell, Book and Candle*. Marshall previously had been wed to Michele Morgan and Micheline Presle. His sixteen-year old son was his best man. He was Ginger's fifth husband, and although their union was to last longer than her previous four mates, they were separated in 1969.

More big television shows followed. On October 22, 1960, Ginger and Perry Como joined Bob Hope for his comedy special *Potomac Madness*, a 60-minute taped musical with songs by Sammy Cahn and Jimmy Van Heusen. David Rose conducted. Ginger charmed the viewers with *I've Got Charm*, and, with Como and Hope, sang *Playing Politics* and *Where Else But in the U.S.A.?*

In 1961, at Fox, Ginger filmed a pilot for a situation comedy *Ginger Rogers Show*. She played twins, one a fashion designer, the other a newspaperwoman. Charles Ruggles played their uncle. Norman Z. McLeod directed and Valentine Davies wrote the script. William Self was executive producer. Cesare Danova and Gardner McKay were the guests. At the end, Ginger spoke about the series and told of its endless possibilities. It was a charming bit of frou-frou (and Ginger looked radiant to be sure), but the show was not picked up by a sponsor.

She appeared on the Bell Telephone Hour's *The Songs of Irving Berlin* on March 2, 1962, acting as hostess as well as singing and dancing. She was backed up by John Raitt, Johnny Desmond, Janet Blair, and Mindy Carson. Donald Voorhees conducted the show. Ginger sang *Let's Face the Music and Dance, Puttin' on the Ritz*, and *Steppin' Out With My Baby*.

Also on the agenda was an appearance on the *Red Skelton Show*, where in addition to clowning with Skelton, she did a medley of dances ending up with a terrific charleston.

Ginger toured the Southwest in *Annie Get Your Gun* and played *The Unsinkable Molly Brown* and later *Tovarich!* in Dallas with great success. In 1963, she played a brief engagement in Southern California in Whitfield Cook's play, *More Perfect Union*.

At this juncture, she and her husband got involved with film production in Jamaica, West Indies, where they independently filmed her seventy-second movie, *The Confession* (1964). William Dieterle replaced Victor Stoloff as director practically at the outset, but more

trouble was yet to come. The cast included Ray Milland, Walter Abel, and Cecil Kellaway and such unknowns as Barbara Eden, Michael Ansara, Pippa Scott, and Elliott Gould.

The entire affair was a total mess, and the production went through a great deal of legal hassle over "unauthorized editing," which delayed its commercial release. Ginger, of course, looked good in numerous outfits and got off a wisecrack or two, but, otherwise, was ineffectual as a madam in an Italian bordello.

The Confession was retitled *Seven Different Ways* and played a few honky-tonk theaters around the country, but never in major cities. Once Barbara Eden and Elliott Gould became known, it was again retitled, this time *Quick, Let's Get Married*, and traveled a similar route. It is still a bad picture and much too boring to be of any particular value.

In 1965, Ginger appeared in the Electronovision version of *Harlow*, which was filmed in a studio, like a live television show, in just seven days; It looked it! The quality of the print was grainy, as was the quality of the script, and a look of cheapness prevailed. An otherwise fine cast plodded through their roles with one aim in mind—to get it over with.

When *Harlow* opened in May 1965, critics had a field day. However, Judith Crist in her *New York Herald Tribune* review had this to say: "The only wholly successful performance in the film is given by Ginger Rogers as the gluttonous, self-centered mother. Looking both marvelously ravaged and lushly attractive, Miss Rogers survives the idiotic requirements of the script and makes us wish that she were doing more in movies—other movies, that is."

Back in 1957, CBS Television presented Rodgers and Hammerstein's *Cinderella* with Julie Andrews, Dorothy Stickney, Howard Lindsay, and an all-star cast. The show was recorded on Columbia Records but was not preserved for television. In 1965, CBS restaged the musical with Lesley Ann Warren as Cinderella, Stuart Damon as the Prince, Walter Pidgeon as the King, and Ginger as the Queen. Celeste Holm, Jo Van Fleet, Pat Carroll, and Barbara Ruick completed the new cast. It was a good production, but not as good as the original. It was rerun in 1971.

In July 1965, Ginger appeared on the Bob Hope Chrysler Theater in a suspense drama entitled *Terror Island* by Chester Krumholz. She seemd a little out of place, but the show was well received. The cast included Carol Lawrence, Donnelly Rhodes, Katharine Ross, and Abraham Sofaer. It was rerun in 1972.

Nancy Carroll and Ginger had been close friends ever since Nancy made *Scarlet Dawn* at Warners in 1932, at the time Ginger was making *You Said a Mouthful*. Nancy's close friend, Douglas Whitney, told me how Nancy was especially looking forward to seeing

With David Janssen and Barbara Stanwyck when Ginger won the *Photoplay* Magazine 1967 Editor's Award

Ginger in *Hello, Dolly!* On August 9, 1965, it was Ginger who went to see Nancy instead. Her friend had died three days earlier and was buried on the day Ginger was to open in *Dolly.* Ginger attended the funeral services in the afternoon and returned to Broadway that evening, replacing Carol Channing in the musical hit *Hello, Dolly!*

Ginger stayed in the show for eighteen and one-half months as the toast of Broadway and later toured with the show for one year.

John Canaday, the musical critic of *The New York Times*, found Ginger

a sweet and wonderful Dolly Gallagher Levi in her first performance of that role before an audience. The audience put on a pretty good performance itself, greeting with such a loving ovation that she could have lived on it for the rest of the evening. But she didn't have to. The audience kept it up and she kept giving them good reason. . . . *Hello Dolly!* is a wonderful showcase for any star, and as a

showcase for the eccentric, strident genius of Carol Channing it suffered, overall, from a kind of central violence that laid everything else low before it. Miss Rogers's quieter performance keeps everything in key, and *Hello, Dolly!* is much closer to *The Matchmaker* than it was.

The night I saw her, you could feel the warmth and affection between audience and star. It was an experience in the theater that does not happen often. The people loved her and Ginger loved the people, and even when she teased into a "little" step or two (with no intentions of going much further), the crowd ate it up. She was something else.

During and after *Dolly*, Ginger appeared on more television programs. *The Ed Sullivan Show* beckoned, as did *The David Frost Show.* More recently, she shared the spotlight with Merv Griffin as his co-hostess. *The Dean Martin Show, Here's Lucy* and *Hollywood Squares* have kept her busy during the last year.

Ginger returned to London, where she had appeared on BBC–TV in the late fifties in Eric Maschwitz's and Hans May's *Carissima*, which had failed miserably. This time, she came to open the London company of Angela Lansbury's notable success, *Mame*, the musical version of Patrick Dennis's *Auntie Mame*. She opened at the Drury Lane Theatre in London's West End on February 20, 1969, with a cast that included Margaret Courtenay, Barry Kent, and Ann Beach. It was one of London's biggest theatrical events of the season. Ginger was the highest paid star in British theatrical history—£5,000 per week.

Irving Wardle, in his London *Times* review reported that "she glows and radiates a blend of sensual magic and athletic power of a kind I have never seen before in one performer." She stayed on in London after the close of *Mame* because there was talk of two different films that producers wanted her to make, but nothing came of these projects.

Ginger ventured into the world of television commercials in 1970. She first did a perfume-gram bit for Western Union and then did a music pitch for *Music of the 30's* for Columbia House.

Recently, Ginger has had a successful straw-hat tour of *Coco*, the Alan Jay Lerner-Andre Previn show that Katharine Hepburn did so beautifully on Broadway. Ginger's interpretation was less strident, but still full of energetic bazazz.

On November 14, 1971, Ginger joined Ethel Merman and Benny Goodman for a benefit called "The Gershwin Years" at Philharmonic Hall, Lincoln Center. The proceeds were equally divided between the American Academy of Dramatic Arts and the George Junior Republic. Ginger sang *But Not for Me* and *Embraceable You*, and Ethel belted out *I Got Rhythm*. Benny Goodman and his current sextet played a mixture of Gershwin tunes. All this—just forty-one years after Ginger, Ethel, and Benny were at the Alvin Theatre in *Girl Crazy*.

In 1972, as part of the dedicatory production festivities, Ginger played the traditionally male role of the Stage Manager in Thornton Wilder's *Our Town* on April 24–29 for the benefit opening of the Ida Green Communications Center of Austin College, Sherman, Texas, sixty miles north of Dallas.

She added another career to her already impressive list when, in the great tradition of Joan Crawford and Cary Grant, she became fashion consultant to the nationwide J. C. Penney chain. Ginger visits some of this chain's 1,700 stores across the country with a twenty-piece wardrobe.

Whatever her future holds for her, Ginger always approaches each new venture with wide-eyed enthusiasm and awareness. Her girlish energy seems to infect everyone around her. It seems doubtful that she will make another film, in view of the fact that the show-everything, say-everything school of moviemaking, sadly, has replaced all of the richness that Hollywood helped create, but she has her memories of those days, and we have our memories of her.

With fashion coordinator Lois Ziegler in her new role as fashion consultant for the J. C. Penney Company

Gallery of Portraits

The Short Films

In *Campus Sweethearts* with Jane and Joe McKenna, Rudy Vallee, and Joey Ray

AS A DIRECT RESULT of her vaudeville tours in 1925 and 1926, Ginger was signed to a three-year contract with Paramount to appear in vaudeville sketches for the then-famous stage shows in Paramount theaters throughout the major cities of the U.S. In 1929, when talkies were definitely here to stay, Ginger began appearing in short subjects for numerous releasing units in the East. Most of these shorts were rehashes of vaudeville routines with added songs and dances.

It is estimated that Ginger appeared in approximately a dozen such films during the period 1929–1931 while she was beginning to make a name for herself on the stage and in feature motion pictures. Besides these story-line shorts, Ginger—like her contemporaries—appeared in compilation films, trailers for charities, candid shorts, and wartime service shorts. This is not a complete listing of Miss Rogers' short subjects (she appeared in at least one Paramount-Christie Comedy which has been difficult to track down) but it is hoped that all her major ones are here.

CAMPUS SWEETHEARTS.   (Radio Pictures). July 1929. 2 reels. Directed by Leo Meehan. Music Arranged and Conducted by Alfred Sherman. Art Director: Ernest Fegte.

Cast: Rudy Vallee, Joe and Jane McKenna, Joey Ray, Leon Leonard, Ginger Rogers, Anne Franklin and Joe Sawyer. The first picture (filmed at the Gramercy RCA Phototone Studios in New York) to be made in the Spoor Berggren three-dimensional widescope 70 millimeter film.

A NIGHT IN A DORMITORY.   (Pathe). September 1929. 2 reels. Produced and Directed by Harry Delmar. Production Supervisor: Philip Tannura. Written by Benny Ryan. Edited by E. Pfitzenmeier. (A Melody Comedy).

Cast: Ginger Rogers, Morgan Morley (also known as Si Wills, Joan Davis's husband), Ruth Hamilton, Thelma White, and Eddie Elkins and his orchestra. Musical numbers: *Stay With It, Song of the Volga; I Love a Man in a Uniform; Where the Sweet Forget-Me-Nots Remember; Why Can't You Love That Way;* and *Dormitory Number.* The adventures of a schoolgirl in a nightclub as related by her to her dormitory sisters. Ginger sang two songs.

A DAY OF A MAN OF AFFAIRS.   (Columbia). November 1929. 1 reel. Directed by Basil Smith. Written by Paul Porter. A Columbia-Victor Gems short subject (produced by Columbia Pictures Corp. and the Victor Company).

Cast: Maurice Holland, Ginger Rogers and Mell Ray.

In an unknown short subject circa 1929

In one of the Paramount-Christie comedies, 1930

40

OFFICE BLUES. (Paramount). November 1930. 1 reel. Directed by Mort Blumenstock. Written by Walton Butterfield. Music and lyrics by Vernon Duke and E.Y. Harburg. Orchestrations and vocal arrangements by John W. (Johnny) Green. Ensemble staged by Maria Gambarelli.

Cast: Ginger Rogers, Clayborne Bryson, and E.R. Rogers. Ginger plays a secretary in love with her young boss, who does not seem to show any interest in her. She ignores an office admirer and while at work indulges in fanciful daydreams. Eventually she discovers that the boss had his eye on her all the time. Ginger sang *We Can't Get Along* and *Dear Sir*. Clayborne Bryson sang *Dear Miss*.

HOLLYWOOD ON PARADE, NO. 1. (Paramount-Publix). July 1932. 10 min. Produced by Lewis Lewyn. A series of revues featuring movie, stage and radio personalities. Fredric March was master of ceremonies. Mitzi Green sang *Was That the Human Thing to Do?* while Ginger and Jack Oakie did a burlesque number, *The Girl Who Used to Be You.* The Brox Sisters did a triple imitation of Dietrich singing *Falling in Love Again.* Eddie Peabody did the finale with a group of banjo-playing girls.

SCREEN SNAPSHOTS. (Columbia). August 1932. A bevy of stars appear at the rodeo: Hoot Gibson, Ginger Rogers, Mary Pickford, William Powell, Tom Mix, Sally Eilers, Mitzi Green, Jackie Searl, Lew Cody, William S. Hart, Tim McCoy, Billie Dove, Clark Gable, Joan Crawford, Will Rogers, Mary Brian, Lina Basquette, Lois Wilson, and Dorothy Jordan.

HOLLYWOOD ON PARADE, NO. 9. (Paramount-Publix). April 1933. Produced by Louis Lewyn. In the studio of artist Willy Pogany, portraits on the wall come to life. Johnny Mack Brown, Harry Green, Bebe Daniels, and Mary Pickford (accepting the honor of being the grand marshal of the 44th Annual Tournament of Roses.) John Boles, Buster Collier, and Robert

In *A Day of a Man of Affairs* with Maurice Holland

With Clayborne Bryson in *Office Blues*

In *Hollywood on Parade, No. 9.* with all the other 1933 Wampas Baby Stars. Seated: Dorothy Wilson, Mary Carlisle, Lona Andre, Eleanor Holm, and Dorothy Layton. Standing: Toshia Mori, Boots Mallory, Ruth Hall, Gloria Stuart, Patricia Ellis, Lilian Bond, Evalyn Knapp, and Marion Shockley

In Office Blues

With Clayborne Bryson in Office Blues

Woolsey did a vaudeville routine. Then the 1932 Wampas Baby Stars each spoke to the camera: Ruth Hall, Patricia Ellis, Lilian Bond, Boots Mallory, Dorothy Layton, Dorothy Wilson, Mary Carlisle, Marion Shockley, Toshia Mori, Gloria Stuart, Eleanor Holm, Ginger Rogers, Lona Andre, and Evalyn Knapp.

HOLIDAY GREETINGS. (1937) from many stars appeared on the screen for Christmas and New Years at theaters all over the United States. Besides director Cecil B. DeMille, the following appeared: Carole Lombard, Ginger Rogers, Gary Cooper, Gene Autry, John Boles, and Bob Burns.

PICTURE PEOPLE, NO. 1. (RKO-Radio). No Date. 10 min. Cinema celebrities caught in a candid mood included Ginger Rogers, Stuart Erwin, June Collyer, Jean Parker, Jack Oakie, Dick Powell, Henry Fonda, and Bob Hope.

SAFEGUARDING MILITARY INFORMATION. (Dept. of the Army). No Date. 10 min. In this army training film, Ginger appeared with Walter Huston.

SHOW BUSINESS AT WAR. (The March of Time: Issue #10; Volume IX). 20th Century-Fox. 1943. 23 min. Compilation film concerning stars entertaining, or working toward entertaining, U.S. servicemen; radio broadcasts, troop shows, the two Canteens (Hollywood and New York) were covered. Ginger Rogers, Humphrey Bogart, Bette Davis, James Cagney, Rita Hayworth, Myrna Loy, Kay Francis, Frank Sinatra, Alexis Smith, Gertrude Lawrence, the Mills Brothers, Jack Benny, Bob Hope, Fred MacMurray, and Ginny Simms.

BATTLE STATIONS. (20th Century-Fox). 1943–4. Produced for the U.S. Coast Guard. 9 min. Music played by the Manhattan Beach Coast Guard Band. About the SPARS, the women's Coast Guard, illustrating the fact that women were taking over more jobs previously held by men during World War II. Music by Vernon Duke. Narrators: James Cagney and Ginger Rogers.

GINGER ROGERS FINDS A BARGAIN. No Date. A 5-minute trailer for the Fourth War Loan Drive.

Filmography

Young Man of Manhattan A Paramount Picture, 1930

With Claudette Colbert, Norman Foster, and John MacDowell

CAST: Claudette Colbert, (Ann Vaughn); Norman Foster, (Toby McLean); Ginger Rogers, (Puff Randolph); Charles Ruggles, (Shorty Ross); Leslie Austin, (Dwight Knowles); The 4 Aalbu Sisters: Lorraine, Aileen, Fern & Harriet Aalbu, (Sherman Sisters); H. Dudley Hawley, (Doctor); Tommy Reilly, (Referee); with John Mac-Dowell

CREDITS: Director, Monta Bell; Scenarist, Robert Presnell; Dialogue Director, Daniel Reed. Novel by Katherine Brush. Photographer, Larry Williams; Art Director, William Saulter; Editor, Emma Hill; Sound Recorder, Ernest F. Zatorsky; Musical Director, David Mendoza; Costumer, Caroline Putnam; Hair Stylist, Fred Graf; Casting, Frank Heath.

SONGS: *I've Got 'It' But 'It' Don't Do Me No Good, I'll Bob Up With The Bob-O-Link, Good 'N' Plenty, If You Can Just Forgive and Forget,* by Irving Kahal, Pierre Norman, Sammy Fain.

SYNOPSIS: Metropolitan newspaper people at work and at play. Puff Randolph, a charming, wisecracking flapper, has a hard time getting her reporter-boyfriend, Shorty Ross, to think about her instead of his assignments at sporting events.

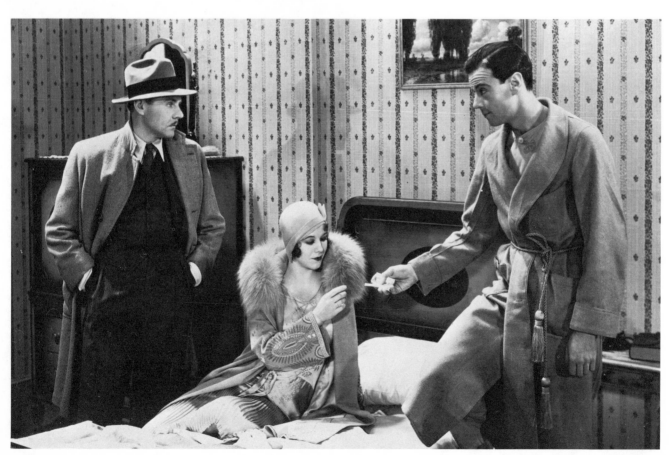

With Charles Ruggles and Norman Foster

REVIEWS

"Ginger Rogers, as Puff, is not quite as addle-brained as she might be but is diverting nonetheless."

Motion Picture Herald

"Charles Ruggles and Ginger Rogers, a newcomer, both also do excellent work."

Screen Play

"Ginger Rogers does the best she can with a flapper role. Miss Rogers is not exactly a century plant, but she is more than 16, and is miscast, though she makes much of the part."

Zit's Weekly

". . . And you simply must see Ginger Rogers and Charles Ruggles; they alone are worth the admission fee!"

Movies

"Ginger Roger's Puff Randolph out Kaned Helen at her best. She came within an ace of purloining the picture and filching the film."

Hollywood Filmograph

"Monta Bell's direction is splendid—there are delightful touches and he has directed the players most intelligently . . . . Ginger Rogers in her interpretation of a modern flapper who talks baby-talk will make a big hit. She is not annoying like Helen Kane, the Boop-A-Doop lady. Ginger Rogers makes no effort to be cute—but gives a legitimate characterization of a predatory college girl."

The Film Mercury

" . . . Ginger Rogers, in the part of Puff, the young girl who chases Toby about with 'irritating regularity' . . . . is attractive and bright and sings well."

Mordaunt Hall
The New York Times

NOTES: While appearing on Broadway in Kalmar and Ruby's musical-comedy *Top Speed,* Ginger began her film career on a Paramount sound stage in Astoria, Queens, as the sassy flapper Puff Randolph in *Young Man of Manhattan.* Although the stars were Claudette Colbert and her husband, Norman Foster, Ginger made a vivid impression in her scenes with Charles Ruggles making flip wisecracks like "Cigarette me, Big Boy!" and a cute song, *I've Got 'It' But 'It' Don't Do Me No Good.*

Director Monta Bell shot the exterior scenes in and around New York City and added pace and dash to an otherwise routine newspaper yarn. The film was punctuated with newsreel shots of sporting events, like the Dempsey-Tunney fight, to lend authenticity.

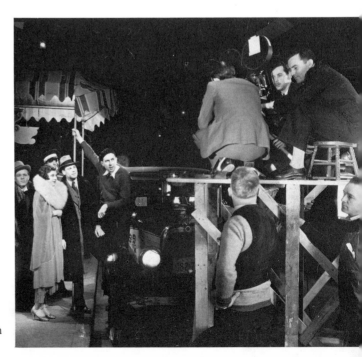

Location shooting in New York City with John MacDowell, Norman Foster, director Monta Bell (in beret), and production crew

Queen High A Paramount Picture, 1930

CAST: Charles Ruggles, (T. Boggs Johns); Frank Morgan, (Mr. Nettleton); Ginger Rogers, (Polly Rockwell); Stanley Smith, (Dick Johns); Helen Carrington, (Mrs. Nettleton); Rudy Cameron, (Cyrus Vanderholt); Betty Garde, (Florence Cole); Theresa Maxwell Conover, (Mrs. Rockwell); Nina Olivette, (Coddles), Tom Brown, (Jimmy); Edith Sheldon, (Dancer); with Theresa Klee and Dorothy Walters

CREDITS: Director, Fred Newmeyer; Producers, Lawrence Schwab & Frank Mandel; Scenarist, Frank Mandel; Dialogue, Frank Mandel; Dialogue Director, Daniel Reed. Based on the play *A Pair of Sixes* by Edward H. Peple. Adapted from the musical comedy by Lawrence Schwab, Lewis Gensler, B.G. DeSylva. Photographer, William Steiner; Operating Cameraman, George Weber; Art Director, William Saulter; Editor, Barney Rogan; Editorial Supervisor, James Sweeney; Sound Recorder, C.A. Tuthill; Synchronizer & Score Supervisor, Max Manne; Musical Arrangements, Johnny Green; Musical Director, Al Goodman; Costumer, Caroline Putnam; Hair Stylist, Fred Graf.

SONGS: *Everything Will Happen for the Best*, by B.G. DeSylva, Lewis Gensler; *Brother, Just Laugh It Off* by Arthur Schwartz, Ralph Rainger; *It Seems to Me* by Dick Howard, Ralph Rainger; *I Love the Girls in My Own Peculiar Way*, by E.Y. Harburg, Henry Souvain; *I'm Afraid of You* by Dick Howard, Ralph Rainger

SYNOPSIS: T. Boggs Johns and Nettleton, partners in a garter business, are constantly unable to agree about their business affairs. To settle their differences, they play a hand of draw poker. The winner manages the business for one year; the loser becomes his personal servant.

REVIEWS

"Ginger Rogers, who has obvious intelligence, though she is not always exactly cast, lends spirited aid in this melange of music, her first endeavour being when she bursts into rhythmic melody in the office of Nettleton and Johns to the terpsichorean accompaniment of the very scantily robed mannequins of the garter department."

Today's Cinema

"Fred Newmeyer, who directed several of Harold Lloyd's comedies, has handled the scenes of this production in an effective fashion . . . . Miss Rogers does nicely by her role and Stanley Smith serves his part satisfactorily. The singing of these two is a good deal better than that in the average musical film."

Mordaunt Hall
The New York Times

NOTES: Ginger's second film again teamed her with Charles Ruggles, but this time she was little more than the romantic young ingenue opposite Stanley Smith. Together, the pair sang *I'm Afraid of You* and *It Seems to Me*, while Ginger and Frank Morgan sang *Everything Will Happen for the Best* and *Brother, Just Laugh It Off*.

Based on the play and musical comedy, *A Pair of Sixes, Queen High* was just a filmed stage play. Frank Mandel's stale screenplay and Fred Newmeyer's pedestrian direction were a definite handicap for the actors. Charles Ruggles and Nina Olivette were in the stage production, which advance publicity said would be filmed entirely in Technicolor.

With Rudy Cameron

With Nina Olivette and Stanley Smith

With Charles Ruggles and Stanley Smith

47

With Jack Oakie

The Sap from Syracuse
A Paramount Picture, 1930

With Jack Oakie and George Barbier

CAST: Jack Oakie, (Littleton Looney); Ginger Rogers, (Ellen Saunders); Granville Bates, (Nycross); George Barbier, (Senator Powell); Sidney Riggs, (Nick Pangolos); Betty Starbuck, (Flo Goodrich); Verree Teasdale, (Dolly Clark); J. Malcolm Dunn, (Captain Barker); Bernard Jukes, (Bells); Walter Fenner, (Henderson); Jack Daley (Hopkins); with Kathryn Reese

CREDITS: Director, A. Edward Sutherland; Scenarist, Gertrude Purcell; Dialogue Director, Daniel Reed; Based on the play by John Wray, Jack O'Donnell, and John Hayden. Photographer, Larry Williams; Art Director, William Saulter; Editor, Helene Turner; Sound Recorder, Edwin Schabbehar; Musical Arrangements, Johnny Green; Ginger Roger's Costumes, Aileen Hamilton; Hair Stylist, Fred Graf; Script Girl, Eve St. John.

SONGS: *Ah, What's the Use, How I Wish I Could Sing a Love Song, Capitalize That Thing Called IT,* by E.Y. Harburg, Johnny Green

SYNOPSIS: Littleton Looney, a day laborer on the Erie Canal, boards a liner for Europe and is mistaken by all the passengers for a prominent mining engineer, reportedly traveling incognito. Enjoying the adulation he receives, he has the time of his life chasing heiress Ellen Saunders around the deck. In the pursuit, he foils two crooks trying to get her out of the way, and finally wins her love.

REVIEWS

"The love interest is Ginger Rogers, very competent ingenue. She is traveling to Macedonia to inspect her gigantic mining properties. She mistakes Oakie for a mining engineer or something of the sort and expects him to save her mines from the Octopodean clutches of her guardian."

Douglas Hodges
Motion Picture Herald

"Ginger Rogers gets her first real chance in this picture."

Zit's Weekly

"One of the saving graces of the picture is the charming personality of Ginger Rogers whose performance is flawless in every detail. When Paramount acquired the services of this youthful stage star the studio scored a beat on other film producers. However, Miss Rogers is little known to Western film fans, but it is the prediction of the writer that she will soon become a popular screen player with the movie folks on the Coast."

Eddie Granville
Hollywood Daily Screen World

NOTES: In her third picture, Ginger had a much bigger part, but the singing was left to Jack Oakie and Betty Starbuck (who gave punch to *Capitalize That Thing Called IT* by E.Y. Harburg and Johnny Green). The leading role of Ellen Saunders, a millionaire's daughter, required that Ginger merely be charming and pretty, which she did with ease. The comedy and the wisecracks were all left to Oakie.

The Sap from Syracuse, an average Oakie picture, was well directed by A. Edward Sutherland, who did the best he could to breathe life into Gertrude Purcell's limp script. When released in England, it was called *The Sap from Abroad*.

With Jack Oakie

Follow the Leader

A Paramount Picture, 1930

CAST: Ed Wynn, (Crickets); Ginger Rogers, (Mary Brennan); Stanley Smith, (Jimmie Moore); Lou Holtz, (Sam Platz); Lida Kane, (Ma Brennan); Ethel Merman, (Helen King); Bobby Watson, (George White); Donald Kirke, (R.C. Black); William Halligan, (Bob Sterling); Holly Hall, (Fritzie Devere); Preston Foster, (Two-Gun Terry); James C. Morton, (Mickie); Tammany Young, (Bull); Jack La Rue, William Gargan, (Hoods); with Bill Black, Richard Scott, Jules Epailly, C. Henderson.

CREDITS: Director, Norman Taurog; Scenarists, Gertrude Purcell, Sid Silvers, Dialogue Director, Al Parker. Based on the play *Manhattan Mary* by William K. Wells, George White, Lew Brown, B.G. DeSylva, and Ray Henderson. Photographer, Larry Williams; Art Director, William Saulter; Editor, Barney Rogan; Sound Recorder, Ernest Zatorsky; Musical Arrangements, Johnny Green; Music Score, Max Manne, Adolph Deutsch; Costumer, Caroline Putnam; Hair Stylist, Fred Graf; Assistant Director, Richard Blaydon.

SONGS: *Broadway (The Heart of the World),* by Lew Brown, B.G. DeSylva, and Ray Henderson. *Satan's Holiday,* by Irving Kahal, Sammy Fain.

SYNOPSIS: Against a gangster background, Crickets, a waiter, struggles to obtain theatrical fame for his employer's daughter. When Helen King, the star of a show, is kidnapped, pert Mary Brennan replaces her.

NOTES: Based on George White's 1927 musical comedy, *Manhattan Mary, Follow the Leader* was revamped for the movies as an Ed Wynn comedy, unfortunately without the music from the play. Wynn re-created the role he did on Broadway, while Ginger played the part Ona Munson originated. Lou Holtz also repeated his Broadway assignment.

One of Paramount's best directors, Norman Taurog, filmed this tiresome comedy in Astoria from a screenplay by Gertrude Purcell and Sid Silvers. He shouldn't have bothered.

Ginger again was cast as the sweet young thing and was totally wasted. Her voice was high-pitched and she was not particularly well photographed. Ethel Merman, who was a last-minute replacement for Ruth Etting, did a jazzy rendition of Irving Kahal and Sammy Fain's *Satan's Holiday.* It is interesting to note that when the film was released (December 1930), Ginger and Ethel were together on Broadway in *Girl Crazy.*

With Ed Wynn

With Lida Kane

With Ed Wynn and Stanley Smith

Honor among Lovers A Paramount Picture, 1931

With Charles Ruggles and Avonne Taylor

CAST: Claudette Colbert, (Julia Traynor); Fredric March, (Jerry Stafford); Monroe Owsley, (Philip Craig); Charles Ruggles, (Monty Dunn); Ginger Rogers, (Doris Blake); Avonne Taylor, (Maybelle); Pat O'Brien (Conroy); Janet McLeary, (Margaret); John Kearney, (Inspector); Ralph Morgan, (Riggs); Jules Epailly, (Louis); Leonard Carey, (Butler); with Grace Kern, Roberta Beatty, Charles Halton, Granville Bates, Si Wills, Betty Morrissey, Dr. Nathan Rozofsky.

CREDITS: Director, Dorothy Arzner; Scenarists, Austin Parker, Gertrude Purcell. Based on a story by Austin Parker. Writer of French version, Peggy Thompson; Photographer, George Folsey; Art Directors, Charles Kirk, J. Franklin Whitman; Editor, Helene Turner; Sound Recorder, C.A. Tuthill; Musical Arrangements, Johnny Green; Costumer, Caroline Putnam; Assistant Director, Arthur Jacobson; Script Girl, Pat Donahue.

SYNOPSIS: Business executive Jerry Stafford loses the love of his pretty secretary, Julia Traynor, to another man, but later gets her back when it becomes apparent that her choice was an unfortunate one. Her girlfriend, Doris Blake, loves reporter Monty Dunn and follows him everywhere.

REVIEWS

"Claudette Colbert and Fredric March in the leading roles have been provided with ideal roles and give finished performances. Other outstanding players are Charles Ruggles and Ginger Rogers."

Motion Picture Herald

"Mr. March makes his part as believable as it is humanly possible. Mr. Ruggles furnished some good comedy when he had the opportunity. Mr. Owsley does good work and Miss Colbert is excellent."

Mordaunt Hall
The New York Times

NOTES: Dorothy Arzner, who was a hit-and-miss director, chalked up another *miss* with *Honor among Lovers,* despite a talented cast: Claudette Colbert, Fredric March, Charles Ruggles and Pat O'Brien, all of whom, like Ginger, went on to become Hollywood stars. However, it was Monroe Owsley who fared well in this sentimental slush, which was simultaneously shot in French and Spanish versions.

Most of the action revolved around Colbert and March, with Ginger and Charles Ruggles around for those occasional breaks in the tension, better known as "comic relief." This trifle had three working titles: *Strictly Business, Sex in Business,* and *Another Man's Wife.*

With Charles Ruggles

The Tip Off

An RKO-Pathe Picture, 1931

CAST: Eddie Quillan, (Tommy); Robert Armstrong, (Kayo McClure); Ginger Rogers, (Baby Face); Joan Peers, (Edna); Ralf Harolde, (Nick Vatelli); Charles Sellon, (Pop Jackson); Mike Donlin, (Swanky); Ernie Adams, (Slug); Jack Herrick, (Joe); Cupid Ainsworth, (Miss Waddums); Frank Darien, (Edna's Uncle); Luis Alberni, (Roadhouse Manager); Ivan Linow, (Kayo's Sparring Partner); Dorothy Granger, (Hatcheck Girl); with John Quillan, Tommy Jordan, Edna Moreno, Swanky Jones

CREDITS: Director, Albert Rogell; Producer, Charles R. Rogers; Associate Producer, Harry Joe Brown; Scenarist, Earl Baldwin; Based on an original story by George Kibbe Turner; Dialogue Director, Ralph Murphy; Photographer, Edward Snyder; Art Director, Carroll Clark; Editor, Charles Craft; Sound Recorders, Charles O'Loughlin, T. Carman; Musical Director, Arthur Lange; Costumer, Gwen Wakeling; Assistant Director, E.J. Babille.

SYNOPSIS: Tommy, an easygoing radio mechanic, blunders into a romance with gangster Nick Vatelli's girl, Edna, but manages to elude danger after he wins the friendship of prizefighter Kayo McClure and his sassy girlfriend, Baby Face.

REVIEWS

"Eddie Quillan will crawl right under your skin like a pet habit . . . . The feminine side is ably upheld by winsome Ginger Rogers and Joan Peers."

Motion Picture Herald

"Ginger Rogers is all that she should be as little spitfire 'Baby Face.'"

Zit's Weekly

"The effervescent Mr. Quillan is completely amusing in his portrayal of starry-eyed innocence. Ginger Rogers makes a clever foil for the comedians in the role of Baby Face. Albert Rogell, the director, deserves a word for the smart pace of the story."

A.D.S.
The New York Times

NOTES: Ginger, who had not been properly utilized at Paramount, got a release from her contract and went straight to RKO-Pathe. *The Tip Off*, her first film after the change, offered her a delightful part as Baby Face. Her sense of humor and well-placed wisecracks helped keep this little comedy moving.

Eddie Quillan and Robert Armstrong were a good screen team and were a pleasure to watch in this flick. Albert Rogell directed with verve. The working titles were *The Lady Killer* and *Eddie Cuts In*.

With Robert Armstrong

With Eddie Quillan and Robert Armstrong

With Robert Armstrong

With Eddie Quillan and Robert Armstrong

Suicide Fleet

A RKO-Pathe Picture, 1931

With Robert Armstrong, James Gleason, and William Boyd

CAST: William Boyd, (Baltimore Clark); Robert Armstrong, (Dutch Herman); James Gleason, (Skeets O'Riley); Ginger Rogers, (Sally); Harry Bannister, (Commander); Frank Reicher, (Captain Holtzmann); Ben Alexander, (Kid, the Lookout); Henry Victor, (Captain Von Schlettow); Hans Joby, (Schwartz); Yola D'Avril, Nanette Faro, (French Girls in Tangiers); James Pierce, (Recruit); Harry Tenbrook, (Jim, Shore Patrolman [Tangiers]); Charles Sullivan, (Sullivan, Sailor); John Kelly, Charles Delaney, (Sailors at Sally's); Tom Keene, (Officer); Harry Strans, (Shore Patrolman [Havana]); Joe Dominguez, Harry Semels, (Havana Merchants); James Burtis, (Sailor).

CREDITS: Director, Albert Rogell; Producer, Charles R. Rogers; Associate Producer, Harry Joe Brown; Scenarist, Lew Lipton. Based on the story *Mystery Ship* by Commander Herbert A. Jones, U.S.N.. Dialogue, F. McGrew Wills; Photographer, Sol Polito; Art Director, Carroll Clark; Editor, Joe Kane; Sound Recorder, Denzil A. Cutler; Musical Director, Arthur Lange; Costumer, Gwen Wakeling; Assistant Director, Jay Marchand; Technical Advisers, Captain W.L. Friedell, Walter Fritzsche.

SYNOPSIS: At sea, seamen Baltimore, Dutch, and Skeets are involved with an American-manned decoy ship, which eventually aids in the demolition of German submarines. On shore, all seek the affection of pert Sally, who works on Coney Island's midway.

REVIEWS

"*Suicide Fleet* tells a story of action at sea and love at home. The romantic element, while woven through the entire story, yet is incidental. Ginger Rogers was well received for her work."

Motion Picture Herald

"The story's about three gobs, who are all that way about the same girl, cute, pert little Ginger Rogers. While the film's not great, it fills in beautifully for an evening's entertainment."

Movie Mirror

"Comedy-drama of surprisingly un-robust proportions . . . . Bill Boyd maintains a wooden dignity in his part, giving a most uninspiring portrayal, while Ginger Rogers is cute enough in the few reels in which she appears."

Zit's Weekly

NOTES: Commander Herbert A. Jones's story *Mystery Ship* was the basis for this rough-and-ready actioner. William Boyd, Robert Armstrong, and James Gleason camped around a great deal with a less than adequate script while Ginger, as Sally, the Salt Water Taffy girl on shore, sang (without the benefit of musical background), *Cream Kisses Only a Dime*.

Albert Rogell handled the directorial chores with little imagination, but Sol Polito contributed some fine shots of New York and Coney Island. It was minor fare indeed, but pleasant entertainment.

With James Gleason and Robert Armstrong

Carnival Boat

A RKO-Pathe Picture, 1932

CAST: William Boyd, (Buck Gannon); Ginger Rogers, (Honey); Fred Kohler, (Hack); Hobart Bosworth, (Gannon); Marie Prevost, (Babe); Edgar Kennedy, (Baldy); Harry Sweet, (Stubby); Charles Sellon, (Lane); Walter Percival, (DeLacey); Jack Carlyle, (DeLacey's Assistant); Joe Marba, (Windy); Eddie Chandler, (Jordan); Bob Perry, (Bartender); James Mason, Charles Sullivan (Loggers); Hal Price, (Observer); with Sam Harris

CREDITS: Director, Albert Rogell; Associate Producer, Harry Joe Brown; Scenarist, James Seymour. Based on a story by Marion Jackson and Don Ryan. Photographer, Ted McCord; Art Director, Carroll Clark; Editor, John Link; Sound Recorder, L. John Myers; Musical Director, Arthur Lange; Costumer, Gwen Wakeling; Assistant Director, Frank Shaw; Still Photographer, Adolph L. Schafer.

With William Boyd

SONGS: *How I Could Go for You* by Bernie Grossman and Howard Lewis. *Run Around* (cut from released print) by Max Steiner.

SYNOPSIS: Honey, a perky young entertainer from a carnival boat, comes between handsome lumberjack Buck Gannon and his domineering father, who hopes his son will take over as manager of a profitable lumber camp.

REVIEWS

"This fast-moving story of a life in a logging camp, the first of its type since talking pictures were introduced, is a splendid film offering Bill Boyd, Hobart Bosworth and Ginger Rogers, and an interesting sight of actual happenings in the land of the big trees. It is a picture well worth seeing . . . . Ginger Rogers shows a new flair for dramatics."

J.C. McNeil
Winnipeg Free-Press

"Boyd, no longer the insufferable smart aleck, plays sincerely, with Ginger Rogers seen to better advantage as the girl from the boat than in her earlier screen efforts. The acting average of the entire cast is unusually good; a well-directed performance which does much to help over a plot which has been developed with plenty of action and better than usual dialogue. The photography is excellent and the sound matches it."

Variety

NOTES: Albert Rogell directed Ginger for the third time in this two-fisted tale of lumberjacks, which was shot on location at Sugar Pine Hill in the High Sierras. Again, action and fast-paced direction dominated the film, but Ginger, as Honey, a snappy little carnival-boat entertainer, added plenty of zest and charm throughout.

Her rendition of *How I Could Go for You* was delightful. Originally called *Timber Beast* and then *Bad Timber, Carnival Boat* remains a good little actioner with some beautiful location photography by Ted McCord.

With William Boyd and Hobart Bosworth

With Hobart Bosworth, William Boyd, Fred Kohler, Marie Prevost, Edgar Kennedy, and Harry Sweet

Singing *How I Could Go for You*

The Tenderfoot

A First National & Vitaphone Picture, 1932

CAST: Joe E. Brown, (Peter Jones); Ginger Rogers, (Ruth); Lew Cody, (Joe Lehman); Vivien Oakland, (Miss Martin); Robert Greig, (Mack); Spencer Charters, (Oscar); Ralph Ince, (Dolan); Marion "Peanuts" Byron, (Kitty); Douglas Gerrard, (Stage Director); Walter Percival, (Depot Slicker); Wilfred Lucas, (Patterson); George Chandler, (Depot Bum); Jill Dennett, (Cafe Cashier); Mae Madison, (Cafe Maid); John Larkin, (Depot Porter); Harry Seymour, (Newsstand Proprietor); Zita Moulton, Charlotte Merriam, (Actresses); Theodore Lorch, Allan Lane, (Actors); Richard Cramer, (Racketeer); Joe Barton, (The Hebrew); Edith Allen, (Tart at Depot); Lee Kohlmar, (Waiter).

CREDITS: Director, Ray Enright; Scenarists, Arthur Caesar, Monty Banks, Earl Baldwin; Based on the story by Richard Carle. Based on the play *The Butter and Egg Man* by George S. Kaufman. Photographer, Gregg Toland; Art Director, Esdras Hartley; Editor, Owen Marks; Makeup Artist, Perc Westmore; Still Photographer, Scotty Welbourne.

SYNOPSIS: Young stenographer Ruth discovers that her boss, Joe Lehman, is about to swindle mild Texas cowboy Peter Jones out of a fortune. She comes to his aid, and he eventually pulls a successful *coup d'etat*, producing *Her Golden Sin* with her in the lead.

With Joe E. Brown, Lew Cody, and Robert Greig

REVIEWS

"George S. Kaufman's gimlet-like wit in his stage comedy, *The Butter and Egg Man*, is knocked sky-high in the screen version, and in its place is blacksmithean buffoonery . . . . Mr. Brown gives quite a humorous showing in some of the sequences. Ginger Rogers impersonates the loyal and loving stenographer in an acceptable fashion. Lew Cody portrays Sam Lehman, an impecunious theatrical producer, quite competently. Vivien Oakland makes the most of the role of the stellar light of *Her Golden Sin*, and Ralph Ince is effective as Dolan."

Mordaunt Hall
The New York Times

"Ginger Rogers is the heart appeal. Her work is outstanding; she takes acting honors next to Brown."

Hollywood Herald

"Chiefly aiding Brown are Ginger Rogers, attractive, always appealing, doing well, although her role calls for but little real effort."

Motion Picture Herald

NOTES: Ginger Rogers again found herself as a romantic leading lady opposite a comedian in this film. This time it was Joe E. Brown, one of the biggest money-making comics of the early talkies. His appeal was widespread and Ginger needed exposure of this kind.

The Tenderfoot was loosely based on George S. Kaufman's play *The Butter and Egg Man*, but was tailored to suit the talent of Joe E. Brown. Ray Enright's sprightly direction and Gregg Toland's photography gave this production a classy look. The cast was excellent, especially Vivien Oakland, a veteran of screen comedies.

With Joe E. Brown and Vivien Oakland

With Joe E. Brown

The Thirteenth Guest
A Monogram Picture, 1932

CAST: Ginger Rogers, (Marie Morgan); Lyle Talbot, (Winston); J. Farrell MacDonald, (Captain Ryan); James Eagles, (Harold Morgan); Eddie Phillips, (Thor Jensen); Erville Alderson, (Adams); Robert Klein, (Barksdale); Crauford Kent, (Dr. Sherwood); Frances Rich, (Marjorie); Ethel Wales, (Mrs. Thornton); Paul Hurst, (Grump); William Davidson, (Captain Brown); Phillips Smalley, (Uncle Dick Thornton); Tom London, (Detective Carter); Harry Tenbrook, (Cabby); John Ince, (John Morgan); Allan Cavan, (Uncle Wayne Seymour); Alan Bridge, (Policeman); Henry Hall, (Sergeant-Jailer); Tiny Sandford, (Mike-Jailer); Kit Guard, (Prisoner).

CREDITS: Director, Albert Ray; Producer, M.H. Hoffman; Scenarists, Frances Hyland, Arthur Hoerl; Dialogue, Armitage Trail. Based on the novel by Armitage Trail. Photographers, Harry Neumann, Tom Galligan; Sound Recorders, Balsley and Phillips; Production Manager, Sidney Algier. Moustaches by Ince of London. Assistant Director, Gene Anderson.

SYNOPSIS: Thirteen years after a fatal dinner party for thirteen guests, during which the host died suddenly, it becomes apparent that the murderer intends to kill all of those who were there that night. Marie Morgan, one of the relatives, almost gets electrocuted.

REVIEWS

"Armitage Trail, the author of *Scarface*, wrote this mystery thriller, which, though farfetched, is fairly well worked out on 'creepy creepy' lines. Ginger Rogers and J. Farrell MacDonald head the cast. Fair entertainment."

Film Weekly

"Ginger Rogers is the girl and looks very cute."

Los Angeles Times

"J. Farrell MacDonald as the police captain gives a 100% performance. Paul Hurst is strangely, although comically, cast as a stupid stooge detective. Most of the laughs are provoked by Hurst, who this time is as timid as he is usually tough.

"Others are in comparatively minor roles, including Ginger Rogers, although she is proven to be the occupant of the title chair."

Variety

NOTES: *The Thirteenth Guest* provided Ginger with her first melodrama. Filmed at Monogram Studios in Hollywood, it was hardly an "A" production, but it was valuable experience for her. Lyle Talbot was good as the detective, while J. Farrell MacDonald and Paul Hurst supplied the lame-brained humor producers believed necessary to murder mysteries.

Albert Ray's direction plodded along at a grim pace, although Harry Neumann's photography tried for the imaginative touch despite the small budget. In England, the title was *Lady Beware*.

With J. Farrell MacDonald and Lyle Talbot

With Lyle Talbot, Frances Rich, Ethel Wales, and Phillips Smalley

With Sally Eilers

Hat Check Girl A Fox Picture, 1932

With Sally Eilers and Monroe Owsley

With Lee Moran and Sally Eilers

CAST: Sally Eilers, (Gerry Marsh); Ben Lyon, (Buster Collins); Ginger Rogers, (Jessie King); Monroe Owsley, (Tod Reese); Arthur Pierson, (Felix Cornwall); Noel Madison, (Dan McCoy); Dewey Robinson, (Tony Carlucci); Harold Goodwin, (Walter Marsh); Eulalie Jensen, (Mrs. Marsh); Purnell Pratt, (Collins); Lee Moran, (Man on Subway); Iris Meredith, (Saleslady); Eddie "Rochester" Anderson, (Waiter); Snowflake (Fred Toones), (Bellman); Henry Armetta, (Water Wagon Driver); Betty Elliott, Bert Roach, Astrid Allwyn, Greta Granstedt, Arthur Housman, Joyce Compton, (Party Guests); Richard Carle, (Professor); Richard Tucker, (Mr. Reynolds); Manya Roberti, (Dancer).

CREDITS: Director, Sidney Lanfield; Scenarists, Philip Klein, Barry Conners; Dialogue Director, Arthur Kober. Based on the novel by Rian James. Photographer, Glenn MacWilliams; Art Director, Gordon Wiles; Editor, Paul Weatherwax; Sound Recorder, W.D. Flick; Musical Score, Arthur Lange; Musical Director, George Lipschulta; Costumer, Rita Kaufman.

SONG: *You're Worth While Waiting For* by L. Wolfe Gilbert, James Hanley.

SYNOPSIS: Young hat-check girl Gerry Marsh is surrounded by nightclub habitues, bootleggers, and blackmailers before she becomes romantically involved with millionaire playboy Buster Collins. Sharing many of her trials and tribulations is Jessie King, her jazzy chum behind the counter.

REVIEWS

"Ginger Rogers, her former prettiness lost in plumpness, speaks her wisecracks with more charm than lies in the words."

Los Angeles Times

"Ginger Rogers supplies a variety of wisecracks and nightclub philosophy that keeps the audience bellowing."
Hollywood Screen World

"Fast, smooth and spicy entertainment for the sophisticated, with a good secondary performance by Ginger Rogers."

Film Weekly

"Sally Eilers in the name part . . . and Ginger Rogers, as her companion of the coat-hangers, carry the brunt of the hauteur, aided and abetted by Monroe Owsley, Purnell Pratt, Dewey Robin n, Richard Carle, Bert Roach, Henry

Armetta and enough others to fill a penthouse—or even a repenthouse!"

Nelson B. Bell
Washington Post

NOTES: Ginger's first film at Fox put her in support of Sally Eilers as her wisecracking, but much bolder, chum. The pre-Code script gave Ginger a marvelous opportunity to demonstrate what she could do with apt wisecracks and risque situations. Her glib Jessie King became the first of many worldly-wise girlfriend roles that would hold her in good stead until stardom came along.

Sidney Lanfield directed this yarn with great style and pace. It is to the credit of this fine director that the actors worked so well together; whether star or extra, they responded well to his guidance.

With Ben Lyon

You Said a Mouthful

A First National & Vitaphone Picture, 1932

With Joe E. Brown

CAST: Joe E. Brown, (Joe Holt, a shipping clerk); Ginger Rogers, (Alice Brandon); Preston Foster, (Ed Dover); Sheila Terry, (Cora); Farina, (Sam); Guinn Williams, (Joe Holt, a swimming champion); Harry Gribbon, (Harry Daniels); Oscar Apfel, (Armstrong); Edwin Maxwell, (Dr. Vorse); Walter Walker, (Tom Brandon); William Burress, (Colby); Frank Hagney, (Holt's Manager); Selmer Jackson, (Jones); Mia Marvin, (Armstrong's Secretary); Harry Seymour, (Announcer); James Eagles, (Messenger); Arthur S. Byron, (Elliott); Anthony Lord, (Bookkeeper); Bert Morehouse, (Office Manager).

CREDITS: Director, Lloyd Bacon; Scenarists, Robert Lord, Bolton Mallory. Based on a story by William B. Dover. Photographer, Richard Towers; Art Director, Jack Okey; Editor, Owen Marks; Makeup Artist, Perc Westmore; Technical Director, Harold Kruger.

SYNOPSIS: Socialite Alice Brandon mistakes Joe Holt, a sappy shipping clerk who has invented an unsinkable swimming suit, for another Joe Holt, a famous champion Canadian swimmer. The wrong Holt is then forced into entering a twenty-mile swimming race.

REVIEWS

"Your old friend, Farina, at last out of the pigtail stage and allowed to play regular he-boy roles, affords much of the comedy in the Brown picture, and Ginger Rogers has a nice part as Alice, the leading lady who makes the great

mistake about the champ and falls in love with the shipping clerk."

San Antonio News

"Ginger Rogers strikes just the right note in her supporting role, giving her ingenue the touch of sophistication and playful spoofing desirable."

Marguerite Tazelaar
New York Herald-Tribune

"And the herione, Ginger Rogers, continues to be one of the most attractive young women on the screen."

World Telegram

"Ginger Rogers was made for a bathing suit."

Photoplay

"Mr. Brown does quite well with this ludicrous role. Ginger Rogers is lively as Alice Brandon, the girl who is fully in sympathy with Joe."

Mordaunt Hall
The New York Times

NOTES: In her second Joe E. Brown picture, Ginger had more to do and looked most becoming as Alice Brandon, a role originally assigned to Gloria Shea. Joe E. was the whole show.

Lloyd Bacon, one of the better directors on the First National lot, directed with style and pace, always knowing how to accent a comic situation. It was Ginger's good luck to have been cast in *You Said a Mouthful*, for Bacon used her to advantage in his next picture, *Forty-second Street*.

With Walter Walker, Joe E. Brown, Farina, and Edwin Maxwell

Forty-second Street   A Warner Bros. & Vitaphone Picture, 1933

With Ruby Keeler and Una Merkel

CAST: Warner Baxter, (Julian Marsh); Bebe Daniels, (Dorothy Brock); George Brent, (Pat Denning); Una Merkel, (Lorraine Fleming); Ruby Keeler, (Peggy Sawyer); Guy Kibbee, (Abner Dillon); Dick Powell, (Billy Lawler); Ginger Rogers, (Ann Lowell [Anytime Annie]); George E. Stone, (Andy Lee); Robert McWade, (Al Jones); Ned Sparks, (Thomas Barry); Eddie Nugent, (Terry Neil); Allen Jenkins, (Mac Elory); Harry Akst, (Jerry); Clarence Nordstrom, (Groom, *Shuffle off to Buffalo*); Henry B. Walthall, (The Actor); Al Dubin, Harry Warren, (Songwriters); Toby Wing, ("Young and Healthy" Girl); Pat Wing, (Chorus Girl); Tom Kennedy, (Slim Murphy); Wallis Clark, (Dr. Chadwick); Jack La Rue, (A Mug); Louise Beavers, (Pansy); Dave O'Brien, (Chorus Boy); Patricia Ellis, (Secretary); George Irving, (House Doctor); Charles Lane, (An Author); Milton Kibbee, (News Spreader); Rolfe Sedan, (Stage Aide); Harry Seymour, (Aide), Gertrude Keeler, Helen Keeler, Geraine Grear, Ann Hovey, Renee Whitney, Dorothy Coonan, Barbara Rogers, June Glory, Jayne Shadduck, Adele Lacy, Loretta Andrews, Margaret La Marr, Mary Jane Halsey, Ruth Eddings, Edna Callaghan, Patsy Farnum, Maxine Cantway, Lynn Browning, Donna Mae Roberts, Lorena Layson, Alice Jans, Eve Marcy, Evelyn Joice, Agnes Ray, Grace Tobin, (Chorus Girls); Kermit Maynard, (Dancer Who Catches Girl).

CREDITS: Director, Lloyd Bacon; Scenarists, James Seymour, Rian James, Whitney Bolton. Based on the novel *Forty-second Street* by Bradford Ropes. Photographer, Sol Polito; Art Director, Jack Okey;

With Warner Baxter

Editors, Thomas Pratt, Frank Ware. Dances by Busby Berkeley. Orchestra Conducted by Leo F. Forbstein, Costumer, Orry-Kelly. Silks by Cheyney Brothers. Makeup Artist, Perc Westmore; Assistant Director, Gordon Hollingshead.

SONGS: *Forty-second Street, Shuffle Off to Buffalo, Young and Healthy, You're Getting to Be a Habit With Me,* by Al Dubin, Harry Warren.

SYNOPSIS: Broadway producer Julian Marsh is forced to use an unknown chorine, Peggy Sawyer, when Dorothy Brock, the lead in the show, sprains her ankle the night of the dress rehearsal. The chorus line includes Ann Lowell, a snappy society-conscious broad known as Anytime Annie, who enlivens the backstage atmosphere with her wisecracks.

REVIEWS

"Ginger Rogers is cute as a chorus girl who affects an English accent and a monocle. Una Merkel is quite funny as another chorus girl."

New York Sun

"One may wish that it were funnier and not quite so conventional as to story without overlooking the quiet charm of Miss Ruby Keeler, the attractive playing of Miss Bebe Daniels and the nonchalant gayety of Miss Ginger Rogers . . . . Miss Rogers, in a minor role, is both amusing and attractive."

Richard Watts, Jr.
New York Herald Tribune

"Guy Kibbee, Una Merkel, Dick Powell and Ginger Rogers are all swell."

Modern Screen

"She got her movie start in *Young Man of Manhattan*, and though she had plenty of movie work after that, her career didn't seem to be getting anywhere—until *Forty-Second Street* came along. She popped a monocle in her eye and ran off with the show, along with Ruby Keeler."

Movie Classic

NOTES: One of the greatest Hollywood musicals, *Forty-second Street*, helped, more than any other film, to revive the screen musical by totally incorporating music into a thin, but somewhat plausible, script. Lloyd Bacon directed the actors, while Busby Berkeley handled the singers and dancers in the various production numbers.

Ginger was sheer bliss as Anytime Annie—a chorine with class—complete with phony accent, monocle, and Pekingese. Warner Baxter was excellent as producer Julian Marsh; Bebe Daniels was properly haughty as star Dorothy Brock (her rendition of *You're Getting to Be a Habit With Me* was lovely); and Dick Powell and newcomer Ruby Keeler (then Mrs. Al Jolson) became Warner's musical lovers. Keeler's rendition of the title song was delightful fun, while Powell pleased the ladies with *Young and Healthy*. Ginger and Una Merkel joined Keeler in the *Shuffle Off to Buffalo* number—and very funny.

After repeated viewings, *Forty-Second Street* is still one of the special pleasures of the thirties—or, for that matter, any Hollywood decade.

Shuffling off to Buffalo with Guy Kibbee

With George E. Stone and Una Merkel

With Una Merkel, Ruby Keeler, George E. Stone, and Warner Baxter

Broadway Bad   A Fox Picture, 1933

With Joan Blondell and Adrienne Ames

CAST: Joan Blondell, (Tony Landers); Ricardo Cortez, (Craig Cutting); Ginger Rogers, (Flip Daly); Adrienne Ames, (Aileen); Allen Vincent, (Bob North); Phil Tead, (Joe Flynn); Francis McDonald, (Charley Davis); Spencer Charters, (Lew Gordon); Ronald Cosby, (Big Fella); Frederick Burton, (Robert North, Sr.); Margaret Seddon, (Bixby); Donald Crisp, (Darrall); Max Wagner, Harold Goodwin (Reporters); Eddie Kane, (Jeweler); John Davidson, (The Prince); Larry Steers, (Business Associate); Matty Roubert, (Newsboy); Henry Hall, (Bailiff).

CREDITS: Director, Sidney Lanfield; Scenarists, Arthur Kober, Maude Fulton. Based on a story by William Lipman, A.W. Pezet. Photographer, George Barnes; Art Director, Gordon Wiles; Editor, Paul Weatherwax; Sound Recorder, Donald Flick; Musical Score, Arthur Lange; Orchestrator, Hugo Friedhofer; Costumer, Earl Luick; Assistant Director, Lester Selander.

SONGS: *Little Man,* by L. Wolfe Gilbert, and James Hanley. *Forget the Past,* by Sidney Mitchell, Harry Akst.

SYNOPSIS: Showgirl Tony Landers becomes disappointed in her rich marriage and places all her affection and hope in her son, keeping him carefully guarded from the tinsel world in which she lives. When she seeks a divorce and has to fight for the custody of her child, Flip Daly, a fellow chorine, stands by her through thick and thin.

With Joan Blondell

REVIEWS

"*Broadway Bad* is a weak little chorus girl picture."

John Cohen, Jr.
New York Sun

" . . . The happy ending mostly concerns Miss Blondell and Mr. Cortez, with hisses for Miss Ames and Mr. Vincent. The role is one of Miss Blondell's best, and she is ably supported by Mr. Cortez, Miss Ames and Ginger Rogers in parts of varying importance."

New York American

" . . . Mr. Cortez is the most amusing of the players as the pleasantly cynical playboy with the evil reputation. Miss Blondell suffers the double burden of a foolish part and uncomplimentary photography. Ginger Rogers appears as a chorus girl with a sentimental streak."

The New York Times

NOTES: After finishing her role in *Forty-second Street*, Ginger returned to Fox to play another girlfriend part. This time it was in support of Joan Blondell, who had replaced Joan Bennett in this tearjerker about a chorus girl who wanted the best for her kid.

Sidney Lanfield directed the Arthur Kober-Maude Fulton screenplay deftly, while Blondell's husband, George Barnes, photographed it. When the plot wasn't sticky with the trials and tribulations of Blondell and Ricardo Cortez, there were fun moments with Ginger as Flip Daly and Adrienne Ames as Aileen.

With Ronald Cosby,
Joan Blondell,
and Margaret Seddon

Ginger's cut number from the nightclub sequence

Ginger's pig-latin rendition of *We're in the Money*—Busby Berkeley's opening number

With Aline MacMahon and Guy Kibbee

With Aline MacMahon, Guy Kibbee, Joan Blondell, and Warren William

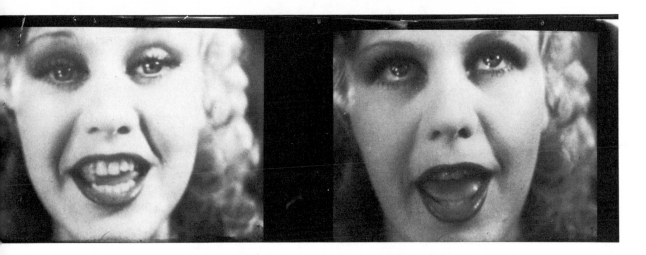

CAST: Warren William, (J. Lawrence Bradford); Joan Blondell, (Carol); Aline MacMahon, (Trixie Lorraine); Ruby Keeler, (Polly Parker); Dick Powell, (Brad Roberts); Guy Kibbee, (Thaniel H. Peabody); Ned Sparks, (Barney Hopkins); Ginger Rogers, (Fay Fortune); Clarence Nordstrom, (Don Gordon); Robert Agnew, (Dance Director); Tammany Young, (Gigolo Eddie); Sterling Holloway, (Messenger Boy); Ferdinand Gottschalk, (Clubman); Lynn Browning, (Gold Digger Girl); Charles C. Wilson, (Deputy); Billy Barty, (*Pettin' in the Park* Baby); Snowflake [Fred Toones], Theresa Harris, (Black Couple); Joan Barclay, (Chorus Girl); Wallace MacDonald, (Stage Manager); Wilbur Mack, Grace Hayle, Charles Lane, Sam Godfrey, (Society Reporters); Hobart Cavanaugh, (Dog Salesman); Jay Eaton, (Diner); Bill Elliott, (Dance Extra); Dennis O'Keefe, (Extra During Intermission); Busby Berkeley, (Call Boy); Billy West, (Medal of Honor Winner); Fred Kelsey, ("Detective Jones"); Etta Moten, ("Forgotten Man" Singer); Frank Mills, (First Forgotten Man); Renee Whitney, Gloria Faythe, Bonnie Bannon, Maxine Cantway, Alice Jans, Loretta Andrews, Margaret Cathew, Muriel Gordon, Pat Wing, Ann Hovey, Kitty Cunningham, June Glory, Lorena Layson, Monica Bannister, Amo Ingraham, Jayne Shadduck, Ebba Hally, Anita Thompson, Adrien Brier, Dorothy Coonan, Bee Stevens, (Gold Diggers).

SONGS: *The Gold Diggers Song (We're in the Money), I've Got to Sing a Torch Song, Remember My Forgotten Man, Pettin' in the Park, The Shadow Waltz,* by Al Dubin, Harry Warren.

CREDITS: Director, Mervyn Le Roy; Producer, Jack L. Warner; Scenarists, Erwin Gelsey, James Seymour; Dialogue, David Boehm, Ben Markson. Based on the play *The Gold Diggers* by Avery Hopwood. Photographer, Sol Polito; Art Director, Anton Grot; Editor, George Amy. Dances by Busby Berkeley. Musical Conductor, Leo F. Forbstein; Costumer, Orry-Kelly; Makeup Artist, Perc Westmore.

SYNOPSIS: Millionaire-turned-composer Brad Roberts provides both music and money to rescue out-of-work actors, singers and dancers. One of them, Fay Fortune, a gold digger par excellence, kicks up her heels.

REVIEWS

"Miss Keeler, Mr. Powell, Mr. Kibbee and Miss Rogers are, for this type of amusement, altogether admirable, and for sheer comedy the film proper is very swell stuff."

Lucius Beebe
New York Herald Tribune

"It is an imaginatively staged, breezy show, with a story of no greater consequence than is to be found in this type of picture . . . . Miss MacMahon adds another fine performance to her list of Hollywood efforts. Miss Blondell is lively as the temporarily distressed Carol. Ruby Keeler does quite well as the heroine. Mr. Powell pleased the audience enormously with his singing and also his acting . . . . Ginger Rogers makes her numbers count for their full worth."

Mordaunt Hall
The New York Times

NOTES: Ginger's offscreen romance with director Mervyn LeRoy was, it is generally conceded, the reason she got the part of Fay Fortune in this musical. She made the most of her opportunity. LeRoy had Ginger open the film in a gold coin dress singing *The Gold Diggers Song (We're in the Money)*—and, in full screen close-up, she sang a chorus in the then-popular pig latin. It was a hoot, and it set the tone for the wild kaleidoscopic Busby Berkeley dance ensembles that were to follow.

Mervyn LeRoy's handling of the mediocre script, the group of fine performers and such great talents as Sol Polito (photography), Anton Grot (art direction), and George Amy (editing) kept the pace throughout. However, *Gold Diggers of 1933* is not remembered as a LeRoy film so much as it is a "Busby Berkeley picture." The famed dance director went mad staging *Pettin' in the Park*, with Powell and Keeler, and *The Shadow Waltz* and *Remember My Forgotten Man*, with Joan Blondell.

Ginger had one other number, dressed in a black sequin dress standing in front of (and atop) a white piano in the nightclub sequence, but it was cut, probably because the picture had grown too long, and Berkeley's giant numbers took precedence.

Professional Sweetheart

An RKO-Radio Picture, 1933

With Norman Foster

CAST: Ginger Rogers, (Glory Eden); Norman Foster, (Jim Davey); ZaSu Pitts, (Esmeralda de Leon); Frank McHugh, (Speed); Allen Jenkins, (O'Connor); Gregory Ratoff, (Ipswich); Edgar Kennedy, (Kelsey); Lucien Littlefield, (Announcer); Franklin Pangborn, (Childress); Frank Darien, (Appleby); Betty Furness, (Reporter); Sterling Holloway, (Scribe); Theresa Harris, (Maid); Grace Hayle, (Reporter).

CREDITS: Director, William Seiter; Producer, H.N. Swanson; Executive Producer, Merian C. Cooper; Scenarist, Maurine Watkins. Based on a story by Maurine Watkins. Photographer, Edward Cronjager; Art Directors, Van Nest Polglase, Carroll Clark; Editor, James Morley; Sound Recorder, Clem Portman; Musical Director, Max Steiner; Makeup Artist, Mel Burns; Still Photographer, John Miehle.

SONGS: *My Imaginary Sweetheart* by Edward Eliscu, Harry Akst.

SYNOPSIS: Glory Eden, a radio entertainer publicized as America's "Purity Girl of the Air," has a difficult time living up to the image. She wants to give it all up and have fun, but her manager chooses a "professional sweetheart" for her from her fan mail. Her dream man is Jim Davey, a hick from Kentucky, who believes the purity stuff at first, but, wised-up, eventually tames the lady.

With Theresa Harris

78

REVIEWS

"Radio's sacred cows, the sponsors of commercial broadcasts and the entertainers featured therein, are taken for a midsummer's sleigh ride in *Professional Sweetheart* .... A competent cast, headed by Ginger Rogers and Norman Foster, has found much that is amusing in the industry to which Radio City was dedicated .... Miss Rogers has rarely been more entertaining."

The New York Times

"Ginger Rogers plays the Purity Girl with pleasing humor."

Thornton Delehanty
New York Evening Post

"More fun than *Once In A Lifetime* .... The story is Maurine Watkins at her satirical best .... With that cute and clever comedienne, Ginger Rogers, to romp in the leading role of radio's "Purity Girl" .... *Professional Sweetheart* is a riot of laughter."

Regina Crewe
New York American

"All in all, it cannot be said that *Professional Sweetheart* is a miracle of freshness, but, thanks chiefly to Miss Rogers, it has its moments. As the radio girl who must be sweet and coy all over the place while she is busting with desire for a little venom, Miss Rogers is genuinely amusing, reminding us that she is, when properly cast, a really skillful and attractive comedienne."

Richard Watts, Jr.
New York Herald Tribune

NOTES: Ginger's first film at RKO-Radio was originally called *Careless*, but was later changed to *The Purity Girl* and then to *Professional Sweetheart* (the British labeled it *Imaginary Sweetheart*). It was a funny satire on the love life of temperamental radio star Glory Eden, delightfully played by Ginger. Norman Foster, who had appeared with her in *Young Man of Manhattan*, was her co-star.

William Seiter handled the direction efficiently, and the supporting cast included such fine comic performers as ZaSu Pitts, Frank McHugh, Allen Jenkins, Edgar Kennedy, Franklin Pangborn, and Grace Hayle. Etta Moten dubbed Ginger's song, *My Imaginary Sweetheart*.

With Gregory Ratoff, Franklin Pangborn, Frank Darien, and Frank McHugh

A Shriek in the Night

An Allied Picture, 1933

CAST: Ginger Rogers, (Patricia Morgan); Lyle Talbot, (Theodore Rand); Arthur Hoyt, (Wilfred); Purnell Pratt, (Inspector Russell); Harvey Clark, (Janitor); Lillian Harmer, (Augusta); Maurice Black, (Martini); Louise Beavers, (Black Maid); Clarence Wilson, (Editor Perkins).

CREDITS: Director, Albert Ray; Producer, M.H. Hoffman; Scenarist, Frances Hyland. Based on a story by Kurt Kempler. Photographers, Harry Neuman, Tom Galligan; Art Director, Gene Hornbistel; Editor, L.R. Brown; Sound Recorder, Homer C. Ellmaker; Musical Supervisor, Abe Meyer; Production Manager, Sydney Algier; Costumer, Alfreda.

SYNOPSIS: Rival newspaper reporters Patricia Morgan and Theodore Rand, who are always trying to outscoop each other, become involved in a series of murders which are committed in a modern apartment building.

Together the dauntless reporters uncover the killer, but not before Patricia is almost thrown into a blazing furnace!

With Purnell Pratt

NOTES: Ginger returned to melodramas with this Allied Production, which was shot on the RKO lot. Her producer, director and co-star (Lyle Talbot) of *The Thirteenth Guest* were back to haunt her, and the results were just about the same—a mild potboiler.

The entire production suffered from a low budget, and one wonders how (or why) Ginger got involved with this effort at all. It is one of the low points of her career, but not quite as low as *Follow the Leader*. In addition to the fact that most first-string reviewers ignored this picture (ditto for audiences), Ginger looked plain in unattractive hairstyles and costumes by Alfreda.

With Harvey Clark

With Lillian Harmer and Purnell Pratt

Don't Bet on Love   A Universal Picture, 1933

With Lew Ayres

CAST: Lew Ayres, (Bill McCaffery); Ginger Rogers, (Molly Gilbert); Charles Grapewin, (Pop McCaffery); Shirley Grey, (Goldie); Merna Kennedy, (Ruby); Tom Dugan, (Scotty); Robert Emmett O'Connor, (Sheldon); Lucille Gleason, (Mrs. Gilbert); Henry Armetta, (Caparillo); Brooks Benedict, (Cunningham); Clay Clement, (Ross); Alfred White, (Rosenbaum); Pepe Sinoff, (Mrs. Rosenbaum); with Charley Lee, Tyler Brooke, Eddie Kane, Craig Reynolds.

CREDITS: Director, Murray Roth; Producer, Carl Laemmle; Scenarists, Murray Roth, Howard Emmett Rogers. Based on a story by Murray Roth. Photographer, Jackson Rose; Art Director, Charles D. Hall; Editor, Robert Carlisle; Editorial Supervisor, Maurice Pivar; Sound Recorder, Gilbert Kurland; Production Supervisor, E.M. Asher.

SYNOPSIS: Bill McCaffery, a young plumber, experiences phenomenal betting luck at the racetrack, but almost ruins his business when his luck runs out. Molly Gilbert, his manicurist sweetheart, stands by him through all and helps him readjust to the simple life of a plumber.

REVIEWS

"Ayres and Miss Rogers appear to advantage as a team, although there is not much for either of them in the way of acting opportunities. They are a good-looking couple, and it's a pity they weren't married right at the start of the story, for Ginger's charm would undoubtedly have caused Ayres to go straight right away."

John Slott
Los Angeles Times

"Miss Rogers tones her performance down to suit the character and proves a versatility unsuspected in her recent acting."

M. Tazelaar
New York Herald Tribune

"With Lew Ayres and Ginger Rogers in the leads, it is well acted, never assumes pretentiousness and stays right in character all the way through."

Motion Picture Herald

"Lew Ayres, as the plumber, and Ginger Rogers, as the manicurist, make a pleasant team."

The New York Times

NOTES: This tame comedy-drama, originally called *In the Money*, dealt with horse racing. Murray Roth, who also co-scripted, directed this hodgepodge badly. Lew Ayres gave a good account of himself despite the script, while Ginger, as a manicurist, had little more to do than to follow the dreary moods of the piece. The good cast, which included Charles Grapewin, Shirley Grey, Merna Kennedy and Lucille Gleason, was generally wasted.

The film has been unavailable for rescreening for many years.

On the set with Lew Ayres

With Charles Grapewin and Lucille Gleason

With Lew Ayres

Sitting Pretty

A Paramount Picture, 1933

CAST: Jack Oakie, (Chick Parker); Jack Haley, (Pete Pendleton); Ginger Rogers, (Dorothy); Thelma Todd, (Gloria Duval); Gregory Ratoff, (Tannenbaum); Lew Cody, (Jules Clark); Harry Revel, (Pianist); Jerry Tucker, (Buzz); Mack Gordon, (Song Publisher); Hale Hamilton, (Vinton); Walter Walker, (George Wilson); Kenneth Thomson, (Norman Lubin); William B. Davidson, (Director); Lee Moran, (Assistant Director); Art Jarrett, (Singer); Anne Nagel, (Girl at Window); Joyce Matthews, (Blond Chorus Girl); Irving Bacon, Stuart Holmes, (Dice Players); Fuzzy Knight, (Stock Clerk); Harvey Clark, (Motorist); Wade Boteler, (Jackson); Frank La Rue, (Studio Gateman); Sidney Bracey, (Manager); Jack Mower, (Clark's Aide); Frank Hagney, (Bar Manager); Larry Steers, Henry Hall, (Party Guests); Russ Powell, (Counterman); Charles Williams, George Brasno, Olive Brasno, (Neighbors); Rollo Lloyd, (Director); Lee Phelps, (Studio Aide); Harry C. Bradley, (Set Designer); Phil Tead, (Aide); Dave O'Brien, (Assistant Cameraman); Charles Coleman, (Butler); James Burtis, (Mover Foreman).

CREDITS: Director, Harry Joe Brown; Producer, Charles R. Rogers; Scenarists, Jack McGowan, S.J. Perelman, Lou Breslow. Based on an original story by Nina Wilcox Putnam. Photographer, Milton Krasner; Art Director, David Garber. Dances by Larry Ceballos. Orchestrator, Howard Jackson; Costumer, Travis Banton; Assistant Director, David Garber.

SONGS: *Did You Ever See a Dream Walking, I Wanna Meander With Miranda, You're Such a Comfort to Me, Good Morning Glory, Many Moons Ago, Lucky Little Extras, There's a Bluebird at My Window, And Then We Wrote, Lights, Action, Camera, Love, Blonde Blase and Beautiful, Ballad of the Southland,* by Mack Gordon, Harry Revel.

SYNOPSIS: Two songwriters, Chick Parker and Pete Pendleton, hitchhike from New York City to Hollywood to seek fame and fortune in movies. They are joined along the way by a pert young lunchwagon proprietress, Dorothy, who sings and dances well.

With Jack Oakie

With Jack Haley

With Jack Haley

REVIEWS

"Ginger Rogers is the heroine and she is sittin' pretty again as to looks and general capability."

John Cohen, Jr.
New York Sun

"The girls help lots, too, with the attractive Ginger having an edge over the curvaceous Thelma."

Regina Crewe
New York American

"Ginger Rogers plays the feminine lead in capable fashion, providing the romantic interest and singing several tunes in her most vivacious manner."

John Slott
Los Angeles Times

"Miss Rogers is always one of the pleasures of the cinema; a girl who combines looks, grace and an unaffected wit."

Richard Watts, Jr.
New York Herald Tribune

"Ginger Rogers deserves a bouquet for the excellent way she puts over a song in close-up. A difficult feat, which she accomplishes amazingly, without awkwardness or grimacing."

Hollywood Screen World

NOTES: This moderately amusing musical marked Ginger's return to filmmaking under the Paramount banner, although it was her first time at their West Coast studio. As the lunchwagon proprietress who joins a pair of eager young songwriters, Ginger got to sing *Did You Ever See a Dream Walking*, *Good Morning Glory* and *There's a Bluebird At My Window*, in addition to joining Jack Oakie and Jack Haley in *You're Such a Comfort to Me*.

Besides the Gordon and Revel songs, *Sitting Pretty* boasted good photography by Milton Krasner, and the satisfying presence of Thelma Todd.

et with chorus girls, Art Jarrett, and lyricist Mack Gordon

Flying Down to Rio An RKO-Radio Picture, 1933

With Gene Raymond and Fred Astaire

CAST: Dolores Del Rio, (Belinha de Rezende); Gene Raymond, (Roger Bond); Raul Roulien, (Julio Rubeiro); Ginger Rogers, (Honey Hale); Fred Astaire, (Fred Ayres); Blanche Frederici, (Dona Elena); Walter Walker, (Senor de Rezende); Etta Moten, (Black Singer); Roy D'Arcy, Maurice Black, Armand Kaliz, (Greeks); Paul Porcasi, (Mayor); Reginald Barlow, (Banker, Alfredo) Alice Gentle, (Concert Singer); Franklin Pangborn, (Hammerstein, Hotel Manager); Eric Blore, (Assistant Manager); Luis Alberni, (Rio Casino Manager); Ray Cooke, (Banjo Player); Wallace MacDonald, (Pilot); Gino Corrado, (Messenger); Lucille Browne, Mary Kornman, (Belinda's Friends); Clarence Muse, (Caddy in Haiti); Harry Semels, (Sign Poster); Jack Rice, Eddie Borden, (Musicians); Movita Castaneda, (Singer);

Martha La Venture, (Dancer); The Brazilian Turunas, The American Clippers Band, (Bands); Sidney Bracey, (Rodriguez, Chauffeur); Harry Bowen, (Airport Mechanic); Manuel Paris, (Man at Aviators' Club); Adrian Rosley, (Club Manager); with Howard Wilson, Margaret Mearing, Betty Furness, Francisco Moran, Helen Collins, Carol Tevis, Eddie Tamblyn, Alice Ardell, Rafael Alvir, Barbara Sheldon, Douglas Williams, Alma Travers, Juan Duval, Eddie Boland, Julian Rivero, Pedro Regas.

CREDITS: Director, Thonton Freeland; Associate Producer, Louis Brock; Executive Producer, Merian C. Cooper; Scenarists, Cyril Hume, H.W. Haneman, Erwin Gelsey. Based on a play by Anne Caldwell. Based

With Gene Raymond

On the *Carioca* set with associate producer Louis Brock, Dolores Del Rio, Gene Raymond, dance director Dave Gould, Raul Roulien, executive producer Merian C. Cooper, Fred Astaire, and director Thornton Freeland

Setting up a close-up shot on the *Carioca* set

on an original story by Louis Brock. Photographer, J. Roy Hunt; Art Directors, Van Nest Polglase, Carroll Clark; Editor, Jack Kitchin. Dances by Dave Gould. Sound Recorder, P.J. Faulkner, Jr.; Musical Director, Max Steiner; Music Recorder, Murray Spivack; Miniatures, Don Jahraus; Costumer, Walter Plunkett; Makeup Artist, Mel Burns; Research Director, Elizabeth McGaffey; Special Photographic Effects, Vernon Walker; Associate Director, George Nicholls, Jr.; Still Photographer, John Miehle.

SONGS: *The Carioca, Music Makes Me, Orchids in the Moonlight, Flying Down to Rio,* by Gus Kahn, Edward Eliscu, Vincent Youmans.

SYNOPSIS: Young orchestra leader Roger Bond and a talented group of entertainers get their big break by flying down to Rio to work at a large resort hotel. While Bond romances beautiful Belinha de Rezende, Honey Hale and Fred Ayres dance up a storm to *The Carioca.*

REVIEWS

"The inspired music of Vincent Youmans, the grace of Fred Astaire, the dark beauty of Dolores Del Rio, Raul Roulien's singing, the comedy of Ginger Rogers and the love-making of Gene Raymond combine to make a glorious Hollywood holiday."

New York American

"Neither Miss Rogers nor Mr. Roulien have much to do, but both have a song apiece and both acquit themselves creditably."

New York Journal

With Ray Cooke (banjo player), Fred Astaire, and Gene Raymond

Dancing "The Carioca" with Fred Astaire and ensemble

"Ginger Rogers, whose talents are highlighted admirably in song and dance, is effectively teamed with Astaire."

Los Angeles Times

"An impressive series of scenes are devoted to a dance known as the Carioca. During this interlude that nimble-toed Fred Astaire and the charming Ginger Rogers give a performance of this Carioca. The music is delightful, and besides Mr. Astaire and Miss Rogers many other persons dance the extraordinarily rhythmic Carioca, one feature of which happens to be that of the couples pressing their foreheads together as they glide around the floor . . . . Both Miss Rogers and Mr. Astaire give splendid performances. Miss Del Rio is alluring and sufficient, and Mr. Raymond does well as the handsome hero."

B.R.C.
The New York Times

"To play the lead in *Flying Down to Rio*, RKO wisely persuaded handsome Dolores Del Rio to come out of a years' retirement . . . . Fred Astaire, who had a brief bit in *Dancing Lady*, appears to much better advantage in his second cinema role. Good shot: Ginger Rogers watching his amazing version of the rhumba-like dance, Carioca."

Time

NOTES: RKO-Radio had originally planned *Flying*

Down to Rio as a vehicle for Dolores Del Rio and Joel McCrea, since that attractive pair won wide audience approval in King Vidor's *Bird of Paradise*. Raul Roulien and Arline Judge had been signed for supporting roles when the studio managed to get Fred Astaire. It was obvious that Miss Judge would hardly be a suitable partner for the masterful Astaire, who had years of stage experience behind him (and specialty numbers in M-G-M's *Dancing Lady*), so Ginger got the part. Gene Raymond replaced Joel McCrea, and production started.

Ginger sang *Music Makes Me*, while Astaire and Del Rio danced to *Orchids in the Moonlight*. The memorable title song was presented by gold-garbed girls strapped on the wings of airplanes (led by Ginger) flying over a South American resort hotel.

However, it was *The Carioca*, which Fred and Ginger had worked hours to perfect, that stunned audiences the world over. Not only did this elegant pair dance away with the picture, they opened up a whole new career for themselves as the screen's foremost dancing stars. They were to have no equals.

Flying Down to Rio was directed with verve by Thornton Freeland; musical direction by Max Steiner was superb.

Chance at Heaven
An RKO-Radio Picture, 1933

CAST: Joel McCrea, (Blacky Gorman); Ginger Rogers, (Marje Harris); Marian Nixon, (Glory Franklyn); Andy Devine, (Al); Virginia Hammond, (Mrs. Franklyn); Lucien Littlefield, (Mr. Harris); Ann Shoemaker, (Mrs. Harris); George Meeker, (Sid Larrick); Herman Bing, (Chauffeur); Betty Furness, (Betty); Harry Bowen, (First Reporter); with Helen Freeman, Thelma Hardwick, Alden Chase, Robert McWade.

CREDITS: Director, William Seiter; Producer, Merian C. Cooper; Associate Producer, H.N. Swanson; Scenarists, Julian Josephson, Sarah Y. Mason. Based on a story by Vina Delmar. Photographer, Nick Musuraca; Art Directors, Van Nest Polglase, Perry Ferguson; Editor, James B. Morley; Sound Recorder, Forrest Perley; Musical Director, Max Steiner; Makeup Artist, Mel Burns; Still Photographer, John Miehle.

SYNOPSIS: Blacky Gorman, a young service station owner, marries rich debutante Glory Franklyn, believing it to be his "chance at heaven," only to return to his former sweetheart, Marje Harris, after a turbulent marriage.

With Marian Nixon

REVIEWS

"The cast is a pleasant one, with Joel McCrea, Ginger Rogers and Marian Nixon playing the featured roles, and helps to make this *Chance at Heaven* much more palatable than it essentially is."

New York World Telegram

"If this picture gets by with the average audience, it will be on Ginger Rogers' account. I understand some expert told her she'd been given bad 'camera angles' in the film. If that's so, I suggest she stick to bad ones in the future, because they resulted in the most convincing job she's done to date."

Hollywood Spectator

"Joel McCrea gives quite a satisfactory performance as Blacky. Ginger Rogers, who dances so nicely in *Flying Down to Rio*, assumes here the role of Marje, and she acts the part better than it deserves."

Mordaunt Hall
The New York Times

NOTES: This was a tender little programmer with a good script by Julian Josephson and Sarah Y. Mason, and smooth direction by William Seiter. Ginger was natural and appealing as Marje Harris, the hometown girl who loses handsome Joel McCrea to a rich girl but remains friends with them both, only to get the man she loves back in the end. Marian Nixon, who replaced Dorothy Wilson, was also quite good. This is a picture of which Ginger can be justly proud.

With Joel McCrea

Rafter Romance An RKO-Radio Picture, 1934

CAST: Ginger Rogers, (Mary Carroll); Norman Foster, (Jack Bacon); George Sidney, (Max Eckbaum); Robert Benchley, (Hubbell); Laura Hope Crews, (Elise); Guinn Williams, (Fritzie); Ferike Boros, (Rosie Eckbaum); Sidney Miller, (Julius).

CREDITS: Director, William Seiter; Producer, Alexander McKaig; Executive Producer, Merian C. Cooper; Associate Producer, Kenneth MacGowan; Scenarists, Sam Mintz, H.W. Haneman; Adaptation, Glenn Tryon. Based on a novel by John Wells. Photographer, David Abel; Art Directors, Van Nest Polglase, John J. Hughes; Editor, James Morley; Sound Recorder, Hugh McDowell, Jr.; Music Director, Max Steiner; Costumer, Bernard Newman; Makeup Artist, Mel Burns; Still Photographer, John Miehle.

SYNOPSIS: Mary Carroll, a young working girl, shares a Greenwich Village attic with Jack Bacon, an artist-night watchman, the pair occupying the apartment in shifts. She begins to develop a hearty dislike for her "roommate" until she meets him, after which all is bliss.

REVIEWS

"Essentially a comedy, it is light and pleasant all the way through. A well-developed love interest angle is worked in. Good old-fashioned hokum is effectively used. There is just a trace of contrasting drama that concentrates audience sympathy on the central characters . . . .

"Situations being evenly balanced, the main theme is continually predominant. The cast's best names are Ginger Rogers and Laura Hope Crews. The show itself rather than names probably will be the most effective selling material."

Motion Picture Herald

"This entertainment with barely enough strength to stand in the rear rank of a double feature bill despite a fair group of cast names. Just about enough material to make a two-reeler . . . . Considering the players involved it's all quite disappointing."

Variety

NOTES: Ginger and Norman Foster (who replaced Dorothy Wilson and Joel McCrea) were the peppery sweethearts who hated one another when apart and loved each other when together in this *More the Merrier-*type romance.

William Seiter, who had directed Ginger in *Professional Sweetheart* and *Chance at Heaven,* gave the picture fluidity. The supporting cast, headed by George Sidney, Robert Benchley, and Laura Hope Crews, helped this programmer along.

With Guinn Williams

With Norman Foster

With Norman Foster, George Sidney, and Laura Hope Crews

Finishing School

An RKO-Radio Picture, 1934

With Frances Dee

CAST: Frances Dee, (Virginia Radcliff); Billie Burke, (Mrs. Radcliff); Ginger Rogers, (Cecelia(Pony)Ferris); Bruce Cabot, (Ralph MacFarland); John Halliday, (Frank Radcliff); Beulah Bondi, (Miss Van Alstyn); Sara Haden, (Miss Fisher); Marjorie Lytell, (Ruth Wallace); Adalyn Doyle, (Madeline Kelly); Dawn O'Day [Anne Shirley], (Billie); Rose Coghlan, (Miss Garland); Ann Cameron, (Miss Schmidt); Claire Myers, Susanne Thompson, Edith Vale, (Girls); Caroline Rankin, (Miss Weber); Jack Norton, (Drunk); Joan Barclay, (Short Girl); Helen Freeman, (Dr. Hewitt); with Irene Franklin, Florence Roberts, John David Horsley, Eddie Baker.

CREDITS: Directors, Wanda Tuchock, George Nicholls, Jr.; Executive Producer, Merian C. Cooper; Associate Producer, Kenneth MacGowan; Scenarists, Wanda Tuchock, Laird Doyle. Based on the play *These Days* by Katherine Clugston. Based on the story by David Hempstead. Photographer, J. Roy Hunt; Art Directors, Van Nest Polglase, Al D'Agostino; Editor, Arthur Schmidt; Sound Recorder, John L. Cass; Musical Director, Max Steiner; Music Recorder, Murray Spivack; Costumer, Walter Plunkett; Makeup Artist, Mel Burns; Still Photographer, John Miehle.

SYNOPSIS: The trials and tribulations of pupils in a snobbish private girls' school are depicted. Virginia Radcliff, whose pleasure-loving mother never gives her the guidance she needs, finds herself pregnant, while her roommate, Pony Ferris, delights in breaking all the rules she can.

REVIEWS

"Ginger Rogers' role is much more acceptable. As Miss Dee's roommate, Miss Rogers is the unconventional type. Regarding the school's regulations and rules, Miss Rogers says 'you can do anything you like, as long as you don't get caught.' Miss Rogers proceeds to break the rules, wisecracking all the while, and classes as the picture's one and only comic."

Variety

"Ginger Rogers plays a madcap young lady in her usual vivacious fashion."

John Slott
Los Angeles Times

"To Miss Rogers fall most of the snappy lines in the piece, and a couple of her nifties panicked the paying guests."

Regina Crewe

"Ginger Rogers (as usual) nearly walks away with all but the scenery."

Modern Screen

NOTES: It took two directors,—Wanda Tuchock and George Nicholls, Jr.—to bring *Finishing School* to the screen. The scenario was based on two sources: a story by David Hempstead and Katherine Clugston's play, *These Days*, which had served as Katharine Hepburn's Broadway debut in 1928.

As Pony Ferris, Ginger again proved how well she could handle a "girlfriend" part. Frances Dee played the difficult lead role well. Formerly a stand-in for Katharine Hepburn, Adalyn Doyle, who played Madeline Kelly, made her debut in this film.

With Adalyn Doyle, Frances Dee, and Marjorie Lytell

With Frances Dee

Twenty Million Sweethearts
A First National Vitaphone Picture, 1934

With Dick Powell

With Pat O'Brien

CAST: Pat O'Brien, (Rush Blake); Dick Powell, (Clayton); Ginger Rogers, (Peggy); The Four Mills Brothers, (As Themselves); Ted Fiorito & His Band, (As Themselves); The Three Radio Rogues, (As Themselves); Allen Jenkins, (Pete); Grant Mitchell, (Sharpe); Joseph Cawthorne, (Brockman); Joan Wheeler, (Marge); Henry O'Neill, (Tappan); Johnny Arthur, (Secretary); The Debutantes, (As Themselves); Muzzy Marcellino, (As Himself); Grace Hayle, (Mrs. Brockman); Oscar Apfel, (Manager); Billy West, (Bellboy); Gordon (Bill) Elliott, (Gigolo—First Man); Eddie Kane, (Second Man); Larry McGrath, (Third Man); Diane Borget, (Girl); Bob Perry, (Manager); Rosalie Roy, (Girl Operator); Eddie Foster, (First Hillbilly); Billy Snyder, (Second Hillbilly); Matt Brooks, (Third Hillbilly); Morris Goldman, (Fourth Hillbilly); Milton Kibbee, (Announcer); John Murray, (Second Announcer); Sam Hayes, (Peggy's Announcer); Dick Winslow, (Page Boy); Leo Forbstein, (Brusiloff); Harry Seymour, (Announcer); Eddie Shubert, (Reporter); George Chandler, (First Reporter); Sam McDaniel, (Black Waiter); William B. Davidson, (Manager); George Humbert, (Headwaiter); Charles Halton, (Sound Effects Man); Charles Sullivan, (Cabby); Nora Cecil, (Lady in Bed); Charles Lane, (Reporter).

CREDITS: Director, Ray Enright; Production Supervisor, Sam Bischoff; Scenarists, Warren Duff, Harry Sauber; Story by Paul Finder Moss, Jerry Wald. Dialogue Director, Stanley Logan; Photographer, Sid Hickox; Operating Cameraman, Wesley Anderson; Art Director, Esdras Hartley; Editor, Clarence Koster; Sound Recorder, Gordon M. Davis; Unit Manager, Al Alborn. Musical conducted by Leo F. Forbstein. Music Mixer, George R. Groves; Costumer, Orry-Kelly; Makeup Artist, Perc Westmore; Unit Mixer, Clare A. Riggs; Assistant Director, Gordon Hollingshead; Technical Adviser, William Ray.

SONGS: *Fair and Warmer, Out for No Good, What Are Your Intentions, I'll String Along With You, Oh I Heard, Yes I Heard* by Al Dubin, Harry Warren.

SYNOPSIS: Clayton, a singing waiter, is picked up by an agent named Rush Blake, who makes him a big radio discovery. Peggy, an actress who has just lost her own weekly show, helps the new "Golden-Voiced Lochinvar from the West" overcome mike fright, and together they delight millions.

With Dick Powell

REVIEWS

". . . . Brimful of life and vitality . . . . Miss Ginger Rogers is both intelligent and charming."

London *Times*

"The lapses in the story are compensated for by the pleasant vocalizations of Mr. Powell and Miss Rogers."

Thornton Delehanty
New York Evening Post

"Dick Powell is certain to increase his present popularity through his good work in this one, and you have never seen Ginger Rogers look better or play with greater skill."

Regina Crewe
New York American

". . . . Miss Rogers puts an amazing amount of feeling into her interpretation. A growing sensitiveness is visible in her acting."

Edwin Schallert
Los Angeles Times

"Miss Rogers, who always strikes me as being one of the most engaging, natural and attractive of the cinema soubrettes, is of vast help to the proceedings, as she usually is."

Richard Watts, Jr.
New York Herald Tribune

"Ginger Rogers does well as Peggy . . . . Ray Enright's direction is splendid. He reveals originality and freshness in his scenes. It is a happy picture, this *Twenty Million Sweethearts*."

Mordaunt Hall
The New York Times

NOTES: *Twenty Million Sweethearts*, originally called *Hot Air*, was engagingly directed by Ray Enright and remains one of the most enjoyable pictures ever made about radio entertainers. On loan from RKO, Ginger shared top billing with Pat O'Brien and Dick Powell.

Wearing some snazzy outfits designed by Orry-Kelly, Ginger looked great and handled her role with flair. She sang *Out For No Good* and, with Powell, *I'll String Along With You*. Powell soloed with *Man on the Flying Trapeze*, while Ted Fiorito did *Fair and Warmer*. The Mills Brothers did *Oh I Heard, Yes I Heard* and *How'm I Doin'*. The Debutantes did *What Are Your Intentions*, and four Jewish comedians did a takeoff on *The Last Round-Up* called *The Last Wind-Up*.

The whole atmosphere of the particular world of radio was captured.

With Dick Powell, Pat O'Brien, Allen Jenkins, and Sam Hayes

Change of Heart   A Fox Picture, 1934

With Charles Farrell

CAST: Janet Gaynor, (Catherine Furness); Charles Farrell, (Chris Thring); James Dunn, (Mack McGowan); Ginger Rogers, (Madge Rountree); Beryl Mercer, (Harriet Hawkins); Gustav Von Seyffertitz, (Dr. Kurtzman); Fiske O'Hara, (T.P. McGowan); Irene Franklin, (Greta Hailstrom); Kenneth Thomson, (Howard Jackson); Theodore Von Eltz, (Gerald Mockby); Drue Leyton, (Mrs. Gerald Mockby); Nella Walker, (Mrs. Frieda Mockby); Shirley Temple, (Shirley, Girl on Airplane); Barbara Barondess, (Phyllis Carmichael); Jane Darwell, (Mrs. McGowan); Mary Carr, (Mrs. Rountree); Mischa Auer, Jamiel Hassan, (Greenwich Village Sequence); Yolanda Patti, (Waitress); Ed Mundin, (Barker); Nick [dick] Foran, (Singer); Leonid Kinsky, (Guest); Frank Moran, (Moving Man); Nell Craig, (Adoption Assistant); Lillian Harmer, (Landlady); Poppy Wilde, Bess Flowers, (Party Guests); William Norton Bailey, (Man in Street).

CREDITS: Director, John G. Blystone; Producer, Winfield Sheehan; Scenarists, Sonya Levien, James Gleason; Dialogue Director, James Gleason. Based on the novel *Manhattan Love Song* by Kathleen Norris. Additional Dialogue, Samuel Hoffenstein; Photographer, Hal Mohr; Set Decorator, Jack Otterson; Editor, James B. Morley; Sound Recorder, Joseph Aiken; Musical Director, Louis De Francesco; Costumer, Rita Kaufman.

SONG: *So What?* by Harry Akst.

SYNOPSIS: Catherine Furness and Mack McGowan and their close friends, Chris Thring and Madge Rountree, graduate from a West Coast college and fly to New York to seek their fortune. They soon find that looking for jobs is not an easy matter, become discouraged and, eventually, change partners.

With Charles Farrell, Janet Gaynor, and James Dunn

With Charles Farrell, James Dunn, and Janet Gaynor

"Miss Rogers, less gingery than usual, nevertheless manages to suggest what slight 'menace' is required to persuade the spectator that Mr. Farrell may just possibly desert his own 'fiery' and fly instead to her."

Philip K. Scheur
Los Angeles Times

"*Change of Heart* also boasts a supporting team in James Dunn and Ginger Rogers, but they, too, are on the backs of a nag that never quite gets started."

Variety

"Besides Miss Gaynor and Mr. Farrell, there are in the case James Dunn and Ginger Rogers, who are fortunate in having more virile roles than their colleagues . . . . Miss Gaynor gives a sympathetic portrayal. Mr. Farrell scarcely seems always at home in his role. Mr. Dunn affords laughter by his lines and action and Miss Rogers is attractive as the careless young woman."

Mordaunt Hall
The New York Times

"Like figures on an Egyptian bas-relief, they love in profile: Dunn loves Gaynor who loves Farrell who loves Rogers who loves all the boys. When Ginger Rogers marries a rich Broadwayite, Farrell goes into a sickly decline. Miss Gaynor nurses him back to health, marries him, keeps him from sinning with sprightly Ginger Rogers, who finds consolation in breezy Jimmy Dunn."

Time

NOTES: For the filming of Kathleen Norris's *Manhattan Love Song*, Fox borrowed Ginger from RKO to support Janet Gaynor and Charles Farrell. James Dunn completed the quartet.

John G. Blystone directed competently from a script by Sonya Levien and actor James Gleason, the latter also served as dialogue director. Hal Mohr, who was to win an Academy Award the following year for co-photographing Warner's *A Midsummer Night's Dream*, handled the camera for *Change of Heart*.

Like most Gaynor-Farrell pictures, this routine love story was popular. It is surprising how good they were together. Ginger played an altogether different role for her—a mantrap—with precision and conviction. Ginger replaced Sally Eilers, who was originally set for the role of Madge Rountree. The working titles were *In Love With Life* and *The World Is Ours*.

With Charles Farrell, Janet Gaynor, and James Dunn

On the runway singing *Shake Your Powder Puff*

Upperworld
A Warner Bros. Vitaphone Picture, 1934

CAST: Warren William, (Alexander Stream); Mary Astor, (Mrs. Hettie Stream); Ginger Rogers, (Lilly Linder); Theodore Newton, (Rocklen); Andy Devine, (Oscar, the Chauffeur); Dickie Moore, (Tommy Stream); J. Carrol Naish, (Lou Colima); Robert Barrat, (Commissioner Clark); Robert Greig, (Caldwell, the Butler); Ferdinand Gottschalk, (Marcus); Willard Robertson, (Captain Reynolds); Mickey Rooney, (Jerry); John M. Qualen, (Chris, the Janitor); Henry O'Neill, (Banker); Sidney Toler, (Officer Moran); Frank Sheridan, (Inspector Kellogg); Nora Cecil, (Housekeeper); Lester Dorr, (Steward); Wilfred Lucas, (Captain); Cliff Saum, (Sailor); William Jeffrey, (Bradley); Edward Le Saint, (Henshaw); John Elliott, (Crandall); Armand Kaliz, (Maurice); Milton Kibbee, (Pilot); Marie Astaire, Joyce Owen, Lucille Collins, (Chorus Girls); Jay Eaton, (Salesman); James P. Burtis, Henry Otho, (Cops); Douglas Cosgrove, (Johnson); Guy Usher, (Carter); Clay Clement, (Medical Examiner); James Durkin, Monte Vandergrift, Jack Cheatham, (Detectives); William B. Davidson, (City Editor); Edwin Stanley, (Fingerprint Expert); Howard Hickman, (Judge); Frank Conroy, (Attorney); Tom McGuire, (Bailiff); Bert Moorhouse, (Court Clerk); Sidney De Gray, (Foreman); Harry Seymour, (Passerby).

CREDITS: Director, Roy Del Ruth; Scenarist, Ben Markson. Based on a story by Ben Hecht. Production Supervisor, Robert Lord; Photographer, Tony Gaudio; Art Director, Anton Grot; Editor, Owen Marks; Sound Recorder, Gordon M. Davis; Musical Conductor, Leo F. Forbstein; Costumer, Orry-Kelly; Makeup Artist, Perc Westmore; Assistant Director, Lee Katz.

SYNOPSIS: Wealthy businessman Alexander Stream, lonely because his social wife Hettie neglects him, innocently becomes entangled with burlesque queen Lilly Linder. Her shady employer, Lou, sets Stream up for blackmail, and both become involved in Lilly's murder.

REVIEWS

"Ginger Rogers is gaily spontaneous as the revue beauty. She dances with grace and delicacy and maintains her wistful southern charm although cast in a supposedly 'hard-boiled' part."

Katherine T. Von Blon
Los Angeles Times

"Roy Del Ruth, the director, has given the script a lively and engrossing production. The actors, perhaps, are too agreeable for satire. The audience can resent none of these. Warren William, as the millionaire, is friendly, human and deserving of sympathy. It is impossible to dislike either Mary Astor, as the thoughtless wife, or Ginger Rogers as the showgirl."

A.D.S.
The New York Times

"*Upper World* represents a successful triumph of acting over material. Not that its plot lines are particularly undistinguished; it is simply that they do not measure up to the standards of the acting Warren William, Mary Astor and Ginger Rogers bring to them . . . . "

William Boehnel
New York World-Telegram

NOTES: A splendid cast and neat direction turned an otherwise familiar story of the eternal triangle into a fine film. Roy Del Ruth handled his players and situations, sensitively, and his direction was aided by Tony Gaudio's expert camera work and Owen Marks's superb editing.

Ginger was alternately warm, appealing, and funny as a jazzy chorus girl who falls for Warren William; their scenes together were excellent. Mary Astor was properly aristocratic as William's neglectful wife, but what a pity that someone—somewhere—did not have the perspicacity to give Astor and Rogers a scene together!

The title has appeared in two forms: *Upperworld* (One word) and *Upper World* (two words); the studio is to blame—every other release carried a different version.

With J. Carrol Naish

With Warren William

With Warren William

With J. Carrol Naish and Warren William

The Gay Divorcee An RKO-Radio Picture, 1934

Dancing "The Continental" with Fred Astaire

CAST: Fred Astaire, (Guy Holden); Ginger Rogers, (Mimi Glossop); Alice Brady, (Aunt Hortense); Edward Everett Horton, (Egbert Fitzgerald); Erik Rhodes, (Rodolfo Tonetti); Eric Blore, (Waiter); Betty Grable, (Dancer); Charles Coleman, (Guy's Valet); William Austin, (Cyril Glossop); Lillian Miles, (Guest); George Davis, Alphonse Martel, (French Waiters); Paul Porcasi, (French Headwaiter); Charles Hall, (Call Boy at Dock); E.E. Clive, (Chief Customs Inspector); with Art Jarrett

CREDITS: Director, Mark Sandrich; Producer, Pandro S. Berman; Production Associate, Zion Myers; Scenarists, George Marion, Jr., Dorothy Yost, Edward Kaufman. Based on the Broadway musical and novel *The Gay Divorce* by Dwight Taylor. Photographer, David Abel; Art Directors, Van Nest Polglase, Carroll Clark; Editor, William Hamilton; Dance Director, Dave Gould; Sound Recorder, Hugh McDowell, Jr.; Musical Director, Max Steiner; Musical Adaptation, Kenneth Webb, Samuel Hoffenstein; Music Recorders, Murray Spivack, P.J. Faulkner, Jr.; Costumer, Walter Plunkett; Makeup Artist, Mel Burns; Special Photographic Effects, Vernon Walker; Research Director, Elizabeth McGaffey; Assistant Director, Argyle Nelson; Still Photographer, John Miehle.

SONGS: *Night and Day*, by Cole Porter, *Don't Let It Bother You, Let's K-Nock K-Nees*, by Mack Gordon, Harry Revel, *A Needle in a Haystack, The Continental*, by Con Conrad, Herb Magidson.

SYNOPSIS: Egbert Fitzgerald, a dense attorney, sends his client Mimi Glossop to a resort hotel to await a hired co-respondent, Rodolfo Tonetti. Hoofer Guy Holden makes advances toward Mimi, who, thinking him to be the co-respondent, despises him accordingly.

With Edward Everett Horton and Alice Brady

REVIEWS

"Ginger Rogers is also excellent."

Variety

"Ginger Rogers, who developed into a charming comedienne as well as the screen's most able song-and-dance entertainer, has no little to do with the picture's merriment."

Eileen Creelman
New York Sun

"As in *Flying Down to Rio*, Miss Rogers proves herself the nearest thing that Astaire has had to a partner since sister Adele took leave of him. Her dancing in *Night and Day* and in a seductive number called *Continental* is distinguished in its grace and felicitous rhythm."

Thornton Delehanty
New York Evening Post

"Last season it was the Carioca which persuaded the foolhardy to bash their heads together. Now the athletic RKO-Radio strategists have created the Continental, an equally strenuous routine in which you confide your secret dreams to your partner under the protective camouflage of the music . . . . Both as a romantic comedian and as a lyric dancer, Mr. Astaire is an urbane delight, and Miss Rogers keeps pace with him even in his rhythmic flights over the furniture."

Andre Sennwald
The New York Times

NOTES: After *Flying Down to Rio*, Ginger made six more pictures (three for RKO; three on loan-out) while Fred Astaire fulfilled a previous committment by appearing on Broadway (and later in London) in Cole Porter's *The Gay Divorce*. Meanwhile, RKO readied a working script for this musical which, because of U.S. censorship problems, was to be called *The Gay Divorcee*.

The plot was typical French farce, and a cast of expert farceurs was employed, but only one of Cole Porter's original songs was retained: *Night and Day*. The seductive lyrical dance Astaire and Rogers do to this haunting melody still lingers with audience long after the rest of the film is forgotten. Ginger sang *Don't Let It Bother You*, while Edward Everett Horton and pert Betty Grable clowned to *Let's K-Nock K-Nees*. Astaire sang and danced to *A Needle in a Haystack*.

The big production number was *The Continental* which ran a full 22 minutes. Ginger and Astaire were magnificent throughout the number, which Max Steiner musically varied with Latin, waltz and broken rhythms. There were also interpolations by Lillian Miles and Erik Rhodes.

With Fred Astaire

In England the original title was retained

107

The "Night and Day" sequence with Fred Astaire

With Fred Astaire and Erik Rhodes

Romance in Manhattan An RKO-Radio Picture, 1934

CAST: Francis Lederer, (Karel Novak); Ginger Rogers, (Sylvia Dennis); Arthur Hohl, (Attorney Pander); Jimmy Butler, (Frank Dennis); J. Farrell MacDonald, (Officer Murphy); Helen Ware, (Miss Anthrop); Eily Malyon, (Miss Evans); Oscar Apfel, (The Judge); Lillian Harmer, (Landlady); Reginald Barlow, (Customs Inspector); Donald Meek, (Minister); Sidney Toler, (Sergeant); Harold Goodwin, (Doctor).

CREDITS: Director, Stephen Roberts; Producer, Pandro S. Berman; Scenarists, Jane Murfin, Edward Kaufman. Based on a story by Norman Krasna, Don Hartman. Photographer, Nick Musuraca; Art Directors, Van Nest Polglase, Charles Kirk; Editor, Jack Hively; Sound Recorder, John Tribby; Musical Director, Al Colombo; Miniatures, Don Jahravs; Research Director, Elizabeth McGaffey; Makeup Artist, Mel Burns; Special Photographic Effects, Vernon Walker; Assistant Director, Dewey Starkey; Still Photographer, John Miehle.

SYNOPSIS: Young Sylvia Dennis and her kid brother, Frank, "adopt" a Czechoslovakian immigrant whose romantic dream of America as a land of promise is put to the test when he becomes a taxi driver. Not only does Sylvia help Karel Novak, she also falls in love with him in the process.

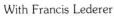
With Francis Lederer

With Sidney Toler, Francis Lederer, and J. Farrell MacDonald

REVIEWS

"Ginger Rogers, one of the more realistic Hollywood blondes, keeps the picture somewhere near the ground in spite of Mr. Lederer's effect of sending it soaring off into space."

New York Sun

"Ginger Rogers, portraying a hard-hit chorus gal, gets into the swing of the tale and handles her role naturally and sympathetically."

Irene Thirer
New York Evening Post

"By expert trouping, Ginger Rogers and Francis Lederer, co-starred, lend considerable credibility to otherwise shallow roles."

Variety

"With Ginger Rogers for his romantic partner, the pride of the Czechs (Francis Lederer) makes a generally engaging

light entertainment out of the slightly anemic materials of *Manhattan Romance* . . . . Miss Rogers continues to be among the most pleasing of the younger Hollywood actresses."

Andre Sennwald
The New York Times

NOTES: Ginger was never one to turn down an opportunity to temporarily hang up her dancing shoes for a dramatic or comic part. In fact, she insisted on these changes of pace. The role of Sylvia Dennis in this movie offered both. Czech star Francis Lederer played the part of friendless immigrant Karlel Novak well. His adventures and misadventures in a new country provided a genial and human story. Stephen Roberts directed this Pandro S. Berman production with his usual foresight.

With Francis Lederer

Roberta An RKO-Radio Picture, 1935

Rehearsing with Fred Astaire

CAST: Irene Dunne, (Stephanie); Fred Astaire, (Huck); Ginger Rogers, (Countess Scharwenka [Lizzie Gatz]); Randolph Scott, (John Kent); Helen Westley, (Roberta) [Aunt Minnie]; Victor Varconi, (Ladislaw); Claire Dodd, (Sophie); Luis Alberni, (Voyda); Ferdinand Munier, (Lord Delves); Torben Meyer, (Albert); Adrian Rosley, (Professor); Grace Hayle, (Lady Reporter); Bodil Rosing, (Fernando); Mike Tellegen, Sam Savitsky, (Cossacks); Zena Savine, (Woman); Johnny "Candy" Candido, Muzzy Marcellino, Gene Sheldon, Howard Lally, William Carey, Paul McLarind, Hal Brown, Charles Sharpe, Ivan Dow, Phil Cuthbert, Delmon Davis, William Dunn, (Orchestra); Lucille Ball, Jane Hamilton, Margaret McChrystal, Kay Sutton, Maxine Jennings, Virginia Reid (Lynne Carver), Lorna Low, Lorraine De Sart, Wanda Perry, Diane Cook, Virginia Carroll, Betty Dumbries, Donna Roberts, (Mannequins); with Mary Forbes, William B. Davidson, Judith Vosselli, Rita Gould.

CREDITS: Director, William Seiter; Producer, Pandro S. Berman; Associate Producer, Zion Myers; Scenarists, Jane Murfin, Sam Mintz; Additional Dialogue, Glenn Tryon, Allan Scott. Based on the Story "Gowns by Roberta" by Alice Duer Miller. Based on the Broadway musical *Roberta* by Jerome Kern, Otto Harbach. Photographer, Edward Cronjager; Art Directors, Van Nest Polglase, Carroll Clark; Set Decorator, Thomas K. Little; Editor, William Hamilton; Sound Recorder, John Tribby; Unit Mixer, P.J. Faulkner, Jr.; Musical Director, Max Steiner. Dances by Fred Astaire. Dance ensembles by Hermes Pan. Costumer, Bernard Newman; Makeup Artist, Mel Burns; Research Director, Elizabeth McGaffey; Assistant Director, Edward Killy; Still Photographer, John Miehle.

SONGS: *Let's Begin, I'll Be Hard to Handle, Yesterdays, I Won't Dance, Smoke Gets in Your Eyes, Lovely to Look at.*

SYNOPSIS: John Kent and his sidekick Huck, stranded along with Huck's orchestra, visit John's Aunt Minnie (internationally known dress designer Roberta). There John meets Stephanie, a Russian princess turned designer, while Huck runs into his old sweetheart Lizzie Gatz, posing as the Countess Scharwenka. When Roberta dies, the foursome race to get the newest fashions presented to the public in a musical fashion show.

REVIEWS

" . . . . But the most pleasant moments in *Roberta* arrive when Fred Astaire and Ginger Rogers turn the story upside down and dance on it. On the three occasions when they allow their feet to speak for them, their sleek and nimble scufflings lift *Roberta* out of the class of ordinary entertainment, make it an intermittent masterpiece. The picture establishes Fred Astaire more firmly than ever as the No. 1 hoofer of the cinema and proves what *The Gay*

With Randolph Scott and Helen Westley

The beginning of the *I Won't Dance* number with Fred Astaire

Dancing *Lovely to Look At* with Fred Astaire

Divorcee suggested: that Ginger Rogers is a wholly acceptable partner."

Time

"Ginger Rogers makes a pert and peppy Indiana native posing as Polish nobility."

Modern Screen

"Fred Astaire and Ginger Rogers dancing like gay elves on a sunbeam . . . . And as for delightful Ginger Rogers, well, she hits new high spots, too."

New York American

"In Ginger Rogers, and as long as he can continue dancing on the screen, Astaire has found an ideal partner. Miss Rogers dances well enough to be able to hold her own in the stepping numbers, which is something when dancing with Astaire. Besides which she looks better and works better with each succeeding picture. In *Roberta*, Miss Rogers makes an authoritative bid for the title of No. 1 Hollywood ingenue. Her work here includes an imitation, unannounced, of Lyda Roberti, who played the stage role."

Variety

"You'll forget the plot when Astaire and Rogers dance."

Liberty

"Mr. Fred Astaire and Miss Ginger Rogers lend it their agreeable personalities and decorate it with their amazing dancing which is so perfect in technique that it has more of the ballet than the ballroom about it . . . . Miss Rogers improves with every film and her partnership with Mr. Astaire should not be broken."

London *Times*

"Mr. Astaire's dancing is not only an aesthetic excitement, but also comedy of a unique and lofty order. In one of the best episodes in *Roberta* he engages in a pantomimic dance with Miss Ginger Rogers which is quite as eloquently comic as an acrimonious love scene out of Noel Coward . . . . For the pattering humor of *Let's Begin, Hard to Handle*, and *I Won't Dance*, there are the extraordinarily pleasing song-and-dance duets of Mr. Astaire and Miss Rogers . . . . If there is a flaw in the photoplay, it is the unfortunate circumstance that Mr. Astaire and his excellent partner, Miss Rogers, cannot be dancing during every minute of it."

Andre Sennwald
The New York Times

With Irene Dunne and Fred Astaire

NOTES: RKO produced a sparkling and tasteful filming of Jerome Kern's Broadway show, *Roberta*. Scenarists Jane Murfin and Sam Mintz stuck close to the original, but additional dialogue by Glenn Tryon and Allan Scott was used to jazz up the script.

Irene Dunne who was lovely as Stephanie, the Russian princess turned dress designer, sang *Yesterdays, Smoke Gets in Your Eyes*, and a Russian song. Fred sang and danced to *Let's Begin*, accompanied by Candy Candido and his orchestra. Astaire and Rogers first sang and then danced to *I'll Be Hard to Handle*.

Lovely to Look At was used first as instrumental music during the fashion show, Dunne later sang it, and then Astaire and Rogers danced to it. Ginger and Fred also sang and danced *I Won't Dance*, and later reprised it for the finale.

William Seiter's direction kept things fresh and alive, as did Max Steiner's handling of the musical.

Lovely to Look At, by Jerome Kern and Jimmy McHugh, was added to the screen version and became the title of the 1951 M-G-M remake.

Dancing *I'll Be Hard to Handle* with Fred Astaire

Star of Midnight   An RKO-Radio Picture, 1935

With William Powell and Frank Reicher

With William Powell

CAST: William Powell, (Clay Dalzell); Ginger Rogers, (Donna Mantin); Paul Kelly, (Kinland); Gene Lockhart, (Swayne); Ralph Morgan, (Mr. Classon [Roger]); Leslie Fenton, (Tim Winthrop); Vivien Oakland, (Mrs. Classon [Jerry]); J. Farrell MacDonald, (Doremus); Russell Hopton, (Tommy Tennant); Frank Reicher, (Abe Ohlman); Robert Emmett O'Connor (Cleary); Francis McDonald, (Kinland Gangster); Paul Hurst, (Corbett).

CREDITS: Director, Stephen Roberts; Producer, Pandro S. Berman; Scenarists, Howard J. Green, Anthony Veiller, Edward Kaufman. Based on the serial story *Star of Midnight* by Arthur Somers Roche. Photographer, J. Roy Hunt; Art Directors, Van Nest Polglase, Charles Kirk; Editor, Arthur Roberts; Sound Recorder, John L. Cass; Musical Score, Max Steiner; Costumer, Bernard Newman; Makeup Artist, Mel Burns; Research Director, Elizabeth McGaffey; Assistant Director, James Anderson; Still Photographer, John Miehle.

SYNOPSIS: A masked dancer mysteriously disappears from a theater. Soon a gossip columnist, on the point of telling master-sleuth Clay Dalzell the secret, is killed. Between drinks, Dalzell and society beauty Donna Mantin solve the murder smoothly, pleasantly, but far from plausibly.

REVIEWS

"Ginger Rogers, rapidly becoming one of the screen's most able light comediennes. . . . neither sings nor dances in this, nor does she need to. Even without Fred Astaire and an orchestra playing Jerome Kern music, Miss Rogers gets along very nicely."

Eileen Creelman
New York Sun

"William Powell is splendid as Dalzell, and so, too, is Ginger Rogers as the lady from Park Avenue."

William Boehnel
New York World Telegram

"This time Mr. Powell has Ginger Rogers to help him solve the mystery, and to keep him happily supplied with drinks, and although she lacks the nonchalant wit of Miss Myrna Loy, she has enough life and intelligence to carry her successfully through this part."

London *Times*

"The presence of Miss Ginger Rogers in the cast is among the decided virtues of the entertainment . . . . The versatile Miss Rogers, who is pleasant to watch in screen musical comedy as in mystery melodrama, is as delightful as usual, in the role of the lawyer's helper, admirer and co-drinker."

Richard Watts
New York Herald Tribune

"Myrna Loy, of course, will always be the perfect partner for Mr. Powell, but Ginger Rogers makes a gallant consort for him here as the persistent lady who is determined to keep their friendship platonic."

Andre Sennwald
The New York Times

NOTES: While RKO was preparing another vehicle for their top dance team, Ginger again worked for Director Stephen Roberts in *Star of Midnight*. As society doll

With George Chandler, Gene Lockhart, and William Powell

Donna Mantin, Ginger co-starred with William Powell in what should have been one of the slickest of mystery melodramas—but wasn't.

The fault was in the script, which lacked plausibility and cheated its audience. Roberts's direction lacked pace. The players managed to breathe a little life into the film, but not enough to keep it afloat.

With Vivien Oakland and William Powell

Top Hat An RKO-Radio Picture, 1935

With Helen Broderick and Fred Astaire

CAST: Fred Astaire, (Jerry Travers); Ginger Rogers, (Dale Tremont); Edward Everett Horton, (Horace Hardwick); Helen Broderick, (Madge Hardwick); Erik Rhodes, (Alberto Beddini); Eric Blore, (Bates); Lucille Ball, (Flower Clerk); Leonard Mudie, (Flower Salesman); Donald Meek, (Curate); Florence Roberts, (Curate's Wife); Edgar Norton, (Hotel Manager, London); Gino Corrado, (Hotel Manager, Venice); Peter Hobbes, (Call Boy); Frank Mills, (Lido Waiter); Tom Ricketts, (Thackeray Club Waiter); Dennis O'Keefe, (Elevator Passenger); with Ben Holmes, Nick Thompson, Tom Costello, John Impolite, Genaro Spagnoli, Rita Rozelle, Phyllis Coghlan, Charles Hall.

On the RKO lot with director Mark Sandrich, Fred Astaire, and composer/lyricist Irving Berlin

CREDITS: Director, Mark Sandrich; Producer, Pandro S. Berman; Scenarists, Dwight Taylor, Allan Scott. Based on the musical *The Gay Divorce* by Dwight Taylor and Cole Porter. Based on the play *The Girl Who Dared* by Alexander Farago, Aladar Laszlo. Photographer, David Abel; Art Directors, Van Nest Polglase, Carroll Clark; Set Decorator, Thomas Little; Editor, William Hamilton. Dances by Fred Astaire. Sound Recorder, Hugh McDowell, Jr.; Director of Ensembles, Hermes Pan; Musical Director, Max Steiner; Orchestrator, Edward Powell; Costumer, Bernard Newman; Unit Mixer, P.J. Faulkner, Jr.; Makeup Artist, Mel Burns; Special Photographic Effects, Vernon Walker; Assistant Director, Argyle Nelson; Still Photographer, John Miehle; Research Director, Elizabeth McGaffey.

SONGS: *The Piccolino, Top Hat, White Tie and Tails, Isn't This a Lovely Day (to Be Caught in the Rain), Cheek to Cheek, No Strings (I'm Fancy Free)*, by Irving Berlin.

SYNOPSIS: Jerry Travers, an entertainer on the London stage, meets pretty Dale Tremont on the street and tries in vain to win her affection. Through his continuous pursuits, he finally makes her fall for him.

REVIEWS

". . . . because both Mr. Astaire and Miss Rogers happen to be comedians as well as dancers, there is virtually no moment when they are not causing havoc in one way or another."

Thornton Delehanty
New York Post

"There has been so much justifiable enthusiasm for the genuine brilliance of Mr. Astaire's work that by comparison Miss Rogers has been neglected. She has been proclaimed a graceful and properly docile partner of the great dancer and a pleasingly pictorial young performer. It happens, however, that she is considerably more than that . . . . For it seems to me that Miss Rogers—who, by the way, is the only actress I can think of who could call herself Ginger and not arouse homicidal rages—has just about everything needed for musical comedy excellence. She has grace and attractiveness and comedy skill, and just the proper amount of romantic gaiety. In addition, she is the best listener since George M. Cohan. She can even simulate attention to the lines of a song when a new melody is being tossed at her amorously."

Richard Watts, Jr.
New York Herald Tribune

Rehearsing the *Piccolino* number for director Mark Sandrich and dance director Hermes Pan (partially hidden)

NOTES: In her fourth picture with Fred Astaire, Ginger sang Irving Berlin's *Get Thee Behind Me, Satan*, but it was cut by the time the film was released (and later used as a solo for Harriet Hilliard in *Follow the Fleet*). What was left in the picture, however, was enough to help make it what many consider their finest film together.

For the romantic adagio *Cheek to Cheek*, Ginger wore a gown of light turquoise satin accented with ostrich feathers. When she and Astaire rehearsed this number for the first time in costume, the feathers started flying, but designer Bernard Newman saved the day by having each single strand knotted. All such technical problems aside, the grace with which they approached this number can never be forgotten.

The *Isn't This a Lovely Day (to Be Caught in the Rain)* number had Ginger in a smart riding habit and Fred in a conventional suit, instead of his usual formal attire.

The setting was London's Hyde Park during a rainstorm. Under the protective roof of a convenient bandstand, the pair actually make you forget that you were watching a movie.

For the production number *The Piccolino*, Irving Berlin gave the stars a hot Italian rhythm with which to demonstrate their terpsichorean skills. They rehearsed more than 125 hours to perfect what was to look so easy on film. Astaire's solos were *No Strings (I'm Fancy Free)* and the sensational *Top Hat, White Tie and Tails* number.

Top Hat was nominated for four Academy Awards: Best Picture; Best Art Direction (Van Nest Polglase and Carroll Clark); Best Dance Director, for *The Piccolino* and *Top Hat* numbers (Hermes Pan); and Best Song, *Cheek to Cheek*, by Irving Berlin. Unfortunately, there were no wins.

Dancing *Isn't This a Lovely Day (to be Caught in the Rain)* with Fred Astaire

The incredible finale—Fred and Ginger dance right off the screen

Dancing *Cheek to Cheek* with Fred Astaire

In Person
An RKO-Radio Picture, 1935

Ginger's incognito scenes with George Brent

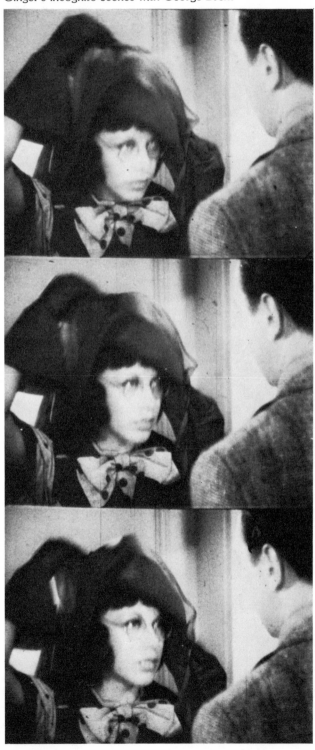

CAST: Ginger Rogers, (Carol Corliss [Clara Colfax]); George Brent, (Emory Muir); Alan Mowbray, (Jay Holmes); Grant Mitchell, (Judge Parks); Samuel S. Hinds, (Dr. Aaron Sylvester); Joan Breslau, (Minna); Louis Mason, (Sheriff Twing); Spencer Charters, (Parson Lunk); Lew Kelly, (Mountain Man); Bob McKenzie, (Theater Manager); Lee Shumway, (Studio Representative); William B. Davidson, (Director Bill Sumner); Tiny Jones, (Woman in Theater); Bud Jamison, (Man in Elevator); George Davis, (Cabbie).

CREDITS: Director, William Siteer; Producer, Pandro S. Berman; Scenarist, Allan Scott. Based on a novel by Samuel Hopkins Adams. Photographer, Edward Cronjager; Art Directors, Van Nest Polglase, Carroll Clark; Editor, Arthur Schmidt; Sound Recorder, Clem A. Portman; Musical Director, Roy Webb. Dances by Hermes Pan. Unit Mixer, P.J. Faulkner, Jr.; Costumer, Bernard Newman; Makeup Artist, Mel Burns; Still Photographer, John Miehle.

SONGS: *Don't Mention Love to Me, Got a New Lease on Life, Out of Sight Out of Mind*, by Oscar Levant, Dorothy Fields.

SYNOPSIS: On a crowded street, Emory Muir comes to the aid of Clara Colfax (actually disguised movie star Carol Corliss), suffering from agoraphobia. Once she learns that Emory is about to retreat to the mountains, Carol joins him and eventually learns to face life—and her own public image.

REVIEWS

"Away from the Fred Astaire partnership, which catapulted Ginger Rogers into radiance as a screen satellite, *In Person* is an unfortunate debut starring effort for her. It may fetch an abnormal amount of negative comment at the expense of Miss Rogers when it's strictly a script fault .... What Miss Rogers does, she does well. She troupes her silly assignment to the hilt. She terps and sings effectively and almost makes the hiding-away screen star role seem real."

Variety

"Remarkable Sight: Miss Rogers in black wig, spectacles, false teeth, which makes her so thoroughly unattractive that RKO's publicity department refused to release 'stills' of her thus disguised."

Time

"Ginger Rogers steps out by herself this week in her first individual starring picture, and steps out very prettily. *In Person* is a slim little comedy, almost too thin for its length; Miss Rogers's twinkling feet and gaiety supply the greater part of the fun. She dances, as she has danced before .... and she sings. If she dances better than she sings, that is hardly news. With the possible exception of her former co-star, Fred Astaire, and of Eleanor Powell, the movies boast no blither dancer than Miss Rogers."

Eileen Creelman
New York Sun

Tapping to *Got a New Lease on Life*
before George Brent

"She seems to have caught from Astaire that pleasantly modest quality that is so rare in the movie stars. She is good anyway, and twice as good because she doesn't seem to think she's anything much."

London *Daily Express*

NOTES: Ginger kept clamoring for her own story—apartfrom her tremendously successful efforts with Fred Astaire—and RKO gave her this little tidbit, taken from a novel by Samuel Hopkins Adams. *In Person* was her first solo starring picture and she worked hard to make this potboiler work, but the story was too mundane.

She was very funny in a black wig and horn-rimmed glasses (complete with pushed-out teeth) in her incognito scenes before co-star George Brent tamed her. Her naturalness of playing was well realized in her later scenes.

Oscar Levant, who was to support Ginger and Fred Astaire in *The Barkleys of Broadway* fourteen years later, wrote three songs with Dorothy Fields. When she and Brent see her latest movie, Ginger sings—onscreen— *Don't Mention Love to Me*, and earlier in the caoin she first sings, on radio, *Got a New Lease on Life*, which she later taps to on a table top. The big production number was the memorable *Out of Sight Out of Mind*. Hermes Pan coached her dances (RKO obviously didn't want the public to forget her musical talents.)

In Person was originally called *Public Property* and then *Tamed*, before it was released.

With Grant Mitchell, George Brent, and Alan Mowbray

With Joan Breslau and George Brent

With George Brent

Follow the Fleet
An RKO-Radio Picture, 1936

CAST: Fred Astaire, (Baker); Ginger Rogers, (Sherry Martin); Randolph Scott, (Bilge Smith); Harriet Hilliard, (Connie Martin); Astrid Allwyn, (Iris Manning); Ray Mayer (Dopey); Harry Beresford, (Captain Hickey); Addison (Jack) Randall, (Lieutenant Williams); Russell Hicks, (Jim Nolan); Brooks Benedict, (Sullivan); Lucille Ball, (Kitty Collins); Betty Grable, Joy Hodges, Jeanne Gray, (Trio); Tony Martin, (Sailor); Maxine Jennings, (Hostess); Jane Hamilton, (Waitress); Frank Mills, Edward Burns, Frank Jenks, (Sailors); Kay Sutton, (Telephone Operator); Doris Lloyd, (Mrs. Courtney); Huntley Gordon, (Touring Officer); James Pierce, (Bouncer); Herbert Rawlinson, (Webber); Thelma Leeds, Lita Chevret, (Girls); Gertrude Short, (Cashier, Dance Joint); George Magrill, (Quartermaster).

CREDITS: Director, Mark Sandrich; Producer, Pandro S. Berman; Scenarist, Dwight Taylor; Based on the play *Shore Leave* by Herbert Osborne, Allan Scott. Photographer, David Abel; Art Director, Van Nest Polglase; Set Decorator, Darrell Silvera; Editor, Henry Berman; Dances by Fred Astaire; Sound Recorder, Hugh McDowell, Jr.; Director of Ensembles, Hermes Pan; Musical Director, Max Steiner; Unit Mixer, P. J. Faulkner, Jr.; Miniatures, Don Jahraus; Costumer, Bernard Newman; Research Director, Elizabeth McGaffey; Makeup Artist, Mel Burns; Special Photographic Effects, Vernon Walker; Assistant Director, Argyle Nelson; Still Photographer, John Miehle; Technical Adviser, Lieutenant Commander Harvey Haislip, U.S.N.

SONGS: *I'm Putting All My Eggs in One Basket, We Saw the Sea, Let's Face the Music and Dance, Let Yourself Go, I'd Rather Lead a Band, Here Am I, But Where Are You?, Get Thee Behind Me, Satan,* by Irving Berlin.

SYNOPSIS: While on shore, two sailors, Baker and Bilge Smith, get involved with two sisters, Sherry and Connie Martin, and end up revamping an old ship into a swank showboat and preparing a musical.

REVIEWS
"Miss Rogers in this one goes beyond the role of dancing vis-a-vis for Astaire and emerges as a corking stepper in her own right. Betty Grable is on and off so quickly it's hardly a screen test."

Variety

"As Sherry, Miss Rogers has never appeared to better advantage. She is more and more lovely to look at. Her

With Jeanne Gray, Betty Grable, and Joy Hodges

Singing *Let Yourself Go*

With Harriet Hilliard

The beautiful production number *Let's Face the Music and Dance* with Fred Astaire

With Astrid Allwyn

Dancing *I'm Putting All My Eggs in One Basket* with Fred Astaire

comedy work and her dancing are superb, and she comes nearer to matching Mr. Astaire in both these departments than ever before. Sherry Martin is the best role she has yet had, and she makes the most of it."

New York World Telegram

"Ginger's dancing has improved immeasurably, and either solo, or partnered by her colleague, she is amazingly good. . . . In addition to their dancing, Fred and Ginger act extremely well, displaying their comedy talents to the full."

Daily Film Renter

"*Follow the Fleet*, the latest Astaire-Rogers music-fest, supplies just what audiences have come to expect from these nimble stars. The picture is well dressed, spirited, and imbued with a lighthearted gaiety. And since Irving Berlin has given it seven new songs, most of which seem definitely in the hit class, *Follow the Fleet* is close to flawless during its lyric moments."

Liberty

"Even though it is not the best of their series, it still is good enough to take the head of this year's class in song and dance entertainment. . . . Comedy, rather than the minor romance of Mr. Scott and Miss Hilliard, would have been a more satisfactory order of the day. We still feel an admiral's salute is due Miss Rogers and Mr. Astaire, with a general broadside of approval for Mr. Berlin, Miss Hilliard, Mr. Scott and Miss Allwyn."

The New York Times

NOTES: Based on the 1922 Herbert Osborne play *Shore Leave*, which also provided the plot for *Hit the Deck*, this was the longest Astaire-Rogers picture—110 minutes. Irving Berlin was on hand again.

Fred and Ginger, in sailor suits, did a jazzy turn or two and some flips to *Let Yourself Go* after Ginger sang. They clowned to the funny *I'm Putting All My Eggs in One Basket*, but it was their finale aboard the showboat that had everybody talking. Performing to the tune of *Let's Face the Music and Dance*, they were the personification of elegance and grace.

Astaire sang and danced to *We Saw the Sea*, which opened the picture and his other solo effort, *I'd Rather Lead a Band*, was reminiscent of his machine-gun tapping to *Top Hat*.

Newcomer Harriet Hilliard sang two numbers, *Here Am I, But Where Are You?* and the song cut from *Top Hat, Get Thee Behind Me, Satan*.

Mark Sandrich again directed with his usual polish and precision, while Hermes Pan worked on the dances with Astaire. Besides Miss Hilliard, the supporting cast included Randolph Scott, Astrid Allwyn, Lucille Ball, Betty Grable and Tony Martin. The total effect of the picture was best summed up by the trade magazine, *Motion Picture Herald*: "All in all, it's grand entertainment."

Unfortunately, the on-again, off-again romance between Hilliard and Scott is a bore, but is difficult to cut out for television showings, so instead the humorous *I'm Putting All My Eggs in One Basket* number gets the editor's ax.

Dancing *Let Yourself Go* with Fred Astaire

With Fred Astaire and Lucille Ball

Swing Time

An RKO-Radio Picture, 1936

CAST: Fred Astaire, (John (Lucky) Garnett); Ginger Rogers, (Penelope (Penny) Carroll); Victor Moore, (Pop [Everett]); Helen Broderick, (Mabel Anderson); Eric Blore, (Gordon); Betty Furness, (Margaret Watson); Georges Metaxa, (Ricardo Romero); Landers Stevens, (Judge Watson); John Harrington, (Dice Raymond); Pierre Watkin, (Al Simpson); Abe Reynolds, (Schmidt); Gerald Hamer, (Eric); Edgar Dearing, (Policeman); Harry Bowen, Harry Bernard, (Stagehands); Donald Kerr, Ted O'Shea, Frank Edmunds, Bill Brand, (Dancers); Frank Jenks, (Red); Frank Mills, (Croupier); Ralph Byrd, (Hotel Clerk); Charles Hall, (Taxi Driver); Jean Perry, (Roulette Dealer); Dale Van Sickel, (Diner); Dennis O'Keefe, Bess Flowers, Ralph Brooks, (Dance Extras *The Way You Look Tonight*); Olin Francis, (Muggsy); Fern Emmett, (Watson's Maid); Floyd Shackleford, (Romero's Butler); Ferdinand Munier, (Minister); Joey Ray, (Announcer); Jack Rice, (Wedding

Dancing to the *Waltz in Swing Time* with Fred Astaire

In costume for the song *A Fine Romance* with Fred Astaire and director George Stevens

Guest); Jack Good, (Dancer); with Blanca Vischer, Sailor Vincent, (Baby) Marie Osborne, Howard Hickman.

CREDITS: Director, George Stevens; Producer, Pandro S. Berman; Scenarists, Howard Lindsay, Allan Scott. Based on a story by Erwin Gelsey. Photographer, David Abel; Art Directors, Van Nest Polglase, Carroll Clark; Set Decorator, Darrell Silvera; Editor, Henry Berman; Dances by Fred Astaire; Sound Recorder, George Marsh; Dance Director, Hermes Pan; Musical Director, Nathaniel Shilkret; Costumer, Bernard Newman; Sets and Costumes for *Bojangles* by John Harkrider; Makeup Artist, Mel Burns; Special Effects, Vernon Walker; Assistant Director, Argyle Nelson; Still Photographer, John Miehle.

SONGS: *The Way You Look Tonight, Bojangles of Harlem, Waltz in Swing Time, Pick Yourself Up, Never Gonna Dance, A Fine Romance,* by Jerome Kern, Dorothy Fields.

SYNOPSIS: John Garnett, a professional dancer, sees pretty young Penelope Carroll on the street and follows her into a dance studio, where, it turns out, she teaches. After many vain attempts at wooing, he begins to make some headway with the girl when Margaret Watson, his old flame, appears on the scene.

REVIEWS

"Miss Rogers at least shares 50-50 with Astaire in *Swing Time* honors, and there will be those who give her an even greater share. Not only does her dancing improve with each appearance, but likewise her acting, and here she shows a distinct flair for delightful comedy."

Regina Crewe
New York American

"Delightful as the Astaire-Rogers combination may be, its twinkling steps and bantering romances are not quite enough to carry an entire production. The stars do better when sharing a picture with some dramatic actors."

Eileen Creelman
New York Sun

"We won't say Fred hasn't ever been as good as he is in *Swing Time* because—well, because he has. But this is certainly Ginger's triumphant vehicle. She's a delectable eyeful and earful!"

Irene Thirer
New York Evening Post

"There's little left to be said about the dancing of this team except that Ginger seems to be getting better. While at first she seemed to be having difficulties trying to keep up with Fred, now she's gotten to the point where she dances just as casually as her partner."

New York Evening Journal

"If, by any chance, you are harboring any fears that Mr. Astaire and Miss Rogers have lost their magnificent sense of rhythm, be reassured. Their routines, although slightly more orthodox than usual, still exemplify ballroom technique at its best. . . . Nothing so intangible as a disappointing score should deter you from enjoying them to the Astaire-Rogers limit."

Frank S. Nugent
The New York Times

"It is high time that Fred Astaire and Ginger Rogers were relieved of the necessity of going through a lot of romantic nonsense in their screen musicales. The vast success of *Swing Time* . . . is more of a tribute to them than to the material of their latest song and dance carnival. They have never performed with more exquisite finish, but the production itself is uneven and definitely disappointing in its conclusion."

New York Herald Tribune

NOTES: This beautifully mounted film owes much of its success to director George Stevens. In their sixth film, Ginger and Fred seemed to be supercharged in the numbers they sang and danced, either separately or together. Ginger benefited from Steven's direction and rapidly dispelled the oft-repeated fiction that she was merely Astaire's lucky dancing partner. Indeed, her acting had improved and her screen image as a down-to-earth girl was further enhanced by her adept handling of this part.

With Victor Moore and Fred Astaire

Jerome Kern and Dorothy Fields provided the delicious dancing duo with some of their finest musical moments. Fred sang and he and Ginger danced eloquently to *Never Gonna Dance*—the film's working title—and they both sang and danced with vigor to *Pick Yourself Up*. Their beautiful rendition of the *Waltz in Swing Time* could not have been bettered. Fred sang and tickled the ivories to, *The Way You Look Tonight*, which won an Oscar for the Best Song of 1936. Together they sang *A Fine Romance*, which also became a popular hit song.

In blackface, Astaire astounded everyone as *Bojangles of Harlem*—one of the peaks of his film career. Hermes Pan won an Academy Award nomination for his work as Dance Director of the Bojangles number.

With Eric Blore and Helen Broderick

Shall We Dance
An RKO-Radio Picture, 1937

Dancing to *They All Laughed* with Fred Astaire

CAST: Fred Astaire, (Petrov [Pete Peters]); Ginger Rogers, (Linda Keene); Edward Everett Horton, (Jeffrey Baird); Eric Blore, (Cecil Flintridge); Jerome Cowan, (Arthur Miller); Ketti Gallian, (Lady Tarrington); William Brisbane, (Jim Montgomery); Harriet Hoctor, (Harriet Hoctor); Ann Shoemaker, (Mrs. Fitzgerald); Ben Alexander, (Bandleader); Emma Young, (Tai); Sherwood Bailey, (Newsboy); Pete Theodore, (Dancing Partner); Marek Windheim, Rolfe Sedan, (Ballet Masters); George Magrill, (Room Steward); Charles Coleman, (Cop in Park); Frank Moran, (Big Man); with Charles Irwin, Jean de Briac, Norman Ainsley, Sam Wren, Pauline Garon, Leonard Mudie, Vasey O'Davoren, Alphonse Martel, Helena Grant, William Burress, Matty Roubert, J. M. Kerrigan, Sam Hayes, Torben Meyer, Spencer Teakle.

CREDITS: Director, Mark Sandrich; Producer, Pandro S. Berman; Scenarists, Allan Scott, Ernest Pagano; Adaptation, P. J. Wolfson. Based on the story *Watch Your Step* by Lee Loeb, Harold Buchman. Photographer, David Abel; Art Directors, Van Nest Polglase, Carroll Clark; Set Decorator, Darrell Silvera; Editor, William Hamilton; Sound Recorder, Hugh McDowell; Dances by Fred Astaire. Musical Score, George Gershwin; Musical Director, Nathaniel Shilkret; Orchestrator, Robert Russell Bennett; Music Arranger, Joseph A. Livingston; Ballet Director, Harry Losee; Makeup Artist, Mel Burns; Special Photographic Effects, Vernon L. Walker; Director of Ensembles, Hermes Pan; Assistant Director, Argyle Nelson; Still Photographer, John Miehle; Wardrobe Attendant, Edith Clark.

SONGS: *Slap That Bass*, *Let's Call The Whole Thing Off*, *They Can't Take That Away from Me*, *Shall We Dance*, *They All Laughed*, *I've Got Beginner's Luck*, by Ira Gershwin, George Gershwin.

SYNOPSIS: Russian ballet star Petrov falls in love with internationally famous hotcha dancer, Linda Keene, but their temperaments clash until her manager, Arthur Miller, cooks up a juicy scandal which eventually brings them together.

REVIEWS
"Miss Rogers' chief virtue remains her lack of ostentation; well-gowned for the occasion, she seems a trifle too lackadaisical, both as actress and singer, but that may merely be the effect of a story which compels her to sulk for most of the time."

Winston Burdett
Brooklyn Daily Eagle

Roller skating with Fred Astaire to *Let's Call the Whole Thing Off*

With Fred Astaire

"The only drawback, if anything of such proved popularity can be so considered, is the familiarity of the Astaire-Rogers act."

Archer Winston
New York Post

"For Miss Rogers, of the gorgeous figure, this picture, at last, marks a decided improvement in dressing. She's still playing around with her hair, though, and not always advantageously according to the camera. The best point about Miss Rogers in these Astaire films continues to be the way she handles herself when he is singing. She rates plenty on this point. It is also a pleasure to watch Miss Rogers sing a song after looking at some of the other Coast girls. No shaking of the shoulders, no weaving hips. Some of the other girls should drop in lest they forget. Her dancing with Astaire is again also good."

Variety

"One of the best things the screen's premier dance team has done, a zestful, prancing, sophisticated musical show. It has a grand score by George Gershwin (lyrics by brother Ira), a generous leavening of comedy, a plot or so and, forever, and ever, the nimble hoofing of a chap with quicksilver in his feet and of a young woman who has leaped to follow him with assurance."

F.S.N.
The New York Times

On the set with director Mark Sandrich

133

With Eric Blore, Ketti Gallian, and Fred Astaire

NOTES: *Shall We Dance* was the seventh Astaire-Rogers picture and was to be their last when it became known that *Swing Time* (their sixth) was running aground at the box office after a marvelous beginning in the large cities.

Mark Sandrich, who had directed them in *The Gay Divorcee*, *Top Hat* and *Follow the Fleet*, handed similar chores here. *Shall We Dance* was graced with songs by George and Ira Gershwin. One of the best, *Let's Call the Whole Thing Off*, was further intensified by Astaire and Rogers dancing it on roller skates. This unusual feat was further proof that RKO felt their top-flight team might run out of steam at the box office.

Besides Ginger's delightful song *They All Laughed*

and Fred's solo *I've Got Beginner's Luck*, Ginger danced with a new partner—Pete Theodore—while Astaire danced with former Ziegfeld ballerina Harriet Hoctor. Fred and Ginger still gave fans plenty to talk about with their superb dance, *They All Laughed*, and the big production number, *Shall We Dance*.

Originally called *Watch Your Step* and then changed to *Stepping Toes* during production, *Shall We Dance*, like other Astaire and Rogers pictures, benefited greatly from a strong supporting cast. The Gershwin song *They Can't Take That Away from Me*, which Fred sang on the ferry, was nominated for an Academy Award but lost out to *Sweet Leilani* from Paramount's *Waikiki Wedding*.

With Pete Theodore

134

Stage Door
An RKO-Radio Picture, 1937

CAST: Katharine Hepburn, (Terry Randall); Ginger Rogers, (Jean Maitland); Adolphe Menjou, (Anthony Powell); Gail Patrick, (Linda Shaw); Constance Collier, (Catherine Luther); Andrea Leeds, (Kaye Hamilton); Samuel S. Hinds, (Henry Sims); Lucille Ball, (Judy Canfield); Pierre Watkin, (Richard Carmichael); Franklin Pangborn, (Harcourt); Elizabeth Dunne, (Mrs. Orcutt); Phyllis Kennedy, (Hattie); Grady Sutton, (Butcher); Jack Carson, (Milbank); Fred Santley, (Dukenfield); William Corson, (Bill); Frank Reicher, (Stage Director); Eve Arden, (Eve); Ann Miller, (Annie); Jane Rhodes, (Ann Braddock); Margaret Early, (Mary); Jean Rouverol, (Dizzy); Norma Drury, (Olga Brent); Peggy O'Donnell, (Susan); Harriet Brandon, (Madeline); Katherine Alexander, Ralph Forbes, Mary Forbes, Huntley Gordon, (Cast of Play); Lynton Brent, (Aide); Theodore Von Eltz, (Elsworth); Jack Rice, (Playwright); Harry Strang, (Chauffeur); Bob Perry, (Baggageman); Larry Steers, (Theater Patron); Mary Bovard, Frances Gifford, Josephine Whittell, Ada Leonard, Mary Jane Shower, Diana Gibson, Linda Gray, Alison Craig, Adele Pearce (Pamela Blake), Lynn Gabriel (Actresses); Jack Gardner, (Script Clerk); Whitey the Cat, (Eve's Cat); Ben Hendricks, Jr., (Waiter); Jack Gargan, Theodore Kosloff, Gerda Mora, Julie Kingdon, (Dancing Instructors); Al Hill, (Taxi Driver); with Byron Stevens, D'Arcy Corrigan, Philip Morris.

CREDITS: Director, Gregory La Cava; Producer, Pandro S. Berman; Scenarists, Morrie Ryskind, Anthony Veiller. Based on the play by Edna Ferber, George S. Kaufman. Photographer, Robert DeGrasse; Art Director, Van Nest Polglase; Set Decorator, Darrell Silvera; Editor, William Hamilton; Sound Recorder, John L. Cass; Musical Score, Roy Webb; Costumer, Muriel King; Jewelry, Trabert & Hoeffer, Inc., Maubonssin; Makeup Artist, Mel Burns; Assistant Director, James Anderson; Still Photographer, John Miehle.

SONG: *Put Your Heart Into Your Feet and Dance*, by Hal Borne, Mort Greene.

SYNOPSIS: The ambitions, dreams and disappointments in a boardinghouse full of stage aspirants. The rich girl trying to make it on her own; the jazzy, flippant girl whose wisecracks protect her from harsh realities; and the oversensitive girl who is hurt deeply by every setback, dominate the scene.

With Adolphe Menjou

With Andrea Leeds

With Gail Patrick

REVIEWS

"Miss Rogers has more to do than Miss Hepburn, but her part is less clearly defined. As a sharpshooter with the snappy reply she scores heavily. Also she does a tipsy scene in Menjou's penthouse which is very amusing. She clearly demonstrates her ability to handle comedy with the same agility she handles her feet. In a slick role she is surefire."

Variety

". . . if you tell me that it is Miss Ginger Rogers who gives the finest performance in the photoplay, I don't believe that I will be able to dispute you. For several years there has been a curious tendency on the part of people who should know better to suggest that Miss Rogers was merely a good-looking dancing girl who was lucky enough to have Fred Astaire for a partner. As a matter of fact, of course, she was a most important contributor to the success of the team and has always had an authentic and original talent as a light comedienne. Now, by her portrayal of the role of Miss Hepburn's sardonic roommate and heckler, a sort of extension of the part Miss Lee Patrick played so well on the stage, she proves conclusively that her gift for comedy playing is deft and delightful. In particular I recommend to you the scene in which she gets slightly in her cups while passing an evening in Adolphe Menjou's penthouse. It is the sort of thing that is rarely done without either excessive vulgarity or a complete lack of credibility. But Miss Rogers succeeds in making the girl seem both alcoholic and entirely charming, and that is nothing short of an epic feat."

New York Herald Tribune

"The real heroine, however, is Ginger Rogers as Jean Maitland, a hard-boiled singer and dancer on whom no one can put anything over. As I have said, I could hear far too little, but I heard enough to know that she was the one candidly-caustic and caustically-candid mistress of every situation."

Punch

On the set with director Gregory LaCava and Katharine Hepburn

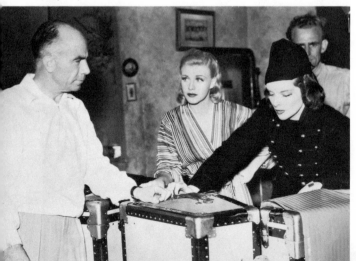

With Ann Miller, Eve Arden, and Lucille Ball

With Katharine Hepburn

"What with Katharine Hepburn, Ginger Rogers, Andrea Leeds, Constance Collier, Gail Patrick, Lucille Ball and all the others, it is a long time since we have seen so much feminine talent so deftly handled. When you think of Miss Rogers' former song-and-dance appearances, it seems as though this is the first chance she has had to be something more than a camera object and stand forth in her own right, pert and charming and just plain nice, her personality flexible in the actor's expression."

Otis Ferguson
The New Republic

NOTES: Ginger had been begging RKO executives for years for a chance to show what a good actress she really was; she proved it in *Stage Door*. Gregory La Cava directed a hand-picked cast with sureness, and managed to evoke the best possible performance from each of his top performers. The result was that rare item: a screenplay that became better than the play on which it was based.

The studio, playing it safe, wrote in a small production number featuring Ginger and Ann Miller. The girls tapped to *Put Your Heart into Your Feet and Dance* in a rehearsal and in a later nightclub sequence.

Katharine Hepburn, winning new laurels for a career that was suffering from costume-itis, gave a splendid account of herself, while Ginger burst forth as a fine comedienne. Jean Maitland remains one of her truly best screen portrayals. The supporting cast was perfect in every way, especially Adolphe Menjou, Constance Collier, and Gail Patrick.

Young Andrea Leeds benefited the most from La Cava's coaching in the difficult role of Kaye Hamilton. She was simply stunning, but she was a shining example of a director's actress—she was never to match this performance again. Her role won her an Academy Award nomination for Best Supporting Actress. The picture was nominated, as were La Cava and Morrie Ryskind and Anthony Veiller, whose witty adaptation made the whole thing possible. Hepburn and Rogers were ignored.

Having Wonderful Time An RKO-Radio Picture, 1938

With Douglas Fairbanks, Jr.

With Jack Carson, Douglas Fairbanks, Jr., Lucille Ball, and Lee Bowman

CAST: Ginger Rogers, (Teddy Shaw); Douglas Fairbanks, Jr., (Chick Kirkland); Peggy Conklin, (Fay Coleman); Lucille Ball, (Miriam); Lee Bowman, (Buzzy Armbruster); Eve Arden, (Henrietta); Dorothea Kent, (Maxine); Richard "Red" Skelton, (Itchy Faulkner); Donald Meek, (P. U. Rogers); Jack Carson, (Emil Beatty); Kirk Windsor, (Henry); Clarence H. Wilson, (Mr. G); Allan (Rocky) Lane, (Mac); Grady Sutton, (Gus); Shimen Ruskin, (Shrimpo); Dorothy Tree, (Frances); Leona Roberts, (Mrs. Shaw); Harlan Briggs, (Mr. Shaw); Inez Courtney, (Emma); Juanita Quigley, (Mabel); Betty Rhodes, (Singer); George Meeker, Ronnie Rondell, (Subway Mashers); Elise Cavanna, (Office Supervisor); Ann Miller (cut from release print), (Vivian); with Mary Bovard, Frances Gifford, Peggy Montgomery, (Baby) Marie Osborne, Mary Jane Irving, Wesley Barry, Dorothy Moore, Stanley Brown, Etienne Girardot, Margaret Seddon, Kay Sutton, Dorothy Day, Lynn Bailey, Tommy Watkins, Cynthia Hobard Fellows, Steve Putnam, Bill Corson, Bob Thatcher, Ben Carter, Russell Gleason, Florence Lake, Vera Gordon and Margaret McWade.

CREDITS: Director, Alfred Santell; Producer, Pandro S. Berman; Scenarist, Arthur Kober. Based on the play by Arthur Kober. Photographer, Robert DeGrasse; Art Directors, Van Nest Polglase, Perry Ferguson; Set Decorator, Darrell Silvera; Editor, William Hamilton; Sound Recorder, John E. Tribby; Musical Director, Roy Webb; Dialogue Director, Ernest Pagano; Miss Rogers's Gowns by Renie; Wardrobe Supervisor, Edward Stevenson; Makeup Artist, Mel Burns; Special Photographic Effects, Vernon L. Walker; Assistant Director, James Anderson; Still Photographer, John Miehle.

SONGS: *Nighty Night*, *My First Impression of You*, by Charles Tobias, Sammy Stept, Bill Livingston.

SYNOPSIS: Teddy Shaw, a bored New York office girl, goes to a camp in the Catskill Mountains for rest and relaxation and finds romance in the form of Chick Kirkland.

REVIEWS

"Ginger Rogers and Douglas Fairbanks, Jr. play the leads as well as anyone but Katherine Locke and Jules Garfield could. . . . It's too bad they couldn't have come from the Bronx instead of Hollywood."

Frank S. Nugent
The New York Times

"The decorative Miss Rogers proves once again that her ability isn't confined solely to dancing. . ."

Rose Pelswick
New York Journal-American

"Ginger Rogers gives one of her very pretty performances, and, whether guarding the feather in her hat or her maidenly honor, presents a picture of elegant womanhood alert to the problems of modern society."

John Mosher
The New Yorker

With Richard "Red" Skelton

With Peggy Conklin

"Both Miss Rogers and Fairbanks have their followings, although neither adds to fame through this picture. . . . The joy, the awakening and the tragic tones of *Having Wonderful Time* are missing. The poetry of its love story is gone. It's just another film."

Variety

"Well, the Will Hays organization—and that, as you know, is the censor with a capital C—first went on record as saying that the play could not be done as a picture. It was too much identified with the Bronx and the Jewish people might create misunderstanding, racial antagonism and all that. Thereupon, RKO very carefully explained that this angle would be entirely eliminated—that the picture would simply be about young people of the lower-middle class. That seemed to be satisfactory. So when I was called in to make the adaptation, the first thing I had to do was turn my Jewish characters into Gentiles. Terry Stern, the little heroine, whom Ginger Rogers played, became Teddy Shaw; Chick Kessler, her sweetheart, played by Douglas Fairbanks, Jr., was given the handle of Chick Kirkland; Fay Fromkin, Teddy's friend, became Fay Coleman; 'Pinkie' Aaronson and Sam Rappaport got completely new names—they became 'Buzzy' Armbruster and Emil Beatty; and even poor 'Itchy' Flexner had to change his proud family name to Faulkner. Only the name of the camp—Camp Carefree—was allowed to remain. And, of course, by some curious contradiction of Hollywood's usual practice, the title of the play went unchanged."

The New York Times

NOTES: Arthur Kober's delightful Broadway play starred Jules Garfield and Katherine Locke with a cast that included Sheldon Leonard and Cornel Wilde in early 1937. Kober's unique understanding and presentation of a Jewish community in the Bronx had everyone howling with laughter. Jules Garfield went to Hollywood shortly thereafter, to become John Garfield, and Arthur Kober reported to RKO to make *Having Wonderful Time* into a *Gentile* soap opera, changing all of the names of his characters!

The studio gave this property to one of its second-string directors, Alfred Santell, who performed his task in an efficient enough manner, but the spark and bite was gone from Kober's original comedy. The result was totally pointless.

Douglas Fairbanks, Jr., was handsome and Ginger was charming, but the supporting cast (Lucille Ball, Lee Bowman, and Eve Arden) provided most of the humor, such as it was. Twenty-three year-old Richard "Red" Skelton, in his movie debut, was so unfunny to the point of boredom that one marvels that he created an entire career out of such nonsense. Ann Miller as Vivian, billed after Skelton, was cut from most of the final print, but can still be spotted in the background of four scenes!

The film contained two forgettable songs (forgettably sung by Betty Rhodes), but did have some beautiful location photography by Robert de Grasse.

Vivacious Lady   An RKO-Radio Picture, 1938

With James Stewart

CAST: Ginger Rogers, (Frances Brent [Francey La Roche]); James Stewart, (Peter Morgan); James Ellison, (Keith Beston); Charles Coburn, (Dr. Morgan); Beulah Bondi, (Mrs. Morgan); Frances Mercer, (Helen); Phyllis Kennedy, (Jenny); Alec Craig, (Joseph); Franklin Pangborn, (Apartment Manager); Grady Sutton, (Culpepper); Hattie McDaniel, (Black Maid); Jack Carson, (Waiter Captain); Willie Best, (Porter); Dorothy Moore, (Hat-Check Girl); Maurice Black, (Headwaiter); Frank M. Thomas, (R. R. Conductor); Spencer Charters, (Husband); Maude Eburne, (Wife); Jane Eberling, (Girl on Bus); Marvin Jones, (Boy on Bus); Bobby Barber, (Italian); Ray Mayer, George Chandler, (Men on Train); with Harry Campbell, June Johnson, Kay Sutton, Phyllis Fraser, Bud Flanagan (Dennis O'Keefe), Edgar Dearing, Helena Grant, Vivian Reid, William Brisbane, Vernon Dent, Katharine Ellis, June Horne, Dorothy Johnson, Phoebe Terbell, Robert Wilson, Stanley Blystone, Barbara Pepper.

CREDITS: Director, George Stevens; Producer, Pandro S. Berman; Scenarists, P. J. Wolfson, Ernest Pagano. Based on a story by I. A. R. Wylie. Photographer, Robert DeGrasse; Art Directors, Van Nest Polglase, Carroll Clark; Set Decorator, Darrell Silvera; Editor, Henry Berman; Sound Recorder, Hugh McDowell, Jr.; Musical Score, Roy Webb; Orchestrator, Robert Russell Bennett; Vocal Arrangements, Roger Edens; Costumers, Bernard Newman, Irene; Makeup Artist, Mel Burns; Assistant Director, Argyle Nelson; Still Photographer, John Miehle.

SONG: *You'll Be Reminded of Me*, by George Jessel, Jack Meskill, Ted Shapiro.

SYNOPSIS: Scintillating nightclub singer Frances Brent meets and marries studious botany professor Peter Morgan, then runs into trouble when he takes her to his small-town home to meet his parents.

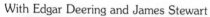

With Edgar Deering and James Stewart

REVIEWS

"*Vivacious Lady* is a pleasant reminder that Ginger Rogers is something more than the other half of a dance team. Without the aid of so much as a time step, she turns in the week's best comedy performance, nicely supported by james Stewart."

Russell Maloney
The New Yorker

"Ginger Rogers's talent for getting into good pictures and managing in surprising little ways to be as good as they are is again demonstrated in *Vivacious Lady* which comes like a veritable deluge of wit in the prevailing drought of comedy. . . . Beulah Bondi, as the prexy's wife whose alleged weak heart is simply a device for keeping peace in the family, is an excellent foil for Mr. Coburn, with his magnificent monocle and intellectual snobbism. James Ellison, formerly of the horse operas, behaves beautifully in a dress suit, and George Stevens directs everybody as they haven't been directed at RKO since *Stage Door*."

Bosley Crowther
The New York Times

"We'd all have to go all the way back to *Nothing Sacred* and *The Awful Truth* for a film comedy that compares with it in sheer fun and broad humor of an adult type. . . . Stewart and Miss Rogers are perfectly matched in their ability to project the nuances of the comedy which are derived from the frustrated efforts of the young lovers to get together. And while Miss Rogers' ardent admirers may miss the twinkling of her clever toes, she makes up for the lack of dance steps by heightening her reputation as a comedienne and by singing prettily, in the introductory scene, the one song number of the picture, *You'll Be Reminded of Me*."

Kate Cameron
New York Daily News

NOTES: George Stevens, who had directed Ginger in *Swing Time*, helped her add another fine protrayal to her ever-growing roster of screen heroines. Her sparkling nightclub singer, Francey La Roche, was indeed a *vivacious lady*. Her knock-down, drag-out fight with Frances Mercer is terribly funny. In the early scenes of the film, Ginger sang *You'll Be Reminded of Me*, but thereafter was content to rely upon her comic expertise.

James Stewart was a perfect co-star for Ginger: the shy, soft-spoken character complemented them both.

Although Stevens's direction was slow and methodical, he concentrated on characterizations and natural developments between his actors. Especially effective were Charles Coburn, Beulah Bondi, Franklin Pangborn, and Grady Sutton. One of the most memorable scenes had Ginger doing the *Big Apple* with Beulah Bondi, James Ellison, and Charles Coburn.

Robert de Grasse received an Academy Award nomination for his splendid photography. RKO's sound department, headed by James Wilkinson, also received a nomination.

With James Ellison, Charles Coburn, and Beulah Bondi

With Maude Eburne, Spencer Charters, and James Stewart

With Hattie McDaniel

With Fred Astaire in the cut number *Let's Make the Most of Our Dream*.

With Fred Astaire,
Ralph Bellamy
and Luella Gear

Carefree
An RKO-Radio Picture, 1938

CAST: Fred Astaire, (Tony Flagg); Ginger Rogers, (Amanda Cooper); Ralph Bellamy, (Stephen Arden); Luella Gear, (Aunt Cora); Jack Carson, (Connors); Clarence Kolb, (Judge Travers); Franklin Pangborn, (Roland Hunter); Walter Kingsford, (Dr. Powers); Kay Sutton, (Miss Adams); Hattie McDaniel, (Hattie); Richard Lane, (Henry); James Finlayson, (Man at Golf Course); with Grace Hayle, Jack Arnold (Vinton Haworth), Phyllis Kennedy, Frank Moran, Edward Gargan, William Carson, and Robert B. Mitchell and His St. Brendan's Boys.

CREDITS: Director, Mark Sandrich; Producer, Pandro S. Berman; Scenarists, Ernest Pagano, Allan Scott; Adaptation, Dudley Nichols, Hagar Wilde. Based on an original story by Marian Ainslee, Guy Endore. Photographer, Robert DeGrasse; Art Directors, Van Nest Polglase, Carroll Clark; Set Decorator, Darrell Silvera; Editor, William Hamilton; Dances by Fred Astaire; Director of Ensembles, Hermes Pan; Sound Recorder, Hugh McDowell, Jr.; Musical Score, Victor Baravalle; Miss Rogers's Gowns by Howard Greer; Wardrobe Supervision, Edward Stevenson; Makeup Artist, Mel Burns; Special Photographic Effects, Vernon L. Walker; Assistant to Producer, Fred Fleck; Assistant Director, Argyle Nelson; Still Photographer, John Miehle.

SONGS: *Change Partners, I Used to Be Color Blind, The Yam, Since They Turned Loch Lomond into Swing,* by Irving Berlin.

SYNOPSIS: Tony Flagg, a psychiatrist, goes out of his way to try to marry off his best friend, Stephen Arden, to a radio star, Amanda Cooper, who cannot make up her mind to marry the guy. As time goes on, Amanda finds herself falling in love with the doctor instead.

With Luella Gear and Hattie McDaniel

Dancing *The Yam* with Fred Astaire

REVIEWS

"Fred has never been more charming, Ginger never more winsome. Their frolics in the dance, including the new invention, 'The Yam,' are, as always, lessons in ease and grace."

New York Post

"It is an expert bit of slapstick nonsense, and as played by Ginger Rogers in the role of Amanda, is as fine a bit of comedy acting as this department has seen in months. Indeed, it confirms what a number of us have felt for a long time, and that is that Miss Rogers is a thoroughly delightful and expert comedienne."

New York World-Telegram

"Mr. Astaire and Ginger never have had a screen play so flawlessly fitted to them. It plausibly introduces the Astaire-Rogers dances in tricky slow-motion. . .Gowned in rather tastelessly extreme costumes, lithe Miss Rogers overcomes them by giving a soundly comic performance. . . . Miss Rogers and Mr. Astaire really should recognize a moral obligation to their fans and refuse to engage in disputes, since they are able together to relieve the sour disposition of the modern mood with such pictures as *Carefree*.

New York Mirror

"More to our taste is *Carefree*, in which the team of Astaire and Rogers becomes the team of Rogers and Astaire. Ginger has taken the lead quite away from her dancing man, except—of course—when they are dancing: Mr. Astaire still seems to be showing her the steps. But otherwise, it is Miss Rogers' comedy and she rules it beautifully."

Frank Nugent
The New York Times

"Coming back into a musical in which I dance, is like putting on a favorite coat or dress which has been laid aside for the time being in favor of newer garments. Everything about it was familiar and easy, and made me feel at home. There is the thrill of newness because I had been away from musicals for more than a year, and there was the charm of variety in changing back and forth from dramatic to musical pictures. It was rather like old home week, too, on the set, with Irving Berlin dropping in to say 'Hello.' . . . This is the eighth joint picture for Fred Astaire and myself. It was as 'Carefree' as one could wish."

Ginger Rogers in the
Brooklyn Daily Eagle

NOTES: *Carefree* clearly demonstrates RKO executives' rethinking process concerning Astaire and Rogers, *i.e*, more concentration on story and character development with songs and dances complementing both, but not becoming an end unto themselves. This was, more than anything else, a delightful spoof on psychiatry (possibly the first), and the finished film included only half of the songs that Irving Berlin composed for it.

Berlin wrote a song called *Care-Free*, but the vocal was scrapped and the music was renamed *Since They Turned Loch Lomond into Swing* for Astaire's golf routine solo. It was his weakest solo number in all their films together.

Ginger was thoroughly charming as a radio singer who could not make up her mind about marriage. Her style was easy, fun-filled and, yes, carefree. Particularly hilarious were Ginger's misadventures while under anesthesia.

In a brief dream sequence, Fred first sang, and then he and Ginger danced in slow-motion to *I Used to Be Color Blind*. It was one of the highlights of their partnership, and the slow-motion idea was inspired and beautifully lyrical. It looks as though the number might originally have been shot in color.

At the country club, Ginger sang and then they danced to the tricky number, *The Yam*. Soon other couples joined them. It is interesting to note that Berlin's song, *The Night Is Filled With Music*, was planned as a song-and-dance routine, but, vocal deleted, it was merely used as instrumental background.

Their biggest hit of this film was *Change Partners*, which was also the working title. Ralph Bellamy and Ginger danced next to Astaire and Luella Gear while Astaire sang the lyrics—and later, on the terrace, he and Ginger danced to it.

Besides these musical numbers, a full-scale dream sequence was filmed. Fred sang, and he and Ginger danced to Berlin's *Let's Make the Most of Our Dream*, but this entire production number was deleted from the final release prints.

Carefree received three Academy Award nominations, but produced no winners: Van Nest Polglase and Carroll Clark for their Art Direction; Victor Baravalle for his musical score; and Berlin's song *Change Partners*—which lost out to *Thanks for the Memory* from Paramount's *Big Broadcast of 1938*.

With Fred Astaire

Dancing *Change Partners* with Fred Astaire

The Story of Vernon and Irene Castle
An RKO-Radio Picture, 1939

CAST: Fred Astaire, (Vernon Castle); Ginger Rogers, (Irene Castle); Edna May Oliver, (Maggie Sutton); Walter Brennan, (Walter); Lew Fields (Himself); Etienne Girardot, (Papa Aubel); Janet Beecher, (Mrs. Foote); Rolfe Sedan, (Emile Aubel); Leonid Kinskey, (Artist); Robert Strange, (Dr. Foote); Douglas Walton, (Student Pilot); Clarence Derwent, (Papa Louis); Sonny Lamont, (Charlie); Frances Mercer, (Claire Ford); Victor Varconi, (Grand Duke); Donald MacBride, (Hotel Manager); Dick Elliott, (Conductor); David McDonald, John Meredith, (Army Pilots); Tiny Jones, (Lady in Revolving Door); Marjorie Belcher (later Marge Champion), (Irene's girlfriend); with Roy D'Arcy, Don Brodie, Bill Franey, Joe Bordeaux, Neil Burns, Jack Perrin, Bill Paton, "Buzz" Barton, Neal Hart, Frank O'Connor, D. H. Turner, Bruce Mitchell, Max Darwyn, Leonard Mudie, Hugh McArthur, Esther Muir, Theodore Von Eltz, George Irving, Willis Clare, Russell Hicks, Hal K. Dawson, Adrienne D'Ambricourt, Ethyl Haworth, Kay Sutton, Allen Wood, Armand Cortez, Eugene Borden, Elspeth Dudgeon, Dorothy Lovett.

Doing *The Yama Yama Man*

With Fred Astaire

148

With Edna May Oliver

CREDITS: Director, H. C. Potter; Producer, George Haight; Production Supervisor, Pandro S. Berman; Scenarist, Richard Sherman; Adaptation, Oscar Hammerstein, Dorothy Yost. Based on the books *My Husband* and *My Memories of Vernon Castle* by Irene Castle. Photographer, Robert DeGrasse; Art Directors, Van Nest Polglase, Perry Ferguson; Set Decorator, Darrell Silvera; Editor, William Hamilton; Sound Recorder, Richard Van Hessen; Musical Director, Victor Baravalle; Orchestrator, Robert Russell Bennett; Dances by Hermes Pan; Costumer, Walter Plunkett; Miss Rogers's Costumes by Irene Castle; Makeup Artist, Mel Burns; Special Photographic Effects, Vernon L. Walker, Douglas Travers; Assistant Director, Argyle Nelson; Still Photographer, John Miehle; Director of Additional Scenes, Leigh Jason; Technical Adviser, Irene Castle.

ORIGINAL SONG: *Only When You're in My Arms*, by Con Conrad, Bert Kalmar, Harry Ruby; plus 67 popular songs of the 1911-1917 era.

SYNOPSIS: Young Irene Foote meets and falls in love with vaudeville performer Vernon Castle. After they marry, they became a sensational ballroom dancing duo, known throughout the world. Everyone copies this elegant pace-setting couple in mode of dress, and hairstyles and products are named after them. After World War I, Vernon returns to Texas as a flight instructor and is killed in a freak accident—thus cutting short a brilliant career.

Dancing the *Castle Walk* (Too Much Mustard) with Fred Astaire

With Fred Astaire

Doing the rehearsal number (*Waiting for the Robert E. Lee*) with Fred Astaire

With Janet Beecher, Robert Strange, Fred Astaire, and Walter Brennan

REVIEWS

"... a thoroughly entertaining piece in which the two most delightful dancers of the present day impersonate the most glamorous dancing pair of another generation."

Rose Pelswick
New York Journal

"It's one of the best Astaire-Rogers films. . . . Miss Rogers and Astaire are excellent as the Castles. The illusion is always there; their deportment is more Vernon and Irene Castle than Astaire and Rogers. Their dance sequences are less spectacular but more consistent with the normal plot progression."

Variety

The Story of Vernon and Irene Castle is one of the most graceful biographies ever set out on celluloid. It is true clear through; true to fact, and, what is even better, true to mood and memory. . . . *The Castles* is as pretty a tribute as you could think of from one pair of famous dancers to another. Fred Astaire quite, and Ginger

Rogers nearly, sacrifices a screen individuality to recapture the spirit of an earlier reputation. The story is quite apart from anything these two have tackled before in pictures. There is little comedy in it, and absolutely no satire. Nobody misunderstands anybody. There is no Other Man, no Other Woman. . . ."

C. A. Lejeune
London *Observer*

"They are dancing at the top of their form all the way, and that's high enough to do the Castles no discredit. They have had the charity, too, to modernize the steps just enough to shake the mothballs from the old ballroom routines. The Castle Walk, the first tango, foxtrot and maxixe might have seemed comically unsensational had they been rigidly reproduced. Astaire and Rogers modified them about as much as the Castles themselves might, were they repeating them today."

Frank S. Nugent
The New York Times

On the set with Fred Astaire and director H. C. Potter

NOTES: This was the final Astaire-Rogers picture made for RKO. It provided the pair with an opportunity to demonstrate their skill in a number of exciting dance styles made popular throughout the world prior to World War I by the famous ballroom dancing couple. Irene Castle was the film's technical adviser and must have given Ginger some anxious moments. (She wanted Ginger to be a brunette!)

H. C. Potter beautifully directed this quasi-biographical script based on two stories by Mrs. Castle. It was the smoothest paced of all the Astaire-Rogers pictures. Ginger's acting helped the film's comic, and later somber, moments considerably, and she was aided by such keen supporting talents as the marvelous Edna May Oliver and Walter Brennan. Her imitation of Bessie McCoy doing her famous "Yama-Yama Man" routine was bliss.

Only one song was written especially for this film: the infectious *Only When You're in My Arms*, which was sung by Astaire to Ginger. Otherwise, the graceful couple accurately re-created the tango, The Castle Walk, the maxixe, the foxtrot, the polka and many assorted waltzes. The songs of the period included *Waiting for the Robert E. Lee*, *By the Light of the Silvery Moon*, *The Missouri Waltz*, *Darktown Strutters' Ball* and *When You Wore a Tulip*.

The reproduction was enhanced by Robert de Grasse's superb camera work and William Hamilton's editing expertise. It is interesting to note that this was the film debut of fifteen-year-old Marjorie Belcher (later Marge Champion). She and her husband Gower were a popular dancing team of the 1950s. Interestingly, Gower Champion directed Ginger in Broadway's *Hello, Dolly!* twenty-six years later.

With David Niven

Bachelor Mother   An RKO-Radio Picture, 1939

CAST: Ginger Rogers, (Polly Parrish); David Niven, (David Merlin); Charles Coburn, (J. B. Merlin); Frank Albertson, (Freddie Miller); E. E. Clive, (Butler); Elbert Coplen, Jr., (Johnnie); Ferike Boros, (Mrs. Weiss); Ernest Truex, (Investigator); Leonard Penn, (Jerome Weiss); Paul Stanton, (Hargraves); Gerald Oliver-Smith, (Hennessy); Leona Roberts, (Old Lady); Dennie Moore, (Mary); June Wilkins, (Louise King); Frank M. Thomas, (Doctor); Edna Holland, (Matron); Donald Duck, (Himself); Irving Bacon, (Clerk); Reed Hadley, (Dance Partner); Chester Clute, (Man in Park); Florence Lake, (Woman in Park); Barbara Pepper, (Dance-Hall Hostess); Horace MacMahon, Charles Hall, (Bouncers); with Edythe Elliott, Murray Alper, Dorothy Adams, Charles Halton, Nestor Paiva, Hugh Prosser, Hal K. Dawson.

CREDITS: Director, Garson Kanin; Producer, B. G. DeSylva; Production Supervisor, Pandro S. Berman; Scenarist, Norman Krasna. Based on an original story by Felix Jackson. Photographer, Robert DeGrasse; Art Directors, Van Nest Polglase, Carroll Clark; Set Decorator, Darrell Silvera; Editors, Henry Berman, Robert Wise; Sound Recorder, Richard Van Hessen; Musical Score, Roy Webb; Dances by Hermes Pan; Costumer, Irene; Makeup Artist, Mel Burns; Special Effects, Vernon L. Walker; Assistant Director, Edward Killy; Still Photographer, John Miehle.

SYNOPSIS: Polly Parrish, an ingenious ex-salesgirl, finds an abandoned baby, is tagged as its unwed mother, and is then rehired by the department store's heir, David Merlin. He becomes interested in Polly, who claims she's not the foundling's mother, and they both fall in love, to the delight of David's father, who has always wanted a grandson.

REVIEWS

"Ginger Rogers, who has become one of the finest actresses on the screen, dominates the proceedings from beginning to end with her radiant personality and fine acting."

New York World-Telegram

". . . hits on all sixteen cylinders, becoming a powerhouse of amusement. . . . Ginger Rogers is delightful. . . . If another picture comes along to prove this department a liar, it will be a pleasure to die laughing."

Archer Winsten
New York Post

With Frank M. Thomas, Elbert Coplen, Jr., and Edna Holland

Dancing with Frank Albertson

With Charles Coburn, Elbert Coplen, Jr., and David Niven

On the set with director Garson Kanin and producer Pandro S. Berman

"Miss Rogers displays a surprising capacity for enjoying the manoeuvres of comedy and at no time does she take the wrong dramatic step. She dances in a single scene and then only to illustrate the waywardness of those who ought to be not on the floor but in the nursery."

The London *Times*

"Mr. Kanin has wisely kept his cast in check and, having a wise cast, has seen that the audience enjoys the joke alone. . . the players are capital. Miss Rogers is demonstrating again that she is one of the screen's most knowing comediennes."

Frank S. Nugent
The New York Times

NOTES: Ginger's appearance in *Bachelor Mother* reminded everyone of her early days in films—her adroit handling of sizzling wisecracks as a worldly-wise working girl who has just been fired and stumbles onto an abandoned baby all in the same day. She handled these situations with ease and flair under Garson Kanin's deft direction. *Bachelor Mother* was not only one of the best comedies of 1939, but also contained one of Ginger's best performances. Her co-star was David Niven, while Charles Coburn and Frank Albertson supported.

Other than one exhibition dance number with Albertson, Ginger was totally dependent upon her comic skills, which had become considerable. The banter between her and Niven (especially when he is trying to return a broken Donald Duck toy) was always fun-filled humor—the kind audiences found so natural in Ginger. Her funniest moment, however, came at the New Year's Eve party. Her parting line to June Wilkins brought the house down.

Originally called *Nobody's Wife* and then *Little Mother*, Felix Jackson's original story received an Oscar nomination. The film was badly remade in 1956, in color, with Debbie Reynolds and Eddie Fisher. The charm and wit of the original were missing.

Fifth Avenue Girl

An RKO-Radio Picture, 1939

CAST: Ginger Rogers, (Mary Gray); Walter Connolly, (Mr. Alfred Borden); Verree Teasdale, (Mrs. Martha Borden); James Ellison, (Mike); Tim Holt, (Tim Borden); Kathryn Adams, (Katherine Borden); Franklin Pangborn, (Higgins); Ferike Boros, (Olga); Louis Calhern, (Dr. Kessler); Theodore Von Eltz, (Terwilliger); Alexander D'Arcy, (Maitre D'Hotel); Bess Flowers, (Woman in Nightclub); with Manda Lane, Mildred Coles, Larry McGrath, Robert Emmett Keane, Kerman Cripps, Louis King, Dick Hogan, Earl Richards, Philip Warren, Dell Henderson, Cornelius Keefe, Bob Perry, Dorothy Dilly, Lionel Pape, Max Wagner, Kenny Williams, George Rosener, Aaron Gonzalez and his Tango-Rumba Band.

CREDITS: Director, Gregory La Cava; Producer, Gregory La Cava; Original Screenplay, Allan Scott; Photographer, Robert DeGrasse; Art Directors, Van Nest Polglase, Perry Ferguson; Set Decorator, Darrell Silvera; Editors, William Hamilton, Robert Wise; Sound Recorder, John L. Cass; Musical Score, Robert Russell Bennett; Costumer, Howard Greer; Makeup Artist, Mel Burns; Assistant Director, Edward Killy; Still Photographer, John Miehle.

SONG: *Tropicana*, by Aaron Gonzalez.

SYNOPSIS: Harried tycoon Alfred Borden hires Mary Gray, a young, unemployed girl he meets in the park, to pose as his mistress, in order to elicit some response from his otherwise "bored" family. The experience gives him a new lease on life and reforms his family.

With Walter Connolly

REVIEWS

"In *Fifth Avenue Girl*, Miss Rogers doesn't dance, which is a pity, and she saunters through the whole quite slight but rather comical piece with a nonchalance which is, I have no doubt, the epitome of artistry."

The New Yorker

"Ginger Rogers proved beyond a doubt in *Bachelor Mother* and now in *Fifth Avenue Girl* that she doesn't need to dance in order to pay the piper for whatever pretties she has in mind to acquire. Her talent for delivering lines amusingly, and her perfect timing of them, place her in the front rank of screen comediennes."

New York Daily News

"With Ginger Rogers giving a superb portrayal of the title role, the Merlin of the motion picture directors has worked genuine magic. . . . Mr. LaCava is not the only one responsible for this either. Miss Rogers does her share and something more than that in invigorating the film. . . . In *Fifth Avenue Girl* she plays with such poise, proficiency and persuasion that she holds a poppycock plot together. Mr. LaCava supplies the treatment to make a well known narrative refreshing. Miss Rogers supplies the heart of the dream."

New York Herald-Tribune

"Gregory LaCava's *Fifth Avenue Girl* is a revised version of *My Man Godfrey*, not quite as antic in dialogue and action, but done in the same deft and entertaining manner. This time it's a girl from the other side of town who moves into a millionaire's mansion and transforms the frittery family into human beings."

The Movies

On the set with Walter Connolly and director Gregory LaCava

With Tim Holt

With Kathryn Adams, Tim Holt, and Verree Teasdale

NOTES: Gregory LaCava, who had directed her in *Stage Door*, showcased Ginger in his reworking of his 1936 vehicle, *My Man Godfrey*. As rewritten by Allan Scott, the emphasis was placed solely on Ginger's role, thus reducing the male part. Therefore LaCava did not give Ginger a male co-star of equal standing. This was, possibly, one of the main reasons the picture did not do well at the box office.

Although it is minor LaCava, it is still a well-mounted, well-acted picture to which the expert director gave his all. And it is still fun. The photography of Robert de Grasse was particularly good as was the editing of William Hamilton and Robert Wise. Ginger looked stunning in costumes designed by Howard Greer. The working titles were *My Fifth Avenue Girl* and *She Said I Do*.

Primrose Path An RKO-Radio Picture, 1940

With Henry Travers and Joel McCrea

With Queenie Vassar

CAST: Ginger Rogers, (Ellie May Adams); Joel McCrea, (Ed Wallace); Marjorie Rambeau, (Mamie Adams); Henry Travers, (Gramp); Miles Mander, (Homer); Queenie Vassar, (Grandma); Joan Carroll, (Honeybell); Vivienne Osborne, (Thelma); Carmen Morales, (Carmelita); Gene Morgan, (Hawkins); with Lorin Raker, Charles Lane, Mara Alexander, Herbert Corthell, Charles Williams, Larry McGrath, Jack Gardner, Nestor Paiva, Jacqueline Dalya, Lawrence Gleason, Jr., Ray Cooke.

CREDITS: Director, Gregory LaCava; Producer, Gregory LaCava; Scenarists, Allan Scott, Gregory LaCava. Based on the play *The Primrose Path* by Robert Buckner, Walter Hart. Based on the novel *February Hill* by Victoria Lincoln. Photographer, Joseph H. August; Art Directors. Van Nest Polglase, Carroll Clark; Set Decorator, Darrell Silvera; Editor, William Hamilton; Sound Recorder, John L. Cass; Musical Score, Werner R. Heymann; Costumer, Renie; Makeup Artist, Mel Burns; Special Effects, Vernon L. Walker; Assistant Director, Edward Killy; Still Photographer, John Miehle.

With Marjorie Rambeau

With Joel McCrea

SYNOPSIS: Ellie May Adams, a girl from the wrong side of the tracks, falls in love with and eventually marries Ed Wallace, a promising young man. In the process of trying to escape the unhealthy influences of her mother and grandmother, she learns much about life.

REVIEWS

"As Ellie May Adams, Ginger Rogers plays what may well be remembered as her finest performance. For the girl who was a dancer in *Top Hat*, an ingenue in *Stage Door* and a comedienne in *Having Wonderful Time* now plays an emotional adolescent with such restraint and verity that she qualifies for top Hollywood honors in versatility."

Life

"The performance is generally good, and, if it errs, it is on the side of over-broadening roles that were broad to begin with. Miss Rogers is variably effective and never less convincing than as the tomboy broken to harness by Mr. McCrea's first kiss. Much better are Queenie Vassar's rouged, bewigged, thoroughly evil old Grannie; Miles Mander's gin-soaked Homer; Marjorie Rambeau's flouncing, good-natured, sentimental Mamie Adams and little Joan Carroll's amazingly precocious Honeybell, who obviously was going to be a chippie off the old block. Any resemblance, by the way, between this *Primrose Path* and that staged on Broadway last season is purely coincidental. Mr. LaCava and Allan Scott have rolled their own version."

Frank S. Nugent
The New York Times

With Marjorie Rambeau, Miles Mander, and Joel McCrea

On the set with Joel McCrea, scenarist Allan Scott and director Gregory LaCava

"*The Primrose Path* is a muddy trail that winds through the worst swamplands of Hollywood and where it ends this reviewer does not know. He didn't wait for the finish. We only remember that Ginger Rogers is rather nice."

L. E.
The Daily Worker

"Ginger Rogers who long ago proved she could act as well as do the Carioca, takes the occasion of *The Primrose Path* to demonstrate that she has no more vanity than a Carmelite nun, and that so far as she is concerned, when realism comes into the plot, pulchritude goes out the window. Most glamour girls are willing to ruffle their hair and rub off the lipstick for one scene in a picture for the sake of what they like to call Art. But the valiant Ginger goes from the film's first reel to its last looking as if she had strayed on her way to the makeup department and instead spent the time in the greasing pit of a garage. With her normally golden hair dyed black, her enviable figure cloaked in baggy dresses, and her face as shiny as a ship's stokers, she does an excellent job of acting an underprivileged shantytown ingenue."

New York Journal-American

NOTES: Gregory LaCava hit it just right with his third Ginger Rogers picture. Here was the new Ginger he had told the public about as far back as *Stage Door*. Had *Primrose Path* not been involved with local censors around the country, Ginger might well have been nominated for her performance as Ellie May.

Based on Robert Buckner and Walter Hart's play *The Primrose Path*, the scenario by LaCava and Allan Scott effectively changed the emphasis from the grandmother to the granddaughter. Although much of the play's ribaldry was deleted, the film still ran into censor trouble. However, this remains a brilliant seriocomic study of the psychological effects of prostitution on the second and third generations of a family.

Although the play, produced on Broadway by George Abbott, did not acknowledge the fact that it had been suggested by Victoria Lincoln's novel, RKO took no chances and mentioned both. Helen Westley played Grandma on Broadway with a cast that included Betty Field and Betty Garde. The film version changed the locale from Fall River, Massachusetts, to the Pacific Coast which Joseph H. August's camera captured beautifully.

The film is most noteworthy—especially in today's realistic approach to life—because its people are real, its story is starkly honest, and its language straightforward. The cast LaCava chose worked well in this setting. Their combined effort made *Primrose Path* a profound experience of American folk life.

Lucky Partners

An RKO-Radio Picture, 1940

With Ronald Colman

CAST: Ronald Colman, (David Grant); Ginger Rogers, (Jean Newton); Spring Byington, (Aunt Lucy); Jack Carson, (Freddie Harper); Cecilia Loftus, (Mrs. Sylvester); Billy Gilbert, (Charles); Hugh O'Connell, (Niagara Clerk); Brandon Tynan, (Mr. Sylvester); Harry Davenport, (Judge); Leon Belasco, (Nick #1); Edward Conrad, (Nick #2); Olin Howland, (Tourist); Benny Rubin, (Spieler #1); Tom Dugan, (Spieler #2); Walter Kingsford, (Wendell); Otto Hoffmann, (Clerk); Lucille Gleason, (Ethel's Mother); Helen Lynd, (Ethel); Alex Melesh, (Art Salesman); Dorothy Adams, (Maid in Apartment); Billy Benedict, (Bellboy); Frank Mills, (Bus Driver); Dorothy Vernon, (Woman on Bus); Allen Wood, Murray Alper, Dick Hogan, (Bellboys); Fern Emmett, (Hotel Maid); Bruce Hale, (Bridegroom); Jane Patten, (Bride); Max Wagner, (Waiter); Tommy Mack, (Joseph); Al Hill, (Motor Cop); George Watts, (Plainclothesman); Edgar Dearing, (Desk Sergeant); Grady Sutton, (Reporter); Robert Dudley, (Bailiff); Charles Halton, (Newspaperman); Harlan Briggs, (Mayor); Nora Cecil, (Clubwoman); Lloyd Ingraham, (Chamber of Commerce); Gayne Whitman, (Announcer's Voice).

CREDITS: Director, Lewis Milestone; Producer, George Haight; Executive Producer, Harry Edington; Scenarists, Allan Scott, John Van Druten. Based on the story *Bonne Chance* by Sacha Guitry. Photographer, Robert DeGrasse; Art Directors, Van Nest Polglase, Carroll Clark; Set Decorator, Darrell Silvera; Editor, Henry Berman; Sound Recorder, John E. Tribby; Musical Score, Dimitri Tiomkin; Miss Rogers's Gowns by Irene; Makeup Artist, Mel Burns; Special Effects, Vernon L. Walker; Assistant Director, Argyle Nelson; Property Man, Gene Rossi; Still Photographer, John Miehle.

SYNOPSIS: Artist David Grant shares a sweepstakes ticket with Jean Newton, a girl who brings him luck. They embark on a synthetic honeymoon with the winnings, to the utter consternation of her fiance, Freddie Harper.

REVIEWS

"Ginger Rogers, always a lively and attractive person, has not been well used in *Lucky Partners*. Either by her hairdresser or her couturiere."

Christian Science Monitor

"The people are too real for the fantastic background of events and the events are too prosaic for the basic innuendo of the treatment. The tale of a Greenwich

Village painter, who persuades a girl to go off on an impersonal honeymoon with him, after they have won a sweepstakes ticket, is neither amusingly risque nor humanly funny. . . . Call it bad casting, but both Ronald Colman and Ginger Rogers, as the guinea pig in the experiment, are neither convincing nor amusing for most of the time."

New York Herald-Tribune

"Colman and Miss Rogers work together with smooth blending of talents and romantic warmth. He is at his debonair best in the whimsical situations. She confirms her right to stand amongst the most resourceful of the screen's comediennes."

Variety

NOTES: Sacha Guitry's *Bonne Chance* provided the basis for this hodgepodge. Stranger than that was the preposterous choice of Lewis Milestone as director; this type of nonsense was not his forte.

Ginger and Ronald Colman labored valiantly, but even their talents were incapable of saving the film. It is to their combined credit that the idea played at all.

The working titles were *Good Luck* and *Change Your Luck*, but from the looks of things, upon release, *Lucky Partners* needed more than luck.

With Jack Carson

With Ronald Colman

With Katharine (K.T.) Stevens and Mary Treen

Kitty Foyle

An RKO-Radio Picture, 1940

Kitty and her alter ego

CAST: Ginger Rogers, (Kitty Foyle); Dennis Morgan, (Wyn Strafford); James Craig, (Mark); Eduardo Ciannelli, (Giono); Ernest Cossart, (Pop); Gladys Cooper, (Mrs. Strafford); Odette Myrtil, (Delphine Detaille); Mary Treen, (Pat); Katharine Stevens, (Oolly); Walter Kingsford, (Mr. Kennett); Cecil Cunningham, (Grandmother); Nella Walker, (Aunt Jessica); Edward Fielding, (Uncle Edgar); Kay Linaker, (Wyn's Wife); Richard Nichols, (Wyn's Boy); Florence Bates, ⅝Customer); Heather Angel, (Girl in Prologue); Tyler Brooke, (Boy in Prologue); Hattie Noel, (Black Woman); Frank Milan, (Parry); Charles Quigley, (Bill); Harriette Brandon, (Miss Bala); Howard Entwistle, (Butler); Billy Elmer, (Neway); Walter Sande, (Trumpeter); Ray Teal, (Saxophonist); Joey Ray, (Drummer); Mel Ruick, (Violinist-Leader); Doodles Weaver, (Pianist); Theodore Von Eltz, (Hotel Clerk); Max Davidson, (Flower Man); Charles Miller, (Doctor); Mary Gordon, (Charwoman); Fay Helm, (Prim Girl); Helen Lynd, (irl in Elevator); Dorothy Vaughan, (Charwoman); Mimi Doyle, (Jane); Hilda Plowright, (Nurse); Spencer Charters, (Father); Gino Corrado, (Guest); with Julie Carter, Jane Patten, Renee Haal, Mary Currier, Patricia Maier, Brooks Benedict, Tom Quinn.

CREDITS: Director, Sam Wood; producer, David Hempstead; Executive Producer, Harry E. Edington; Scenarist, Dalton Trumbo; Additional Dialogue, Donald Ogden Stewart. Based on the novel *Kitty Foyle* by Christopher Morley. Photographer, Robert DeGrasse; Art Directors, Van Nest Polglase, Mark-Lee Kirk; Set Decorator, Darrell Silvera; Editor, Henry Berman; Sound Recorder, John L. Cass; Musical Score, Roy Webb; Costumer, Renie; Makeup Artist, Mel Burns; Assistant Director, Argyle Nelson; Still Photographer, John Miehle.

SYNOPSIS: Kitty Foyle, a hard-working white-collar girl from a lower-middle-class family, meets and is romanced by young Philadelphia socialite Wyn Strafford. However, happiness is not to be hers on this high social level, and soon Kitty reverts to her own way of life and finds love with a young man of her social and economic background.

With James Craig

With Ernest Cossart

164

With Dennis Morgan

REVIEWS

"*Kitty Foyle*, as brought to the screen under Sam Wood's masterful direction, and with Ginger Rogers' superb characterization, is first, last and always, a love story. And when did you last see a simple, sincere, unaffected tale of love? Miss Rogers is extraordinarily good as Kitty, and there is a fine performance as the Philadelphia blueblood by Dennis Morgan, who makes the character less a stuffed shirt than a likable weakling."

William Boehnel
New York World-Telegram

"A girl in love is like Ginger Rogers as Kitty Foyle. That's the highest tribute possible to her and the movie—presupposing you're sure that love is something wonderful and difficult and worth it. . . . This job of Miss Rogers' shines with myriad facets, lighted by Sam Woods' direction, by true and sensitive dialogue, by (save for an appeasement of the Hays Office marriage) a logically motivated and richly filled-in script."

Cecilia Ager
PM

"*Kitty Foyle* is a sentimentalist's delight. Ginger Rogers plays her with as much forthright and appealing integrity as one can possibly expect. And Dennis Morgan and James Craig are wholly attractive rivals for her love. But the sharpness and contemporary significance of Mr. Morley's commentary are missing. His Kitty was of real flesh and blood; this one is persuasive but fictitious. His Kitty burned life's candle at both ends; this one burns two candles, and when one goes out she has the other handy."

Bosley Crowther
The New York Times

"*Kitty Foyle* will give few thrills to those who were needled by the book. It will disappoint those who, like this reviewer, were anticipating something far out of the ordinary with Ginger Rogers acting, Sam Wood directing, and Donald Ogden Stewart adding lines of dialogue to those of adapter Dalton Trumbo and author Morley. Between Stewart's additions and Morley's originals some fairly trite dialogue sneaked in and it isn't sufficiently covered by Ginger's deadpan deliveries."

Archer Winsten
New York Post

NOTES: The effectiveness that Ginger had achieved in LaCava's *Primrose Path* was just the beginning of her lower-middle-class working-girl portraits. With *Kitty Foyle*, her characterization of the hopes, fears, desires, romance, and reality of young American womanhood came into full bloom. Her portrayal of Morley's heroine was a knockout.

Producer David Hempstead first gave Ginger the copy of Morley's novel, but, once shooting began on the Dalton Trumbo script (plus Donald Ogden Stewart's additions), the production went into high gear. Director Sam Wood guided his actors well, but his handling of the stream-of-consciousness scenes (with Kitty's alter ego speaking to her from the image in the mirror) were ineffectual.

As Kitty, the poor, hard-working white-collar salesgirl, Ginger gave a flawless performance. It rang true in nearly every scene—a fine bit of acting that won her 1940's Academy Award as Best Actress of the Year. It was her first and only nomination.

The RKO production received four other Academy Award nominations, but, alas, did not produce any winners: Best Picture; Best Director (Wood); Best Screenplay (Trumbo); and Best Sound (RKO's Sound Chief, John Aalberg, received the nomination.)

The supporting cast was superb throughout. Memorable were Ginger's co-stars Dennis Morgan and James Craig, and Eduardo Ciannelli, Ernest Cossart, Gladys Cooper, and Florence Bates.

With Gladys Cooper

With Florence Bates

CAST: Ginger Rogers, (Janie); George Murphy, (Tom); Alan Marshal, (Dick Hamilton); Burgess Meredith, (Harry); Joe Cunningham, (Pop); Jane Seymour, (Ma); Lenore Lonergan, (Babs); Vicki Lester, (Paula); Phil Silvers, (Ice Cream Man); Betty Breckenridge, (Gertrude); Sid Skolsky, (Announcer); Edna Holland, (Miss Schlom); Gus Glassmire, (Music Store Proprietor); Netta Packer, (Salesclerk); Sarah Edwards, (Mrs. Burton); Ellen Lowe, (Matron); William Halligan, (Mr. Burton); Joe Bernard, (Judge); Gertrude Short, (Bridge Matron); Edward Colebrook, (Stalled Car Driver); Gayle Mellott, (Brenda); Dorothy Lloyd, (Gypsy Oracle); Berry Kroeger, (Boy Lead); Lurene Tuttle, (Girl Lead); Knox Manning, (Radio Announcer); William Alland, (Newsreel Announcer); Jack Briggs, (Boy); with Jane Patten and Theodore Ramsey.

CREDITS: Director, Garson Kanin; Producer, Robert Sisk; Original Screenplay, Paul Jarrico; Photographer, Merrit Gerstad; Art Directors, Van Nest Polglase, Mark-Lee Kirk; Set Decorator, Darrell Silvera; Editor, John Sturges; Sound Recorder; Earl L. Wolcott; Musical Score, Roy Webb; Costumer, Renie; Makeup Artist, Mel Burns; Special Photographic Effects, Vernon L. Walker; Assistant Director, Fred A. Flock; Still Photographer, John Miehle.

SONG: *Tom Collins* by Gene Rose, Roy Webb.

On the set with director Garson Kanin and production crew

With Burgess Meredith, Alan Marshal, and George Murphy

SYNOPSIS: Janie, an ordinary working girl, becomes dizzily confused by the presence of three suitors: Tom, a sincere down-to-earth fellow; Dick, a rich boy caught by her charms; and Harry, a nonconformist. She dreams of what life would be with each and finally makes her choice.

REVIEWS

"The airy charm of the picture is in the way it spins along, popping with nifty dialogue and bubbling with visual absurdities. Ginger Rogers plays the girl, as no other actress we know could, with a perfect combination of skepticism and daffiness."

Bosley Crowther
The New York Times

"The title indicates the plot pretty much. Ginger has love dust in her eyes and clouds on her brain as she works out her proposal problems, and she is convincing as ever."

National Board of Review

"This is Ginger Rogers' first assignment since she won the Academy Award for her *Kitty Foyle*, and her impersonation of Janie, the improbable telephone operator, ranks with her best."

Newsweek

With George Murphy

With Burgess Meredith and Phil Silvers

"Even Joe DiMaggio occasionally strikes out. So there is some excuse for Ginger Rogers, 1940 Academy Award winner, who fails to make a hit in the new double-play combination, *Tom, Dick and Harry*. Miss Rogers . . . is hampered throughout by childish dialogue and an even more puerile plot. . . . Miss Rogers is annoyingly coy in this opus, probably because her lines are so coy. Somehow, the sophisticated roles are better suited to her abilities."

New York Morning Telegraph

"Ginger Rogers is at her best in the role of Janie, which means that search where you will, you won't find a more skillful and charming performance."

William Boehnel
New York World-Telegram

"Ginger Rogers is one of the principal reasons, the central and dominating reason, for the picture's entertainment qualities. Miss Rogers keeps the film light at all times, never giving way to sentimentality or dramatics. The film constantly pokes fun at the character she plays, Janie, the belle of the switchboard. Miss Rogers keeps Janie a comedy character always, throwing away lines deftly, pointing up each situation and line. She is not, because of an unfortunate pompadour hairdo, as flatteringly photographed as usual. Her Janie is still a delightful person."

Eileen Creelman
New York Sun

NOTES: Following close on the heels of *Kitty Foyle*, Ginger again got a terrific script—this time Paul Jarrico's original screenplay *Tom, Dick and Harry*. Garson Kanin, with whom she had worked in *Bachelor Mother*, directed. It was as successful as their previous effort and perfect for American audiences who could feel the threat of World War II at their doors.

Ginger delivered a lovable portrait of a dizzy telephone operator who cannot choose between three admirers. She dreams about life with each one to help her in her final decision. She illustrated the foibles and delicious romanticism of young American girls during this period.

Her suitors were all well suited to their chores and characters: George Murphy, Alan Marshal and especially Burgess Meredith. Paul Jarrico received an Academy Award nomination for his original screenplay and it is interesting to note that Ginger's third husband-to-be, Jack Briggs, had a small part in the picture. Phil Silvers scored as an obnoxious Good Humor man.

Roxie Hart

A 20th Century-Fox Picture, 1942

CAST: Ginger Rogers, (Roxie Hart); Adolphe Menjou, (Billy Flynn); George Montgomery, (Homer Howard); Lynne Overman, (Jake Callahan); Nigel Bruce, (E. Clay Benham); Phil Silvers, (Babe); Sara Allgood, (Mrs. Morton); William Frawley, (O'Malley); Spring Byington, (Mary Sunshine); Ted North, (Stuart Chapman); Helene Reynolds, (Velma Wall); George Chandler, (Amos Hart); Charles D. Brown, (Charles E. Murdock); Morris Ankrum, (Martin S. Harrison); George Lessey, (Judge); Iris Adrian, (Two-Gun Gertie); Milton Parsons, (Announcer); Billy Wayne, (Court Clerk); Charles Williams, (Photographer); Leon Belasco, (Waiter); Lee Shumway, (Policeman); Larry Lawson, Harry Carter, (Reporters); Pat O'Malley, (Policeman); Bob Perry, (Prisoner's Bailiff); Jeff Corey, (Orderly); Phillip Morris, (Policeman); Jack Norton, (Producer); Leonard Kibrick, (Newsboy); Frank Orth, Alec Craig, Edward Clark, (Idlers); Frank Darien, (Finnegan); Jim Pierce, (Policeman); Arthur Aylesworth, (Mr. Wadsworth); Margaret Seddon, (Mrs. Wadsworth); Stanley Blystone, (Policeman); Mary Treen, (Secretary).

CREDITS: Director, William A. Wellman; Producer, Nunnally Johnson; Scenarist, Nunnally Johnson. Based on the play *Chicago* by Maurine Watkins. Photographer, Leon Shamroy; Art Directors, Richard Day, Wiard B. Ihnen; Set Decorator, Thomas Little; Editor, James B. Clark; Sound Recorders, Alfred Bruzlin, Roger Heman; Musical Score, Alfred Newman; Costumer, Gwen Wakeling; Dances by Hermes Pan; Makeup Artist, Guy Pearce; Assistant Director, Ad Schaumer.

SYNOPSIS: Roxie Hart, a tawdry, gum-chewing, wisecracking dancer, takes the rap for a murder which her husband Amos committed for publicity's sake. She is defended by Billy Flynn, a melodramatic lawyer who constantly coaches her every move and is always seeing to it that her shapely legs are in view of the jurors.

REVIEWS

"Miss Rogers herself, one of the most accomplished young players on the screen, gives the whole business just the right touch of burlesque. . . . Take it from me, you're going to love this dame, Roxie Hart."

New York Morning Telegraph

"Mr. Johnson and Mr. Wellman, who directed, have squeezed every laugh they could from it. As a matter of fact, one fault is that they have squeezed just a bit too hard. . . . Mr. Johnson and Mr. Wellman didn't know when to quit. The same goes for the performers; little or no restraint was placed upon them. Miss Rogers is a talented actress, but it pains one to see her tossed into a role which requires that she do no more than play a Dumb Dora to excess, swaggering with hands on hips, chewing gum and teasing the hem of her skirt. . . . They

Doing *The Black Bottom*

With Adolphe Menjou

With Lynne Overman, Adolphe Menjou, and George Montgomery

With George Montgomery, Phil Silvers, George Chandler, Nigel Bruce, Lynne Overman and Charles D. Brown

all give the bad impression of working a shade too hard. And the film, between the script and its performance, becomes a raucous and tasteless travesty."

Bosley Crowther
The New York Times

"Ginger Rogers as the gum-chewing, pretty-calfed moron never fails to give just the right flavor and verve to her interpretation. Her rendering of the 'Black Bottom' has all the authority of Mary Garden singing *'Louise'.*"

National Board of Review

"Miss Rogers apparently enjoyed herself portraying Roxie, and her enthusiasm for the attractive little tramp, who can tap dance as expertly as she can fib about approaching motherhood, is contagious. This bolstering of the poet's contention that a rosebud need not have a mind may not result in Miss Rogers having another page in the memory books, but it is a highly colorful part and it is projected to the queen's taste!"

Gilbert Kanour
Baltimore Evening Sun

NOTES: *Roxie Hart* was a staccato-paced burlesque of the 1920s expertly directed by William A. Wellman. Francine Larrimore appeared on Broadway as Roxie in 1926 and, two years later, Phyllis Haver made the silent

film at Warner Brothers. Ginger may not have been everyone's choice for Roxie, but Nunnally Johnson turned the seriocomic play into a rich burlesque, thus giving Ginger every opportunity to be vivacious.

In this framework, Ginger was hilarious as the gum-chewing, wisecracking dancer. As the shyster lawyer who defends her, Adolphe Menjou gave a rousing performance. Lynne Overman, the wacky reporter; Phil Silvers, the outlandish photographer; Iris Adrian, sassy Two-Gun Gertie; Spring Byington, nosy columnist Mary Sunshine; and George Chandler, as Roxie's mousy husband, were all delightfully cast. George Montgomery did well in a role that required him merely to look good.

It was first-class Wellman, and the action—and fun—never lagged. His touches were everywhere, even down to the smallest bit. Typical of the picture's humor: When Roxie calls her folks to tell them that she may be executed, Pa looks at Ma and says, "They're goin' to hang Roxie." Without a trace of concern, Ma replies, "What did I tell you?"

In 1975 director Bob Fosse brought a musical version of *Roxie Hart* called *Chicago* to Broadway as a vehicle for his wife Gwen Verdon. To give her energetic—as well as box-office—support, the script built up the part of Velma for jazzy Chita Rivera.

However, the cast was submerged by an over-stylized and mechanical production. The songs were forgettable. Exit Roxie!

With Spring Byington

With Nigel Bruce and Sara Allgood

Tales of Manhattan   A 20th Century-Fox Picture, 1942

CAST: Charles Boyer, (Paul Orman); Rita Hayworth, (Ethel Halloway); Ginger Rogers, (Diane); Henry Fonda, (George); Charles Laughton, (Charles Smith); Edward G. Robinson, (Avery L. Browne); Paul Robeson, (Luke); Ethel Waters, (Esther); Eddie "Rochester" Anderson, (Rev. Lazarus); Thomas Mitchell, (John Halloway); Eugene Pallette, (Luther); Cesar Romero, (Harry); Gail Patrick, (Ellen); Roland Young, (Edgar); Marion Martin, (Squirrel); Elsa Lanchester, (Mrs. Smith); Victor Francen, (Arturo Bellini); George Sanders, (Williams); James Gleason, ("Father" Joe); Harry Davenport, (Professor Lyons); James Rennie, (Hank Bronson); J. Carrol Naish, (Costello); The Hall Johnson Choir, (Themselves); Frank Orth, (Secondhand Clothes Dealer); Christian Rub, (Wilson); Sig Arno, (Piccolo Player); Harry Hayden, (David); Morris Ankrum, (Judge); Don Douglas, (Henderson); Mae Marsh, (Molly); Clarence Muse, (Grandpa); George Reed, (Christopher); Cordell Hickman, (Nicodemus); Paul Renay, ("Spud" Johnson); Barbara Lynn, (Mary); Adeline DeWalt Reynolds, (Grandmother); Helene Reynolds, (Actress); with Robert Greig, Connie Leon, Will Wright, Frank Darien, Dewey Robinson, Esther Howard, Rita Christiani, Alberta Gary, Tod Stanhope.

CREDITS: Director, Julien Duvivier; Producers, Boris Morros, S. P. Eagle; Original Screenplay by Ben Hecht, Ferenc Molnar, Donald Ogden Stewart, Samuel Hoffenstein, Alan Campbell, Ladislaus Fodor, L. Vadnai, L. Gorog, Lamar Trotti, Henry Blankfort; Photographer, Joseph Walker; Art Directors, Richard Day, Boris Leven; Set Decorator, Thomas Little; Editor, Robert Bischoff; Sound Recorders, W. D. Flick, Roger Heman; Musical Score, Sol Kaplan; Vocal Arrangements, Hall Johnson; Musical Director, Edward Paul; Orchestrators, Charles Bradshaw, Hugo Friedhofer, Clarence Wheeler; Costumers, Dolly Tree, Bernard Newman, Gwen Wakeling, Irene; Makeup Artist, Guy Pearce; Assistant Director, Robert Stillman; Unit Manager, J. H. Vadel.

SONG: *Glory Day* by Leo Robin, Ralph Rainger; Sung by Paul Robeson.

SYNOPSIS: A series of unrelated stories built around a dress suit. The second, and weakest, episode relates the story of Diane, who is engaged to Harry, but, at the same time, is convinced that he is cheating on her. She eventually falls for Harry's shy friend, George.

With Gail Patrick

REVIEWS

"... boasts a cast glittering enough to interest everyone but the lads who have to figure out the electric light bulbs on theatre marquees."

Rose Pelswick
New York Journal-American

"Under the circumstances it may be irrelevant to point out that, although many of the players are excellent, none gives what might be considered the best performance in his career ... and that, although at least ten prominent writers are associated with the screenplay, it is often embarrassingly hokum and pathetic. One of the script's drawbacks is the comparative dearth of compensating humor."

Newsweek

"Of the series, this corner may be put down as preferring the Robinson episode above all else, with Robinson himself giving a superb performance as the Bowery bum and with Jimmy Gleason and Mae Marsh as a pair of mission workers in the lower depths aiding him mightily. The Boyer-Hayworth-Mitchell contretemps is a little on the hammy side, the Ginger Rogers-Henry Fonda bit is cute and titillating, the Laughton symphony is laid on with a shovel and the Robeson-Waters-Rochester finale has been attacked by no less a person than Robeson himself as doing an injustice to his people. We'll let it go at that."

New York Morning Telegraph

NOTES: Originally this film contained six segments, all directed by Julien Duvivier, but the film ran too long and a W. C. Fields section was deleted from the release print.

With Cesar Romero

Even then, it ran 118 minutes! The five unrelated stories were linked together by the passing down of a man's full-dress evening suit, a novel idea.

Obviously, some sequences were better than others, but Ginger got herself involved in the silliest one. Her co-stars were Henry Fonda, Cesar Romero, Gail Patrick (with whom she worked in *Stage Door*), Roland Young, and Marion Martin.

All in all, the stars of each episode made the whole thing worthwhile.

With Roland Young, Marion Martin, Cesar Romero, and Henry Fonda

The Major and the Minor

A Paramount Picture, 1942

CAST: Ginger Rogers, (Susan Applegate); Ray Milland, (Major Kirby); Rita Johnson, (Pamela Hill); Robert Benchley, (Mr. Osborne); Diana Lynn, (Lucy Hill); Edward Fielding, (Colonel Hill); Frankie Thomas, (Cadet Osborne); Raymond Roe, (Cadet Wigton); Charles Smith, (Cadet Korner); Larry Nunn, (Cadet Babcock); Billy Dawson, (Cadet Miller); Lela Rogers, (Mrs. Applegate); Aldrich Bowker, (Reverend Doyle); Boyd Irwin, (Major Griscom); Byron Shores, (Captain Durand); Richard Kiske, (Will Duffy); Norma Varden, (Mrs. Osborne); Gretl Sherk, (Mrs. Shackleford); Stanley Desmond, (Shumaker); Ethel Clayton, Gloria Williams, (Bit Women); Lynda Grey, (Bit Girl); Will Wright, (First Ticket Agent); William Newell, (Second Ticket Agent); Freddie Mercer, (Little Boy in Railroad Station); Carlotta Jelm, (Little Girl in Railroad Station); Tom McGuire, (News Vendor); George Andersen, (Man with Esquire); Stanley Andrews, (First Conductor); Emory Parnell, (Second Conductor); Guy Wilkerson, (Farmer Truck Driver); Milt Kibbee, (Station Agent); Archie Twitchell, (Sergeant); Alice Keating, (Nurse); Ralph Gilliam, Dick Chandlee, Buster Nichols, Stephen Kirchner, Kenneth Grant, Billy Clauson, John Bogden, Bradley Hail, Billy O'Kelly, Jack Lindquist, David McKim, Jim Pilcher, Don Wilmot, (Cadets); Billy Ray, (Cadet Summerville); Marie Blake, (Bertha); Mary Field, (Mother in Railroad Station); Dell Henderson, (Doorman); Ed Peil, Sr., (Stationmaster); Ken Lundy, (Elevator Boy); Tom Dugan, (Deadbeat); with Dickie Jones and Billy Cook.

CREDITS: Director, Billy Wilder; Producer, Arthur Hornblow, Jr.; Scenarists, Charles Brackett, Billy Wilder; Based on the play *Connie Goes Home* by Edward Childs Carpenter; Based on the story *Sunny Goes Home* by Fannie Kilbourne; Photographer, Leo Tover; Art Directors, Hans Dreier, Roland Anderson; Editor, Doane Harrison; Sound Recorders, Harold Lewis, Don Johnson; Musical Score, Robert Emmett Dolan; Costumer, Edith Head; Makeup Artist, Wally Westmore; Assistant Director, C.C. Coleman.

SYNOPSIS: Young Susan Applegate has disguised herself as a child to travel home half-fare when she encounters U. S. Army Major Kirby enroute to his fiancee, Pamela Hill, at a small-town military academy. The major offers to take care of the "little girl," who is falling in love with him.

REVIEWS

"Miss Rogers has turned in any number of versatile screen performances in the past, from assisting Fred Astaire in hoofing routines to playing a bedraggled gamine in *Primrose Path*. She has never plumbed the

With Lela Rogers

With Diana Lynn

With Ray Milland

depth of her artistry to such brilliant ends as she has in *The Major and the Minor*. She has the nerve that few movie stars have—to play straight when a characterization demands it. In her most awkward gangling as a 12-year-old, she is nothing short of magnificent."

Richard Watts, Jr.
New York Herald Tribune

"The appearance of Ginger Rogers as a 12-year-old child would be enough to strike consternation in the heart of any man, but when Miss Rogers in this 12-year-old makeup is plunked right down in the middle of a boys' military school, and has to ward off the advances of teen-year kids with ideas of their own, the results are nothing less than enchanting . . . . Trust a player like Miss Rogers to get every possible ounce out of a business like this . . . . Miss Rogers is naturally splendid, as she always is . . . . Also there's a girl named Diana Lynn, as the sister, on whom you might keep an eye in the future, because she pretty nearly takes the play right straight away from all the stars, in her little part."

Leo Mishkin
New York Morning Telegraph

NOTES: This was Ginger's first Paramount picture in nine years (the last was 1933's *Sitting Pretty* just before she flew down to Rio at RKO), and it could not have been a better picture.

Arthur Hornblow, Jr., produced and assigned one of Paramount's best screenwriters as director. *The Major and the Minor* was Billy Wilder's first directorial effort, and was such a critical and box-office hit that it launched him on his way to becoming one of Hollywood's best directors.

The scenario by Charles Brackett and Wilder cleverly utilized the framework from a play and a story and supercharged it with current events and natural situations. Ginger, as Susan Applegate, was captivating as a fed-up working girl leaving New York for Iowa by posing as a 12-year-old to travel half-fare. Her contretemps with a U.S. Army major, enroute to a boy's military academy, was hilarious cinema.

Diana Lynn as a sassy teen-ager who discovers Ginger's masquerade, was excellent. Rita Johnson was properly bitchy as Milland's fiancee and Mrs. Lela Rogers played Ginger's mother. At one point, Ginger even impersonates her own mother! The military school exteriors were photographed at St. John's Military Academy, Delafield, Wisconsin. Wilder handled all of the young cadets (who were dying to get at Ginger) extremely well. In fact, it was Wilder's technique of placing his actors in risque situations and having them play against the obvious that resulted in top-notch farce.

With Robert Benchley

On the set with director Billy Wilder

With Walter Slezak

With Cary Grant

Once upon a Honeymoon
An RKO-Radio Picture, 1942

CAST: Ginger Rogers, (Katie O'Hara); Cary Grant, (Pat O'Toole); Walter Slezak, (Baron Von Luber); Albert Dekker, (Le Blanc); Albert Basserman, (General Borelski); Ferike Boros, (Elsa); John Banner, (Kleinoch); Harry Shannon, (Cumberland); Natasha Lytess, (Anna); Hans Conried, (The Fitter); Alex Melesh, (Waiter); Walter Byron, Otto Reichow, (Guards); Peter Seal, (Polish Orderly); Hans Wollenberger, (Waiter); Walter Stahl, Russell Gaige, (Guests of Baron); Dina Smirnova, (Traveler-Warsaw); George Irving, (American Consul); William Vaughn, (German Colonel); Dell Henderson, (American Attache); Carl Ekberg, (Hitler); Fred Niblo, (Ship Captain); Oscar Lorraine, (Ship Steward); Bert Roach, (Bartender); Emory Parnell, (Quisling); Boyd Davis, (Chamberlin); Claudine De Luc, (Hotel Proprietor); with Rudolph Myzed, Felix Bosch, Joseph Kamaryt, Leda Nicova.

CREDITS: Director, Leo McCarey; Producer, Leo McCarey; Scenarist, Sheridan Gibney. Based on a story by Leo McCarey, Sheridan Gibney. Photographer, George Barnes; Art Directors, Albert S. D'Agostino, Al Herman; Set Decorators, Darrell Silvera, Claude E. Carpenter; Editor, Theron Warth; Sound Recorder, Steve Dunn; Musical Score, Robert Emmett Dolan; Costumer, Miss Leslie; Makeup Artist, Mel Burns; Montage, Douglas Travers; Special Photographic Effects, Vernon L. Walker; Assistant Director, Harry Scott; Still Photographer, John Miehle.

SYNOPSIS: U.S. foreign correspondent Pat O'Toole tries to prove to Katie O'Hara, an American gold digger, that her Nazi husband, Baron von Luber, is Hitler's advance agent in each of the about-to-be-conquered countries, but he does not count on falling for the lady.

REVIEWS

"It is the quick change in moods that tests Miss Rogers' ability and her successful interpretations are a grand exposition of her merit. An actress of less ability, and a lesser director than Leo McCarey, easily could have failed dismally in attempting to portray such a story as this one. And Mr. Grant, always a smooth delineator lends no little to the tone of the production."

G. E. Blackford
New York Journal-American

"The main part of the acrobatics is a virtuoso performance by Ginger Rogers as a Brooklyn showgirl putting on the dog because she has the scent of a baron with money sticking out of every pocket. She gets an able assist from Cary Grant, a newshound with an almost insane zest for his job and a completely insane zest for pursuing Ginger . . . the picture does stop frequently to

With Cary Grant

let Ginger and Cary sit in close-up for discussions of man, woman and life. That left me a little impatient for the funny stuff and the exciting stuff to begin again."

New York World-Telegram

"This is not to say that Ginger Rogers and Cary Grant fall down in their bravura performances. True, they both spread it on thick, Grant, his careless charm, Rogers, the artless sincerity of a gold digger rising to obloquy as the wife-to-be of a leading Nazi. Frequently they hit the mark and have you with them in their long adventure, but then, too often, they talk you right out of it."

Archer Winsten
New York Post

NOTES: Ginger got fairly close to the realities of America's involvement in World War II in *The Major and the Minor*, but in *Once upon a Honeymoon*, Leo McCarey put her right in the middle of things. As an ex-hoofer who marries a Gestapo agent, she is at first enlightened and then rescued by an American correspondent (Grant).

The film's main problem was that it tried to go in several directions at the same time. The characters and situations, as written by scenarist Sheridan Gibney, were most enjoyable and there were many pokes at Hitler's conquests (all Germans are dunderheads, according to Hollywood films), but not all audiences were laughing. It was a strange mixture of comedy and reality, and the two did not always blend.

Cary Grant was an ideal choice as Ginger's co-star and they worked well together. In fact, the cast itself played well throughout.

Steve Dunn's sound recording received the film's only Academy Award nomination.

With Walter Byron, Cary Grant, and Otto Reichow

Tender Comrade

An RKO-Radio Picture, 1943

CAST: Ginger Rogers, (Jo); Robert Ryan, (Chris); Ruth Hussey, (Barbara); Patricia Collinge, (Helen Stacey); Mady Christians, (Manya); Kim Hunter, (Doris); Jane Darwell, (Mrs. Henderson); Mary Forbes, (Jo's Mother); Richard Martin, (Mike); Richard Gaines, (Waldo); Patti Brill, (Western Union Girl); Euline Martin, (Baby); Edward Fielding, (Doctor); Claire Whitney, (Nurse); Donald Davis, Robert Anderson, (Boys).

With Robert Ryan

CREDITS: Director, Edward Dmytryk; Producer, David Hempstead; Associate Producer, Sherman Todd; Scenarist, Dalton Trumbo. Based on a story by Dalton Trumbo. Photographer, Russell Metty; Art Directors, Al D'Agostino, Carroll Clark; Set Decorators, Darrell Silvera, Al Fields; Editor, Roland Gross; Sound Recorder, Roy Meadows; Musical Score, Leigh Harline; Musical Director, C. Bakaleinikoff; Orchestrator, Maurice DePackh; Miss Rogers's Costumes by Edith Head; Gowns by Renie; Makeup Artist, Mel Burns; Special Effects, Vernon L. Walker; Assistant Director, Harry Scott; Still Photographer, John Miehle.

SYNOPSIS: Jo, a young defense-plant worker whose husband, Chris, is away at war, decides to share a house with three other defense-plant women in the same situation.

REVIEWS

"If *Tender Comrade* were a steak, you could cut it with a cafeteria spoon. Essentially it is mush, covered with an irritating cuteness and hiding one tough tendon of tragedy. . . . Miss Rogers tries hard, too hard perhaps, and Ryan is sensibly subdued, but they cannot work clear of artificially mannered lines and emotions running riot at the expense of solid character building. . . . *Tender Comrade* should be sent back to the kitchen of Director Edward Dmytryk and Author Dalton Trumbo with the reminder that mincemeat belongs in a pie, not a picture about war and wives."

Archer Winsten
New York Post

"Miss Rogers is too cute a good deal of the time, though. For that matter, everybody in the picture has been subjected to direction of a particularly low grade."

The New Yorker

"Slopping over with sentimentality and the most banal of sermonizing, this is the story of four rather dull women whose husbands are off at war. There has seldom been a wordier film, nor can I remember any in which there was less action. Nothing ever happens on screen."

New York Sun

NOTES: Producer David Hempstead and scenarist Dalton Trumbo, who gave Ginger such a good production and material in *Kitty Foyle*, concocted this little wartime romantic melodrama. Edward Dmytryk directed this maudlin bit of "Americana" with an iron hand—it was too heavy.

At this time, Trumbo and Dmytryk were not concealing their Communist sympathies. Ginger soon began to notice little anti-American speeches creeping into her dialogue and, upon complaint (she explained later), these lines were given to other actresses.

With Patricia Collinge, Ruth Hussey, and Kim Hunter

On the set with script girl Mercy Weireter, director Edward Dmytryk, Mady Christians, and Patricia Collinge

With Jane Darwell

With Barry Sullivan

With Warner Baxter

CAST: Ginger Rogers, (Liza Elliott); Ray Milland, (Charley Johnson); Warner Baxter, (Kendall Nesbitt); Jon Hall, (Randy Curtis); Barry Sullivan, (Dr. Brooks); Mischa Auer, (Russell Paxton); Phyllis Brooks, (Allison DuBois); Mary Philips, (Maggie Grant); Edward Fielding, (Dr. Carlton); Don Loper, (Adams); Mary Parker, (Miss Parker); Catherine Craig, (Miss Foster); Marietta Canty, (Martha); Virginia Farmer, (Miss Edwards); Fay Helm, (Miss Bowers); Gail Russell, (Barbara); Marian Hall, (Miss Stevens); Kay Linaker, (Liza's Mother); Harvey Stephens, (Liza's Father); Billy Daniels, (Office Boy); Georgia Backus, (Miss Sullivan); Rand Brooks, (Ben); Pepito Perez, (Clown); Charles Smith, (Barbara's Boyfriend); Mary MacLaren, (Librarian); Paul McVey, (Jack Goddard); Paul Pierce, George Mayon, (Specialty Dancers); Tristram Coffin, Dennis Moore, Jack Luden, (Men); George Calliga, (Captain of Waiters); Frances Robinson, (Girl with Randy); Jan Buckingham, (Miss Shawn); Jack Mulhall, (Photographer); Hillary Brooke, (Miss Barr); Miriam Franklin, (Dancer); Dorothy Granger, (Autograph Hunter); Charles Coleman, (Butler); Lester Sharpe, (Pianist); Bobby Beers, (Charley as a Boy); Phyllis M. Brooks, (Barbara at 7); Marjean Neville, (Liza at 5 and 7); Charles Bates, (David); Audrey Young, Louise LaPlanche, (Office Girls); Murray Alper, (Taxicab Driver); Billy Dawson, (Boy at Circus); Priscilla Lyon, (Little Girl at Circus); Buz Buckley, (Freckle-faced Boy); Herbert Corthell, (Senator).

CREDITS: Director, Mitchell Leisen; Producer, Mitchell Leisen; Associate Producer, Richard Blumenthal; Scenarists, Frances Goodrich, Albert Hackett. Based on the play *Lady in the Dark* by Moss Hart. Photographer, Ray Rennahan; Art Directors, Hans Dreier, Raoul Pene du Bois; Set Decorator, Ray Moyer; Editor, Alma Macrorie; Sound Recorders, Earl Hayman, Walter Oberst; Musical Score, Robert Emmett Dolan; Music Associate, Arthur Franklin; Orchestrator, Robert Russell Bennett; Vocal Arrangements, Joseph J. Lilley; Costumer, Raoul Pene du Bois; Modern Gowns, Edith Head. Dances Staged by Billy Daniels. Makeup Artist, Wally Westmore; Special Photographic Effects, Gordon Jennings, Paul Lerpae, Farciot Edouart; Assistant Directors, Chico Alonso, Richard McWhorter; Technicolor Color Consultant, Natalie Kalmus; Technicolor Associate, Morgan Padelford; Still Photographer, G.E. Richardson.

SONGS: One Life to Live, Girl of the Moment, It Looks Like Liza, This Is New, My Ship, Jenny, by Ira Gershwin, Kurt Weill; *Suddenly It's Spring*, by Johnny Burke, Jimmy Van Heusen; *Artist's Waltz*, by Robert Emmett Dolan; *Dream Lover*, by Clifford Grey, Victor Schertzinger.

SYNOPSIS: Liza Elliott, *Allure* magazine's editor-in-chief, undergoes psychoanalysis to discover why she suffrers from headaches and continuous daydreams. Her security in a man's world is threatened by her enterprising assistant, Charley Johnson, and an old friend, Kendall Nesbitt, who wants to take her away from it all.

REVIEWS

"It was fortunate that the work had Miss Rogers in the starring role. It is difficult to say whether the Hacketts or the actress are chiefly responsible for the signal success of a dubious motion picture enterprise. Certainly Miss Rogers contrives to make Liza Elliott a captivating character. Whether she is being the severely groomed and efficient magazine editor who is the epitome of the career woman, or is imagining herself the glamour girl she might have been had it not been for a series of frustrations, she is wonderful."

Howard Barnes
New York Herald Tribune

"Some of Miss Rogers' dreams seem to be governed not so much by what's on her mind as what the special-effects man would like to have a go at. Maybe I'm backward, but my dreams don't have all that mist or fog or whatever it is that Miss Rogers has been surrounded with in her subconscious state, and I don't know but what somebody just wanted to kid around a little with dry ice. Miss Rogers, by the way, is an easy magazine editor on the eyes, although she is made up a bit too elaborately."

The New Yorker

"Put *Lady in the Dark* down as unique in the annals of the movies. It is one of the few attempts successfully to

With Ray Milland

With Warner Baxter and Jon Hall

analyze mental processes, and the result is gaudy, glamorous and glittering . . . . Technicolor photography is not too kind to Ginger Rogers, but she does an able job in the role, conveying even the *Saga of Jenny* with amazing effectiveness."

Edwin Schallert
Los Angeles Times

"Miss Rogers, giving her complicated role a performance second to none she has ever done, is presented as the business executive of a smart magazine for women . . . . Leisen's direction captures every whit of glamorous delight inherent in the subject and treatment, and balances the entertainment items with a sensitive hand, as well as keeping the psychoanalytical matters completely credible."

Variety

NOTES: *Lady in the Dark* was Ginger's first all-color film. The Frances Goodrich-Albert Hackett script, from Moss Hart's play, stuck fairly close to the original concept. However, under Mitchell Leisen's heavy-handed direction, all the fun went out of the piece and

Ginger was much too grand and not too much fun. Many maintain she was miscast.

The lightness that had given Gertrude Lawrence a perfect stage vehicle was badly needed to uplift this glossy picture. Leisen and a brilliant technical crew spent all their time and energy on the trimmings while the story was ignored.

Liza Elliott was indeed a juicy part, and Ginger did the best she could with it—but, in the final analysis, she got lost in the gloss. Few of the original Ira Gershwin-Kurt Weill songs remained in the release print, although many of them had been filmed!

Despite its shortcomings, *Lady in the Dark* made a bundle for Paramount. It was perfect escapist movie fare. Ray Rennahan's brilliant photography, the art direction of Hans Dreier and Raoul Pene du Bois (the dream sequences) and Ray Moyer's set decorations all were nominated for Academy Awards. According to the picture's publicity crew, Leisen himself designed Ginger's celebrated mink dress.

Lady in the Dark was purchased for the then-record sum of $283,000 and cost $2,000,000 to make.

I'll Be Seeing You

A Vanguard Production

A Selznick International Picture Released thru United Artists, 1944

With Joseph Cotten

With Dorothy Stone, Spring Byington, and Shirley Temple

CAST: Ginger Rogers, (Mary Marshall); Joseph Cotten, (Zachary Morgan); Shirley Temple, (Barbara Marshall); Spring Byington, (Mrs. Marshall); Tom Tully, (Mr. Marshall); Chill Wills, (Swanson); Dare Harris (John Derek); (Lieutenant Bruce); Kenny Bowers, (Sailor on Train); Stanley Ridges, (Warden); Walter Baldwin, (Vendor); Dorothy Stone, (Saleslady).

CREDITS: Director, William Dieterle; Producer, Dore Schary; Scenarist, Marion Parsonnet. Based on the radio drama *Double Furlough* by Charles Martin. Photographer, Tony Gaudio; Art Director, Mark-Lee Kirk; Set Decorators, Earl B. Wooden, Emile Kuri; Editor, William H. Ziegler; Editorial Supervisor, Hal C. Kern; Musical Score, Daniele Amfitheatrof; Costumer, Edith Head; Makeup Artist, William Riddle; Assistant Director, Lowell J. Farrell; Production Assistant, Lou Lusty.

SONG: *I'll Be Seeing You*, by Irving Kahal, Sammy Fain.

SYNOPSIS: Aboard a train, Mary Marshall, on a Christmas furlough from the state penitentiary where she is serving a term for manslaughter, meets U.S. Army Sergeant Zachary Morgan, newly discharged from a mental hospital, and invites him to spend the holidays with her relatives.

REVIEWS

"What distinguishes the story is its general honesty and lack of obvious histrionics, the many fine touches of family life and the performance of the cast . . . . Joseph Cotten gives a fine portrait of the slightly befuddled soldier slowly coming out of his semi-stupor under the influence of a sympathetic family, while Ginger Rogers is again a noteworthy dramatic actress as the embittered but resigned young woman struggling for a dream she

189

With Shirley Temple, Spring Byington, Joseph Cotten, and Tom Tully

once thought forever lost .... William Dieterle's direction is a little slow sometimes, but suitable to the film's mood. Dialog is simple and natural, and performances honest."

Variety

"In the principal roles and under the direction of William Dieterle, Joseph Cotten and Ginger Rogers give performances that are excellent. Mr. Cotten, because his role is obviously the more demanding and tenebrous, deserves the highest honors. He plays the shell-shocked veteran with supreme restraint and with a calm and determined independence that beautifully reveals his pain and pride. Miss Rogers is altogether moving as the girl likewise injured by fate, but her role is plainly old-fashioned for reflection and counterpoint."

Bosley Crowther
The New York Times

NOTES: As *Lady in the Dark* had passed from Gertrude Lawrence to Ginger, from stage to screen, this film involved the same ladies, but passed from radio to screen. Gertrude Lawrence and James Cagney had performed Charles Martin's drama *Double Furlough* on radio.

David O. Selznick got Ginger for this Vanguard Production, with William Dieterle directing after Selznick had replaced director George Cukor. Actually Cukor had directed Ginger at the outset. Later retitled *I'll Be Seeing You*, this was a low-key sentimental drama which benefited greatly from Ginger's sensitive portrayal and Joseph Cotten's expert handling of a difficult role.

Tony Gaudio's camera work and Daniele Amfitheatrof's musical score were added assets. The supporting cast was most effective. The working titles were *Double Furlough* and *With All My Heart*.

Week-End at the Waldorf A Metro-Goldwyn-Mayer Picture, 1945

With Walter Pidgeon

CAST: Ginger Rogers, (Irene Malvern); Lana Turner, (Bunny Smith); Walter Pidgeon, (Chip Collyer); Van Johnson, (Captain James Hollis); Robert Benchley, (Randy Morton); Edward Arnold, (Martin X. Edley); Constance Collier, (Mme. Jaleska); Leon Ames, (Henry Burton); Warner Anderson, (Dr. Campbell); Phyllis Thaxter, (Cynthia Drew); Keenan Wynn, (Oliver Webson); Porter Hall, (Stevens); Samuel S. Hinds, (Mr. Jessup); George Zucco, (Bey of Aribajan); Xavier Cugat, (Himself); Lina Romay, (Juanita); Bob Graham, (Singer); Michael Kirby, (Lieutenant John Rand); Cora Sue Collins, (Jane Rand); Rosemary De Camp, (Anna); Jacqueline De Wit, (Kate Douglas); Frank Puglia, (Emile); Charles Wilson, (Hi Johns); Irving Bacon, (Sam Skelly); Miles Mander, (British Secretary); Nana Bryant, (Mrs. H. Davenport Drew); Russell Hicks, (McPherson); Ludmilla Pitoeff, (Irma); Naomi Childers, (Night Maid); Moroni Olsen, (House Detective Blake); William Halligan, (Chief Jennings); John Wengraf, (Alix); Ruth Lee, (The Woman); William Hall, (Cassidy the Doorman); Rex Evans, (Pianist); Wyndham Standing, (Literary Type); Harry Barris, (Anna's Boyfriend); Byron Foulger, (Barber); Gladden James, (Assistant Manager); Carli Elinor, (Orchestra Leader); Dick Crockett, (Bell Captain); William Tannen, (Photographer); Mel Shubert, Jack Luden, (Clerks); Hal K. Dawson, (First Clerk); Gertrude Short, (Telephone Operator); Mary Icide, (Elevator Girl); Helen McLeod, (Elevator Operator); Dorothy Christy, (Cashier); Gloria Findlay, (Turkish Coffee Girl); Bess Flowers, (Guest).

191

With Xavier Cugat, Van Johnson, Lana Turner, and Walter Pidgeon

CREDITS: Director, Robert Z. Leonard; Producer, Arthur Hornblow, Jr.; Scenarists, Sam Spewack, Bella Spewack; Adaptation, Guy Bolton. Based on the play *Grand Hotel* by Vicki Baum. Photographer, Robert Planck; Art Directors, Cedric Gibbons, Daniel B. Cathcart; Set Decorators, Edwin B. Willis, Jack Bonar; Editor, Robert J. Kern; Dance Director, Charles Walters; Sound Recorder, Douglas Shearer; Musical Score, Johnny Green; Underscoring, Sidney Cutner; Orchestrators, Sidney Cutner, Ted Duncan, Leo Shuken; Choral Arrangement, Kay Thompson; Costumers, Irene and Marion Herwood Keyes; Makeup Artist, Jack Dawn; Hair Stylist, Sydney Guilaroff; Special Effects, Warren Newcombe; Assistant Director, Bill Lewis; Technical Adviser, Ted Saucier.

SONGS: *And There You Are*, by Pepe Guizar; *Guadalajara*, by Sammy Fain, Ted Koehler.

SYNOPSIS: At New York's Waldorf-Astoria Hotel, successful film actress Irene Malvern discovers war correspondent Chip Collyer in her room. Although she mistakes him for a thief, she offers him shelter.

REVIEWS

"*Weekend at the Waldorf* is *Grand Hotel* in modern dress . . . . Because she appears more frequently than the other players, Ginger Rogers attracts the most attention, as a super-tense film celebrity whose fame and fortune has brought her nothing but loneliness. But there are half a dozen other competent performers who plow their way through this three-day ordeal in the rooms and corridors of Manhattan's famed Waldorf-Astoria Hotel."

Time

"*Week-End at the Waldorf* will command potent box office. It's a big, star-packed show that can't miss. It has been given the type of production and direction that best displays the wealth of talent and material. Caliber of the playing makes it difficult to give the edge to any of the star teams that are paired in the story. Ginger Rogers, as the tired picture actress, and Walter Pidgeon, a tired war correspondent, give expert interpretations to the brittle, sophisticated dialog and situations that mark their roles."

Variety

"Miss Rogers is a knowing comedienne who sparks several of the scenes as the lovely star who finds the correspondent in her rooms at night and tries to reform him, thinking him a thief."

Otis Guernsey, Jr.
New York Herald Tribune

NOTES: *Week-End at the Waldorf* was M-G-M's glossy updating of Vicki Baum's *Grand Hotel*, and was Ginger's first film for the company. Under Robert Z. Leonard's slick direction, Ginger gave warmth and laughter to the part of actress Irene Malvern. Her scenes with Walter Pidgeon were delightful and the best, by far, in the film.

Lana Turner was Bunny Smith, stenographer who dreams of a rich man, but finally settles for "ordinary" soldier Van Johnson. The typical gloss that marked this giant studio's pictures was in full evidence here. Ginger and Lana were both dressed by Irene (Ginger got twelve gowns with almost as many hair styles by Sydney Guilaroff).

In the original, Greta Garbo and Joan Crawford were never permitted to meet on film—a mistake that has puzzled cinemagoers ever since. Just passing each other in the hall, without any exchange of dialogue—perhaps a stare and glance—would have been enough. The ladies would have made it play! Similarly, Ginger and Lana never met in this remake.

With Irving Bacon,
Leon Ames,
and Van Johnson

193

Heartbeat

An RKO-Radio Picture, 1946

CAST: Ginger Rogers, (Arlette); Jean Pierre Aumont, (Pierre); Adolphe Menjou, (Ambassador); Basil Rathbone, (Professor Aristide); Eduardo Ciannelli, (Baron Dvorak); Mikhail Rasumny, (Yves Cadubert); Melville Cooper, (Roland Medeville); Mona Maris, (Ambassador's Wife); Henry Stephenson, (Minister); Eddie Hayden, (Fat Thief).

CREDITS: Director, Sam Wood; Producers, Robert Hakim, Raymond Hakim; Scenarists, Hans Wilhelm, Max Kolpe, Michel Duran; Adaptation, Morris Ryskind; Additional Dialogue, Roland Leigh. Based on the French film *Battement de Coeur*. Photographer, Joseph Valentine; Art Director, Lionel Banks; Set Decorator, George Sawley; Editor, Roland Gross; Sound Recorder, John Tribby; Musical Score, Paul Misraki; Musical Director, C. Bakaleinikoff; Costumer, Howard Greer; Makeup Artist, Mel Burns; Assistant Director, John Sherwood; Still Photographer, John Miehle.

SONG: *Can You Guess*, by Paul Misraki, Ervin Drake.

SYNOPSIS: Arlette, a destitute girl, enrolls in a pickpocket school operated by Professor Aristide and, under his strict tutelage, becomes a star pupil. Her first major assignment is to "lift" something from a diplomat, Pierre, with whom she eventually becomes romantically involved.

REVIEWS

"Miss Rogers, as the stray, does all that she is asked to do in her quick changes from a reform school refugee to the supposed niece of a baron, but she is ill at ease throughout most of the production . . . . *Heartbeat* is neither Gallic nor good. It employs Hollywood resources to a minimum of cinematic advantage."

New York Herald Tribune

"*Heartbeat* has Ginger Rogers having quite a time for herself in most of its footage as a French waif who becomes a diplomat's lady . . . . Perhaps a little music would have helped. There were spots where Miss Rogers might even have danced to advantage. A Ginger Rogers song and dance is always a help. *Heartbeat* is light enough to have needed just a bit of music . . . The film is not long. It is still too long, however, for such a frail plot . . . . When suspense is gone, the picture becomes mechanical. And a mechanical fantasy is a heavy dish."

New York Sun

"Picture frequently reaches for its laughs and spontaneity which situations demand is for most part absent. Miss Rogers tries hard, and so does rest of cast, but material simply isn't there for the gay farce this should be. Most memorable performances are delivered by Rathbone, as the professor, and Mikhail Rasumny, an inept pupil who befriends Miss Rogers."

Variety

With Jean Pierre Aumont

With Basil Rathbone

With Jean Pierre Aumont, Adolphe Menjou, and Mona Maris

"Wood contributes a job of polished direction which closer editing would aid. The clever moments are spaced with interludes that are definitely dull. These pauses in story progression also interfere with Ginger Rogers' portrayal of her Cinderella, and no one does these undiscovered beauties better than she. Her utter lack of makeup is good in the beginning, but a couple of her makeups later are unfortunate, despite the ace photography by Joseph Valentine.

Hollywood Reporter

NOTES: For the first time since her Award-winning *Kitty Foyle*, Ginger worked with director Sam Wood. Unfortunately, by this time, Wood had lost most of the insight that had made him a brilliant cinema craftsman (who could forget his splendid *Kings Row*)? The script, which Morris Ryskind had adapted from the French film *Battement de Coeur*, took three scenarists to bring it around—with the added dialogue of Roland Leigh thrown in for good measure. Too many cooks spoiled the broth.

What makes *Heartbeat* worth remembering is the expert way the cast handled improbable dialogue, ludicrous situations and two-dimensional characters. Ginger was delightful as Arlette, a destitute waif who joins a pickpocket school. Jean Pierre Aumont, as the diplomat whose pocket Ginger is assigned to pick, could not have been more charming. Adolphe Menjou, Basil Rathbone, Eduardo Ciannelli, and Mona Maris were all memorable in their respective roles.

With Mikhail Rasumny

Magnificent Doll   A Universal-International Picture   A Hallmark Production, 1946

With Burgess Meredith

CAST: Ginger Rogers, (Dolly Payne); David Niven, (Aaron Burr); Burgess Meredith, (James Madison); Horace (Stephen) McNally, (John Todd); Peggy Wood, (Mrs. Payne); Frances Williams, (Amy); Robert H. Barrat, (Mr. Payne); Grandon Rhodes, (Thomas Jefferson); Henri Letondal, (Count D'Arignon); Joe Forte, (Senator Ainsworth); Erville Alderson, (Darcy); George Barrows, (Jedson); Francis McDonald, (Barber Jenks); Emmett Vogan, (Mr. Gallentine); Arthur Space, (Alexander Hamilton); Joseph Crehan, (Williams); Byron Foulger, (Servant); Larry Blake, (Charles); Pierre Watkin, (Harper); John Sheehan, (Janitor); Ruth Lee, (Mrs. Gallentine); John Hamilton, (Mr. Witherspoon); George Carleton, (Howard); Harlan Tucker, (Ralston); Vivien Oakland, (Mrs. Witherspoon); Al Hill, (Man); Olaf Hytten, (Blennerhassett); Lee Phelps, (Hatch); Joe King, (Jailer); Brandon Hurst, (Brown); Harlan Briggs, (Quinn); Larry Steers, (Lafayette).

CREDITS: Director, Frank Borzage; Producers, Jack H. Skirball, Bruce Manning; Scenarist, Irving Stone. Based on an original story by Irving Stone. Photographer, Joseph Valentine; Art Supervisor, Jack Otterson; Art Director, Alexander Golitzen; Set Decorators, Russell A. Gausman, Ted Offenbecker; Editor, Ted J. Kent; Sound Recorder, Charles Felstead; Technician, Robert Pritchard; Musical Score, H.J. Salter; Orchestrator, David Tamkin; Costumers, Travis Banton, Vera West; Makeup Artist, Jack P. Pierce; Hair Stylists, Carmen Dirigo, Anna Malin; Hats, Lilly Dache; Assistant Director, John F. Sherwood; Production Manager, Arthur Siteman; Set Continuity, Adele Cannon.

SYNOPSIS: After the death of her Quaker husband John Todd, Dolly Payne Todd and her mother open a boardinghouse. She finds herself desired by two men: fiery, impetuous Senator Aaron Burr and gentle philosopher Congressman James Madison. Later Dolly marries Madison, who is elected President. Yet her notorious love affair with Aaron Burr almost alters the course of U.S. history.

REVIEWS

"The Jack Skirball-Bruce Manning production has all the frou-frou charm of a Martha Washington box of candy and the sets and costumes have the appeal of Colonial miniatures. With such good taste in all departments, it is to wonder why so much stuff was piled on Miss Rogers, who wears everything but a Colonial version of the kitchen sink in almost every scene. Yet, behind the frills, Ginger manages to turn in an attractive and spirited performance in a more subtle role than she usually essays."

Los Angeles Examiner

"Ginger Rogers plays Dolly Madison with dignity and conviction, and even sounds forceful enough to sway a mob from violence."

Los Angeles Daily News

"Glorification of Ginger Rogers in the costume manner may be witnessed in the *Magnificent Doll*. It is accomplished with style in this impression of early American life.

Miss Rogers is at her glamorous best and reflects in her portrayal an intelligent approach to the character as screen-depicted."

Edwin Schallert
Los Angeles Times

"In the role of magnificent Dolly, Miss Rogers wears her Lilly Dache hats and her Vera West gowns with more attention than she seems to be giving to her lines—which is not altogether reprehensible, for the lines are distressingly dull."

The New York Times

NOTES: If *Magnificent Doll* proved one thing, it was that Irving Stone should concentrate his efforts on historical novels and not historical screenplays. He did just that.

In this banal treatment of what otherwise should have been pregnant with exciting possibilities—the James Madison-Aaron Burr-Dolly Payne Madison triangle—the characters Stone provided for his actors resembled zombies. Director Frank Borzage, long past his prime, was ineffectual in his direction, and the result was boring and turgid historical drama.

Ginger was mannered and totally miscast as Dolly Madison and seemed out of place in such surroundings. Her fans were pleased she looked so well in costumes by Travis Banton and Vera West but critics and the general public disagreed. David Niven (*Bachelor Mother*) and Burgess Meredith (*Tom, Dick and Harry*) also gave up a losing battle.

With David Niven and Burgess Meredith

It Had to Be You

A Columbia Picture, 1947

CAST: Ginger Rogers, (Victoria Stafford); Cornel Wilde, ("George" Johnny Blaine); Percy Waram, (Mr. Stafford); Spring Byington, (Mrs. Stafford); Ron Randell, (Oliver H.P. Harrington); Thurston Hall, (Mr. Harrington); Charles Evans, (Dr. Parkinson); William Bevan, (Evans); Frank Orth, (Conductor Brown); Harry Hays Morgan, (George Benson); Douglas Wood, (Mr. Kimberly); Mary Forbes, (Mrs. Kimberly); Anna Q. Nilsson, (Saleslady); Gerald Fielding, (Peabody); Nancy Saunders, (Model); Douglas D. Coppin, (Boyfriend); Virginia Hunter, (Maid of Honor); Michael Towne, (First Fireman); Fred Sears, (Second Fireman/ tillerman); Paul Campbell, (Radio Announcer); Carol Nugent,(Victoria [Age Six]); Jerry Hunt, (Indian Boy); Judy Nugent, (Victoria [Age Five]); Mary Patterson, (Victoria [Age Three]); Dudley Dickerson, (Porter); Ralph Peters, (Cab Driver #1); Garry Owen, (Cab Driver #2); Harlan Warde, (Atherton); Myron Healy, (Standish); Jack Rice, (Floorwalker); George Chandler, (Bit Man); Vernon Dent, (Bit Man—Drugstore); Vera Lewis, (Mrs. Brown).

CREDITS: Directors, Don Hartman, Rudolph Mate; Producer, Don Hartman; Assistant Producer, Norman Deming; Scenarists, Norman Panama, Melvin Frank. Based on a story by Don Hartman, Allen Boretz. Photographers, Rudolph Mate, Vincent Farrar; Art Directors, Stephen Goosson, Rudolph Sternad; Set Decorators, Wilbur Menefee, William Kiernan; Editor, Gene Havlick; Camera Operator, Irving Klein; Sound Recorder, Jack Haynes; Musical Score, Heinz Roemheld; Musical Director, W.M. Stoloff; Orchestrator, Herschel Burke Gilbert. Assistant to the Producer, Norman Deming. Costumer, Jean Louis; Hair Styles, Helen Hunt; Makeup Artist, Clay Campbell. Jewels by Lackritz. Assistant Director, Sam Nelson; Still Photographer, Lippman.

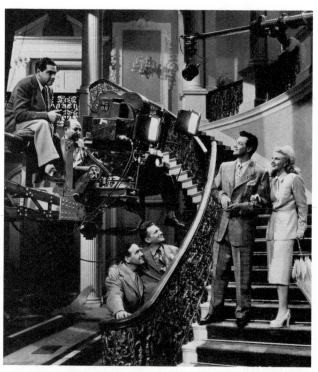

On the set with photographer Vincent Farrar, cameraman Irving Klein (on boom), and co-directors Rudolph Mate and Don Hartman

SYNOPSIS: Socialite Victoria Stafford always gets cold feet at the very last minute of a marriage ceremony, since she is looking for just the right man. When fireman Johnny Blaine appears on the scene, Victoria is sure he is the man of her dreams.

REVIEWS

"Unfortunately, Miss Rogers makes an exaggerated attempt to be cute and coy, and the resultant grimaces are a little embrrassing."

Virginia Wright
Los Angeles Daily News

"The whole business is acted with bounce and enthusiasm, as Ginger Rogers turns in a swiftly paced comedy performance reminiscent of her best films of some years ago, and Cornel Wilde plays his Indian-fireman dual role with quite unexpected farcical skill."

Cue

"Anyone of whom it can be said that she refused to act in Dreiser's *Sister Carrie* because it was too radical should be subjected to pictures like *It Had to Be You* . . . . If this is the kind of picture Hollywood will use from now on to keep itself purged of investigators, censors, religious hatchet men, Communists and thinkers, the cure is clearly worse than any possible evil. In a world where popular entertainment is the first principle and prime mover, *It Had to Be You* is twice removed from its goal."

Archer Winsten
New York Post

NOTES: It took two directors, two photographers, two scenarists and two original story writers to bring *It Had to Be You* to the screen. At best, it is a pleasant but silly comedy. Ginger seemed to be having a good time, but—at the same time—the film did not do anything special for her career. It resembled *Tom Dick and Harry*—a superior comedy-fantasy which required only one director, one photographer, and one writer.

This was Ginger's first picture at Columbia, and without her it would have fallen flat. She worked overtime to make all the nutty situations play. If the script and direction had matched her energy, *It Had to Be You* might have succeeded. Despite criticism, it proved popular with audiences, who were still recovering from World War II.

Cornel Wilde was her handsome co-star and he, too, showed a fine comic sense—a complete change of pace from his popular swashbuckling adventures. The main set, with its sweeping staircase had been previously used in Katharine Hepburn's *Holiday* (1938).

With Cornel Wilde and Ron Randell

With Harry Hays Morgan, Percy Waram, and Cornel Wilde

With Fred Astaire

CAST: Fred Astaire, (Josh Barkley); Ginger Rogers, (Dinah Barkley); Oscar Levant, (Ezra Miller); Billie Burke, (Mrs. Belney); Gale Robbins, (Shirlene May); Jacques Francois, (Jacques Barredout); George Zucco, (The Judge); Clinton Sundberg, (Bert Felsher); Inez Cooper, (Pamela Driscoll); Carol Brewster, (Gloria Amboy); Wilson Wood, (Larry); Jean Andren, (First Woman); Laura Treadwell, (Second Woman); Margaret Bert, (Mary, the Maid); Allen Wood, (Taxi Driver); Forbes Murray, Bess Flowers, Lois Austin, Betty Blythe, (Guests in Theatre Lobby); Bill Tannen, (Doorman at Theatre); Mahlon Hamilton, (Apartment Doorman); Lorraine Crawford, (Cleo Fernby); Dee Turnell, (Blonde); Reginald Simpson, (Husband); Hans Conried, (Ladislaus Ladi); Sherry Hall, (Chauffeur); Frank Ferguson, (Mr. Perkins); Nolan Leary, (Stage Doorman); Joe Granby, (Duke de Morny); Esther Sommers, (Sarah's Mother); Helen Eby-Rock, (Sarah's Aunt); Joyce Matthews, (Genevieve); Roberta Johnson, (Henrietta); Mary Jo Ellis, (Clementine); Jack Rice, (Ticket Man); Roger Moore, (First Man); Wilbur Mack, Larry Steers, Lillian West, (Guests).

CREDITS: Director, Charles Walters; Producer, Arthur Freed; Associate Producer, Roger Edens; Original Screenplay, Betty Comden, Adolph Green; Photographer, Harry Stradling; Operating Cameraman, Sammy Leavitt; Art Directors, Cedric Gibbons, Edward Carfagno; Set Decorators, Edwin B. Willis, Arthur Krams; Editor, Albert Akst; Sound Recorder, Douglas Shearer; Musical Director, Lennie Hayton; Orchestrator, Conrad Salinger; Musical Arrangements, Robert Tucker. Dances by Robert Alton. Costumers, Irene, Valles. Mr. Astaire's Dances by Hermes Pan, Irving G. Reis. Makeup Artist, Jack Dawn; Hair Stylist, Sydney Guilaroff; Special Effects, Warren Newcombe; Assistant Director, Wallace Worsley; Technicolor Color Consultant, Natalie Kalmus; Technicolor Associate, Henri Jaffa.

SONGS: *Shoes With Wings On, My One and Only Highland Fling, You'd Be Hard to Replace, Week-End in the Country, Manhattan Downbeat,* by Ira Gershwin, Harry Warren; *They Can't Take That Away from Me,* by Ira Gershwin, George Gershwin.

SYNOPSIS: Josh and Dinah Barkley are a sensational musical team, but Dinah yearns for a dramatic career and separates from her celebrated partner. After these new endeavors, Dinah teams up with Josh again, and they once again become the sparkling Barkleys of Broadway.

With Jacques Francois and Fred Astaire

With Gale Robbins and Fred Astaire

Dancing *Swing Trot* with Fred Astaire

REVIEWS

"*The Barkleys of Broadway* is a lighthearted Technicolored reunion for Hollywood's best-known dance team: Fred Astaire and Ginger Rogers . . . . For one thing, time—even in Hollywood—has not stood still. Ginger and Fred are no longer quite up to the soaring, smoothly paced routines of the '30s . . . . The important point is that Astaire & Rogers are seasoned showmen—both as dancers and comedians. Their dance numbers, though more sedate than ever before, are enchanting examples of the breezy, sophisticated style which they themselves brought to perfection."

Time

"Ginger and Fred are a couple with incorruptible style, and they've done as much good for the movies as any couple we know. Their teaming throughout the Nineteen Thirties in a series of musical films, beginning with *Flying Down to Rio* in 1933, was one of the most felicitous combinations that the screen has ever known, offering a brand of entertainment which had brilliance, integrity and class. And even though it was repeated in such memorable song-and-dance shows as *Top Hat*, *Swing Time*, and *Carefree*, the combination bloomed, drawing variety and freshness out of its own unique qualities.

"That is why it is quite natural that all of us should be thrilled to see it back in operation after a dreary hiatus of ten years. And that is why it is not surprising that the couple should be as fresh and as slick in *The Barkleys of Broadway* as it was in the days of yore."

Bosley Crowther
The New York Times

NOTES: Although *The Barkleys of Broadway* was conceived as a vehicle for Astaire and Judy Garland, its story line (Comden and Green wrote the original screenplay) bore a striking resemblance to the actual careers of Fred and Ginger. This became apparent once Miss Garland had to bow out of the filming because of ill health. Arthur Freed fortunately was able to secure Ginger's services and, after a ten-year absence, Astaire and Rogers danced together again—this time in color (and at M-G-M).

Together, the stars filled in those ten years as if only a weekend had passed. To help bridge the gap, they danced to *They Can't Take That Away from Me* which Fred had sung (and had danced with Harriet Hoctor) in RKO's 1937 *Shall We Dance*. Harry Warren's *Bouncin' the Blues* was used as a rehearsal tap for the nimble pair while Ginger, in a gold dress, joined Fred for *The Swing Trot (You'll Adore)*. Together they also did *You'd be Hard to Replace*, *My One and Only Highland Fling*, and *Manhattan Downbeat*, a fitting finale indeed.

Astaire's solo was *Shoes With Wings On* and again he proved he was still the master of cinematic dancing. Oscar Levant joined Fred and Ginger in the song *A Week-End in the Country*, and soloed with Khachaturian's *Saber Dance*, and Tchaikowsky's *Concerto in B-Flat Minor*.

With all the high points this film produced, there had to be a low point and, sadly, Ginger reached it with her ludicrous recitation of *La Marseillaise* (Charles Walters directed) in the section where Dinah Barkley goes dramatic.

Originally, there was supposed to be a hillbilly number called *The Courtin' of Elmer and Ella* as a specialty for Fred and Judy, echoing their hilarious *We're a Couple of Swells* number from *Easter Parade*, but it was dropped when Judy became ill.

Harry Stradling's fine photography received an Academy Award nomination.

Dancing *Manhattan Downbeat* with Fred Astaire

On the set with Fred Astaire and visitor Judy Garland

Dancing to *They Can't Take That Away from Me* with Fred Astaire

Perfect Strangers

A Warner Bros. Picture, 1950

With Margalo Gillmore, Frank Conlan, Howard Freeman, Dennis Morgan, George Chandler, Thelma Ritter, Alan Reed, Anthony Ross, Sumner Getchell, Charles Meredith, and Marjorie Bennett

CAST: Ginger Rogers, (Terry Scott); Dennis Morgan, (David Campbell); Thelma Ritter, (Lena Fassler); Margalo Gillmore, (Isobel Bradford); Anthony Ross, (Robert Fisher); Howard Freeman, (Timkin); Alan Reed, (Harry Patullo); Paul Ford, (Judge Byron); Harry Bellaver, (Bailiff); George Chandler, (Lester Hubley); Frank Conlan, (John Brokaw); Charles Meredith, (Lyle Pettijohn); Frances Charles, (Eileen Marcher); Marjorie Bennett, (Mrs. Moore); Paul McVey, (District Attorney); Edith Evanson, (Mary Travers); Whit Bissell, (Defense Attorney); Sumner Getchell, (John Simon); Ford Rainey, (Ernest Craig); Sarah Selby, (Mrs. Wilson); Alan Wood, (Clerk of Court); Ronnie Tyler, (Newsboy); Isabel Withers, (Woman); Max Mellenger, (Official); Boyd Davis, (Judge); Weldon Heyburn, (Man); Ezelle Poule, (Secretary); Mike Lally, (Court Steno); Charles Lind, (Thomas Luscomb); Russell De Vorkin, (Newsboy); Donald Kerr, (Busboy); Ned Glass, (O'Hanlon); Paul Dubov, (Vonderheit); Creighton Hale, John Albright, Frank Marlowe, Ed Coke, (Reporters); Lou Marcelle, (Television Announcer); Frank Pat Henry, (Doctor); Joleen King, (Nurse); Dick Kipling, (Autopsy Surgeon); Sidney Dubin, (Chemist); Art Miles, (Sheriff); Joseph Kerr, (Doctor); Richard Bartell, (Weatherman); Frank Cady, (Geologist); Hugh Murray, (Minister); Pat Mitchell, (Newsboy).

CREDITS: Director, Bretaigne Windust; Producer, Jerry Wald; Scenarist, Edith Sommer. Based on the Play *Ladies and Gentlemen* by Ben Hecht, Charles MacArthur. adaptation by George Oppenheimer. Photographer, Peverell Marley; Operating Cameraman, Ray Ramsey; Art Director, Stanley Fleischer; Set Decorator, George James Hopkins; Editor, David Weisbart; Sound Recorder, Al Riggs; Musical Score, Leigh Harline; Orchestrator, Maurice De Packh; Costumer, Milo Anderson; Hair Stylist, Gertrude Wheeler; Makeup Artist, Eddie Allen; Makeup Supervisor, Perc Westmore; Script Supervisor, Howard Hohler; Grip, Warren Yable; Assistant Director, Chuck Hansen; Production Manager, Eric Stacey; Gaffer, Frank Flanagan; Still Photographer, Mac Julian.

SYNOPSIS: On sequestered jury during a murder trial, divorcee Terry Scott meets, and falls in love with, David Campbell, an unhappily married man, during the hours away from the trial. Both soon realize they must go their separate ways.

REVIEWS

"The best parts of *Perfect Strangers* are those which have almost nothing to do with the script. Miss Ritter, Howard Freeman and Alan Reed contribute comic accents to the tale of a locked-up jury which are frequently delightful. The trouble is that the rueful romance between Miss Rogers and Mr. Morgan, which reflects the trial which they are deliberating, is extremely dull. It is not that Miss Rogers fails to portray an unwilling juror who falls in love with a married man in her same panel. She is as adroit as ever in creating the illusion that she is a Los Angeles matron who discovers that our government presumes a person innocent until proven guilty."

Howard Barnes
New York Herald Tribune

"Miss Rogers plays with brightness, warmth and a clean incisiveness which the less responsive Morgan is unable to match, though he at least makes an effort."

Philip K. Scheuer
Los Angeles Times

"For all of its loose-jointed meandering, its stilted performances with an exception or two, and its faulty script, *Perfect Strangers* is a film more interesting than monotonous. A lot of this is due to Ginger Rogers' skillful trouping in a role she makes more credible than it deserves. She puts a lot of sincerity into some of the script's more philosophical lines, and it emerges from the screen so that it means something."

Lowell E. Redelings
Hollywood Citizen-News

NOTES: Based on Ben Hecht and Charles MacArthur's play *Ladies and Gentlemen*, this xilm became an above-average romantic drama of two jurors who fall in love while deliberating a murder case.

In the specially filmed trailer made for this film, Ginger explained that, ever since *Kitty Foyle*, she and

With Anthony Ross and Dennis Morgan

Dennis Morgan had looked for just the right story in which to appear again. Whether that is fiction or fact does not really matter, because they both brought honesty, sincerity and conviction to their parts.

Under Bretaigne Windust's serviceable direction, a fine cast turned Edith Sommer's screenplay into more than romantic nonsense. Especially effective were Thelma Ritter, Anthony Ross, Margalo Gillmore, and Howard Freeman.

In England the film was called *Too Dangerous to Love*.

Storm Warning

A Warner Bros. Picture, 1950

CAST: Ginger Rogers, (Marsha Mitchell); Ronald Reagan, (Burt Rainey); Doris Day, (Lucy Rice); Steve Cochran, (Hank Rice); Hugh Sanders, (Charlie Barr); Lloyd Gough, (Cliff Rummel); Raymond Greenleaf, (Faulkner); Ned Glass, (George Athens); Walter Baldwin, (Bledsoe); Lynne Whitney, (Cora Athens); Stuart Randall, (Walters); Sean McClory, (Shore); Paul Burns, (Hauser); Dave McMahon, (Hollis); Robert Williams, (Jaeger); Charles Watts, (Wally); Charles Phillips, (Bus Driver); Dale Van Sickle, (Walter Adams); Anthony Warde, (Jute Box Collector); Lloyd Jenkins, (Interne); Paul Brinegar, (First Cameraman); King Donovan, (Ambulance Driver); Tom Wells, (Second Cameraman); Duke Watson, (Ernie); Len Hendry, (First Cop); Frank Marlowe, (Al [Bus Driver]); Ned Davenport, (Second Cop); David Le Grand, (Customer); Leo Cleary, (Barnet); Alex Gerry, (Basset); Charles Conrad, (Jordan); Grandon Rhodes, (Pike); Charles Marsh, (Fowler); Lillian Albertson, (Mrs. Rainey); Eddie Hearn, (Mr. Rainey); Dabbs Greer, (Attendant); Pat Flaherty, (Assistant); Dewey Robinson, Gene Evans, (Klansmen).

CREDITS: Director, Stuart Heisler; Producer, Jerry Wald; Scenarists, Daniel Fuchs, Richard Brooks. Based on a story by Daniel Fuchs, Richard Brooks. Photographer, Carl Guthrie; Operating Cameraman, Lou Jennings; Art Director, Leo K. Kuter; Set Decorator, G.W. Berntsen; Editor, Clarence Kolster; Sound Recorder, Leslie G. Hewitt; Musical Score, Daniele Amfitheatrof; Musical Director, Ray Heindorf; Orchestrator, Maurice De Packh; Costumer, Milo Anderson; Hair Stylist, Ray Forman; Makeup Artists, Perc Westmore, Frank Westmore; Script Supervisor, Howard Hohler; Assistant Director, Chuck Hansen; Grip, Herschel Brown; Gaffer, Vic Johnson; Still Photographer, Eugene Ritchie,

SYNOPSIS: Marsha Mitchell, a traveling dress model, stops in a small Southern town to visit her married sister, Lucy, but first witnesses a murder by the Ku Klux Klan, to which she discovers her brother-in-law, Hank, belongs.

REVIEWS

"Believe me, both Ginger Rogers and Doris Day will surprise you with their fine playing. Both musical comedy queens turn in performances that would stack up with Bette Davis or Olivia De Havilland."

Dorothy Manners
Los Angeles Examiner

With Ronald Reagan and Stuart Randall

With Steve Cochran

With Steve Cochran and Doris Day

"Miss Rogers does well as the model, and the county prosecutor is given a lot of sock by Ronald Reagan, portraying a character who beats his head against the stone wall of prejudice and fear. Unexpected and very good is the offbeat assignment of the sister, as done by Doris Day, and Steve Cochran scores soundly as the stupid, killer husband."

Variety

"Ginger Rogers as the northern girl who witnesses the Klan murder once again shows her mettle as a dramatic actress. She is deeply impressive as the visitor suddenly caught up in the frustration of being put in the position of having to testify against her sister's husband."

Motion Picture Herald

"Nevertheless, under Stuart Heisler's steady pacing, Miss Rogers and company perform with honesty and restraint. Surprise of the occasion is the successful casting of the singer Doris Day in a straight role that calls for considerable dramatic assurance."

Newsweek

"In the role of innocent bystander and key witness, Ginger Rogers—never notable as a great dramatic actress—gives evidence of a hitherto unsuspected dramatic sense. This is her finest performance to date—certainly surpassing her *Kitty Foyle*, for which she received an Academy Award. Miss Rogers gets solid support from Doris Day as her sister."

Cue

NOTES: *Storm Warning* provided Ginger with a fine dramatic part of Marsha Mitchell. Warners had originally wanted to reteam Lauren Bacall and Doris Day (after their appearance in Michael Curtiz's *Young Man With a Horn*), but Bacall backed out in order to accompany husband Humphrey Bogart to Africa for the filming of *The African Queen*.

Director Stuart Heisler expertly handled a fine cast, and his attention to details and atmosphere made this a superior mood piece as well as a topical melodrama. The Daniel Fuchs-Richard Brooks script was meaty and moving.

Ginger sank her teeth into her role, and her adroit blending of humor in the form of wisecracks carried a sting and hit their mark. Doris Day performed very well indeed; in fact, it is her best role prior to *Love Me or Leave Me*. Ronald Reagan was effective on the side of the law, while Steve Cochran gave brute forcefulness to the obnoxious part of Ginger's brother-in-law. In the final analysis, *Storm Warning* is a film which deserves a second or third viewing.

Location footage was filmed in Corona, California.

The Groom Wore Spurs

A Universal-International Picture
A Fidelity Production, 1951

With James Brown, Jack Carson, Franklyn Farnum, and Kate Drain Lawson

CAST: Ginger Rogers, (Abigail Furnival); Jack Carson, (Ben Castle); Joan Davis, (Alice Dean); Stanley Ridges, (Harry Kallen); James Brown, (Steve Hall); John Litel, (District Attorney); Victor Sen Yung, (Ignacio); Mira McKinney, (Mrs. Forbes); Gordon Nelson, (Ricky); George Meader, (Bellboy); Kemp Niver, (Killer); Robert B. Williams, (Jake Harris); Franklyn Farnum, (Reverend); Kate Drain Lawson, (Witness); with Ross Hunter.

CREDITS: Director, Richard Whorf; Producer, Howard Welsch; Scenarists, Robert Carson, Robert Libbott, Frank Burt. Based on the story *Legal Bride* by Robert Carson. Photographer, Peverell Marley; Art Director, Perry Ferguson; Set Decorator, Julia Heron; Editor, Otto Ludwig; Sound Recorder, Victor Appel, Mac Dalgleish; Musical Score, Arthur Lange, Charles Maxwell; Musical Director, Emil Newman; Costumer, Jacie and Eloise Jensson; Hair Stylist, Louise Miehle; Makeup Artist, Frank Westmore; Production Supervisor, Ben Hersh; Assistant Director, Tom Andre.

SONGS: *No More Wand'rin Around,* by Emil Newman, Arthur Lange.

SYNOPSIS: Lady lawyer Abigail Furnival is engaged to keep rich, lamebrain cowboy Ben Castle out of jams. In the course of all their misadventures together, she finally falls for the guy and marries him.

With Jack Carson and Joan Davis

REVIEWS

"The first few minutes of *The Groom Wore Spurs* give promise of a bright comedy, but the film soon degenerates into slapstick . . . . The film's main fault lies in the contrived plot and screenplay. Ginger Rogers, though somewhat miscast, surmounts the contradictions in her role and usually manages to be convincing."

Hollywood Reporter

"*The Groom Wore Spurs* is a rib-tickling dig at Hollywood cowboys who despise horses, hate the wide, open spaces, are slow with their six-guns and use doubles and dubs in the fighting and singing sequences."

Hollywood Citizen-News

NOTES: *The Groom Wore Spurs* was a feather-light comedy which was a complete waste of time for Ginger. It was the type of comedy that Jack Carson and Joan Davis found lucrative, but low-down comedy was never Ginger's forte. It was a mistake.

Direct Richard Whorf tried to inject pace and purpose into a tired script but the results were uneventful.

With Joan Davis and Ross Hunter

We're Not Married A 20th Century-Fox Picture, 1952

CAST: Ginger Rogers, (Ramona); Fred Allen, (Steve Gladwyn); Victor Moore, (Justice of the Peace); Marilyn Monroe, (Annabel Norris); David Wayne, (Jeff Norris); Eve Arden, (Katie Woodruff); Paul Douglas, (Hector Woodruff); Eddie Bracken, (Willie Fisher); Mitzi Gaynor, (Patsy Fisher); Louis Calhern, (Freddie Melrose); Zsa Zsa Gabor, (Eve Melrose); James Gleason, (Duffy); Paul Stewart, (Attorney Stone); Jane Darwell, (Mrs. Bush); Alan Bridge, (Detective Magnus); Harry Goler, (Radio Announcer); Victor Sutherland, (Governor Bush); Tom Powers, (Attorney General); Maurice Cass, (Organist); Maude Wallace, (Autograph Hound); Margie Liszt, (Irene); Richard Buckley, (Mr. Graves); Ralph Dumke, (Twitchell); Lee Marvin, (Pinky); Marjorie Weaver, (Ruthie); O.Z. Whitehead, (Postman); Harry Harvey, (Ned); Selmer Jackson, (Chaplain Hall).

CREDITS: Director, Edmund Goulding; Producer, Nunnally Johnson; Scenarist, Nunnally Johnson; Adaptation, Dwight Taylor. Based on a story by Gina Kaus, Jay Dratler. Photographer, Leo Tover; Art Directors, Lyle R. Wheeler, Leland Fuller; Set Decorators, Thomas Little, Claude Carpenter; Editor, Louis Loeffler; Sound Recorders, W.D. Flick, Roger Heman; Musical Score, Cyril Mockridge; Musical Director, Lionel Newman; Orchestrator, Bernard Mayers; Wardrobe Director, Charles Le Maire; Costumer, Eloise Jensson; Makeup Artist, Ben Nye; Hair Stylist, Helen Turpin; Assistant Director, Paul Helmick.

SYNOPSIS: An elderly justice of the peace discovers he married five couples during a time when his license was invalid. Ramona and Steve Gladwyn, one of the couples, have an early-morning breakfast-type radio program, which is jeopardized when the sponsor learns they are not really married.

NOTES: *We're Not Married* was Ginger's first segment-film since *Tales of Manhattan* in 1942. Of the five couples the film explores, Ginger and Fred Allen were, by far, the most effective. Their portrayals of a radio Mr. and Mrs. were rich in satire and contained more fact than fiction. She and Allen played well together.

Edmund Goulding's direction of Nunnally Johnson's script was zesty. The film remains one of the brightest comedies of the early 1950s, and the slick production was a hit with the public.

REVIEWS

"I personally was fondest of Mr. Allen and Miss Rogers, for their portrayal of those hideously jolly folk who make the radio unbearable in the morning."

The New Yorker

With Fred Allen

"By far the funniest sequence in Nunnally Johnson's script is the first, which involves Miss Rogers and Allen as a breakfasting radio couple—the Glad Gladwyns—who ignore each other in parlor, bedroom and bath, but simper over their bacon and eggs for a national network."

Newsweek

"Far and away the best sequence: baggy-eyed Fred Allen being wed to a bored Ginger Rogers by fuddy-duddy Justice of the Peace Victor Moore in one of the funniest marriage ceremonies ever seen on the screen."

Time

"The prize turn of the picture is contributed by Fred Allen and Ginger Rogers as a Mr. and Mrs. radio act . . . . Miss Rogers is also snappish in her throaty, blonde fashion, and together they prick the bubbles of professional wedded bliss, scattering laughter with each edgy gesture."

Otis Guernsey
New York Herald Tribune

With Jane Darwell, Fred Allen, and Victor Moore

Monkey Business

A 20th Century-Fox Picture, 1952

CAST: Cary Grant, (Barnaby Fulton); Ginger Rogers, (Edwina); Charles Coburn, (Mr. Oxley); Marilyn Monroe, (Lois Laurel); Hugh Marlowe, (Harvey Entwhistle); Henri Letondal, (Siegfried Kitzel); Robert Cornthwaite, (Dr. Zoldeck); Larry Keating, (Mr. Culverly); Douglas Spencer, (Dr. Brunner); Esther Dale, (Mrs. Rhinelander); George Winslow, (Little Indian); Emmett Lynn, (Jimmy); Joseph Mell, (Barber); George Eldredge, (Auto Salesman); Heinie Conklin, (Painter); Kathleen Freeman, (Nurse); Olan Soule, (Hotel Clerk); Harry Carey, Jr., (Reporter); John McKee, (Photographer); Faire Binney, (Dowager); Billy McLean, (Bellboy); Paul Maxey, Mack Williams, (Dignitaries); Forbes Murray, (Bit Man); Marjorie Holliday, (Bit Receptionist); Harry Carter, (Bit Scientist); Harry Seymour, (Clothing Store Salesman); Harry Bartell, Jerry Paris, (Scientists); Roger Moore, (Bit Man); Ruth Warren, Isabel Withers, Olive Carey, (Laundresses); Dabbs Greer, (Cab Driver); Russ Clark, Ray Montgomery, (Cops); Melinda Plowman, (Bit Girl); Terry Goodman, Ronnie Clark, Rudy Lee, Mickey Little, Brad Mora, Jimmy Roebuck, Louis Lettieri, (Bit Boys); Robert Nichols, (Garage Man).

CREDITS: Director, Howard Hawks; Producer, Sol C. Siegel; Scenarists, Ben Hecht, I.A.L. Diamond, Charles Lederer. Based on a story by Harry Segall. Photographer, Milton Krasner; Art Directors, Lyle Wheeler, George Patrick; Set Decorators, Thomas Little, Walter M. Scott; Editor, William B. Murphy; Sound Recorders, W.D. Flick, Roger Heman; Musical Score, Leigh Harline; Orchestrator, Earle Hagen; Wardrobe Director, Charles Le Maire; Costumer, Travilla; Makeup Artist, Ben Nye; Hair Stylist, Helen Turpin; Assistant Director, Paul Helmick.

SYNOPSIS: Professor Barnaby Fulton, a research chemist, develops a formula to make people grow "younger" and his first two guinea pigs are himself and his lovely wife Edwina. Soon his boss, Oliver Oxley, and his boss's sassy secretary, Lois Laurel, join in the fun.

With Cary Grant

REVIEWS

"Grant has never been better than in his part as the absentminded professor in search of the elixir of youth. His extraordinarily agile and amusing performance is matched to the hilt by that of Ginger Rogers as his long-suffering wife. And those who recall that Miss Rogers was once a famous dancing star, will find that she still excels in that department. She obviously delights in her part, which is a demanding one."

Motion Picture Herald

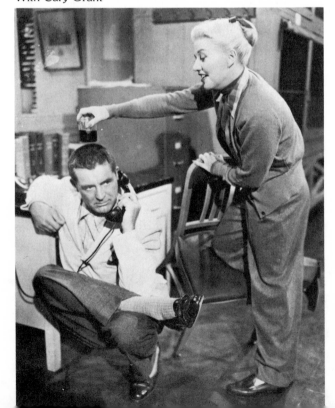

"Grant and Miss Rogers are perfectly matched as the rather settled couple who find new 'youth' temporarily. They are individually swell as comedians, too. Coburn as the head of the chemical company has his moments and Miss Monroe adds plenty of decoration and some comedy."

Los Angeles Times

"Ginger hasn't been so funny since the days she used to do those lighthearted farces. And, well, you know that Grant fellow in a comedy part.

A few words about Miss Monroe, the box-office delight. Apart from her most famous attibutes, she handles the paper-headed siren role with some unexpected touches of comedy."

Los Angeles Examiner

NOTES: Howard Hawks directed *Monkey Business* in much the same screwball manner as some of the 1930s comedies; the result was most satisfying. The gag-lined script by Ben Hecht, I.A.L. Diamond, and Charles Lederer contributed immeasureably.

Ginger had many comic moments, and a few unfortunate ones as the child, but was generally delightful. This film reunited her with Cary Grant, and their scenes together were fun-filled. Charles Coburn was especially funny as Grant's boss, whose dimwitted secretary was given bounce-to-the-ounce by Marilyn Monroe, soon to become 20th Century-Fox's biggest box-office draw. Coburn's classic comment to Monroe at one point: "Get someone to type this."

With Cary Grant, Robert Cornthwaite, and Marilyn Monroe

Dreamboat   A 20th Century-Fox Picture, 1952

With Jay Adler

With Anne Francis and Jeffrey Hunter

With Clifton Webb

CAST: Clifton Webb, (Thornton Sayre); Ginger Rogers, (Gloria); Anne Francis, (Carol Sayre); Jeffrey Hunter, (Bill Ainslee); Elsa Lanchester, (Dr. Coffey); Fred Clark, (Sam Levitt); Paul Harvey, (Harrington); Ray Collins, (Timothy Stone); Helene Stanley, (Mimi); Richard Garrick, (Judge Bowles); George Barrows, (Commandant); Jay Adler, (Desk Clerk); Marietta Canty, (Lavinia); Laura Brooks, (Mrs. Gunther); Emory Parnell, (Used Car Salesman); Helen Hatch, (Mrs. Faust); Harry Cheshire, (Macintosh); Everett Glass, (George Bradley); Paul Maxey, (Clarence Bornay); Sandor Szabo, (Giant Arab); Leo Cleary, (Court Clerk); Lee Turnbull, (Denham); Helen Brown, (Dorothy); Al Herman, (Drunk); Howard Banks, (Hotel Clerk); Jack Mather, (Hotel Detective); Matt Mattox, Frank Radcliffe, (Men in Commercial); Gwyneth Verdon, (Girl in Commercial); Robert Easton, (T.V. Commercial); Donna Lee Hickey, (Cigarette Girl); Richard Allan, (Student); Clive Morgan, (French Captain); Crystal Reeves, (Secretary); Vici Raaf, Barbara Wooddell, (Receptionists); Don Kohler, Robert B. Williams, (Photographers); Tony De Mario, (Waiter); Joe Recht, (Busboy); Steve Carruthers, Warren Mace, (Bit Men); Victoria Horne, (Waitress); Bob Nichols, (Student); Paul Kruger, (Doorman); Alphonse Martel, (Maitre D'); Fred Graham, (Bartender); Jean Corbett, (Bit Girl); Mary Treen, (Bit Wife); Richard Karlan, (Husband).

CREDITS: Director, Claude Binyon; Producer, Sol C. Siegel; Scenarist, Claude Binyon. Based on a story by John D. Weaver. Photographer, Milton Krasner; Art Directors, Lyle R. Wheeler, Maurice Ransford; Set Decorators, Thomas Little, Fred J. Rode; Editor, James B. Clark; Sound Recorder, E. Clayton Ward, Roger Heman; Musical Score, Cyril Mockridge; Music Director, Lionel Newman; Orchestrator, Bernard Mayers; Costumer, Travilla; Wardrobe Director, Charles LeMaire; Makeup Artist, Ben Nye; Hair Stylist, Helen Turpin; Special Effects, Ray Kellogg; T.V. Animation, UPA (United Productions of America); Assistant Director, Ad Schaumer.

SYNOPSIS: Highly respected college professor Thornton Sayre is suddenly plagued by his old movies being shown on television and sets out, with his daughter Carol, to prevent any further showings. However, his former co-star, Gloria, who is hostess of the embarrassing series of films on television, has other plans.

REVIEWS

"Webb is smooth as ever in the kind of role at which he has no peer. Miss Rogers' portrayal of the renovated leading lady is a joy to watch."   *Los Angeles Daily News*

"A devastating satire on television, *Dreamboat* is a merry comedy filled with uproarious laughter from beginning to end . . . . Webb does his usual beautiful job as the pompous professor, skillfully getting every detail nuance out of the role. Ginger Rogers has a lot of fun—which will be shared by audiences—as the old-time movie queen still carrying on as though her reign had never ended."   *Hollywood Reporter*

"The silent movies have been speeded and hoked up and are performed with the expected abandon by Mr. Webb and Miss Rogers, who assume a variety of disguises and survive the most horrendous escapades before winding up in the final passionate clinch."   *Los Angeles Times*

NOTES: Claude Binyon's lightweight spoof on television's use of old movies and commercials was given considerable assistance by Clifton Webb and Ginger in the leads. The byplay of these two stars (especially the silent-film episodes) brought the script off its knees. Troupers like Elsa Lanchester and Fred Clark also contributed to the gaiety.

Dreamboat was also distinguished by its superb mounting: art direction, set decoration, and photography. Ginger looked especially good in Travilla's costumes. Anne Francis and Jeffrey Hunter, up and coming stars of the 1950s, were fine in their roles. It is interesting to note that the girl in the commercial was Gwyneth (Gwen) Verdon, just prior to her sensational rocket to stardom on Broadway. A cigarette girl was played by Donna Lee Hickey (later May Wynn in *The Caine Mutiny*.)

With Clifton Webb

With William Holden and Pat Crowley

With Jesse White and William Holden

Forever Female
A Paramount Picture, 1953

CAST: Ginger Rogers, (Beatrice Page); William Holden, (Stanley Krown); Paul Douglas, (E. Harry Phillips); Pat Crowley, (Sally Carver); James Gleason, (Eddie Woods); Jesse White, (Willie Wolfe); Marjorie Rambeau, (Herself); George Reeves, (George Courtland); King Donovan, (Playwright); Vic Perrin, (Scenic Designer); Russell Gaige, (Theatrical Producer); Marion Ross, (Patty); Richard Shannon, (Stage Manager); Sally Mansfield, Kathryn Grandstaff, Rand Harper, (Young Hopefuls); Henry Dar Boggia, (Felix); Victor Romito, (Maitre D'); Hyacinthe Railla, Alfred Paix, (Waiters); Walter Reed, (Leading Man); Josephine Whittell, (Katherine); Almira Sessions, (Mother); Joel Marston, (Photographer); Grace Hampton, (Olga O'Brien); David Leonard, (Bill Forrest); Maidie Norman, (Emma); Richard Garland, (Clerk); Michael Darrin, (Jack); William Leslie, (Bill); Dulce Daye, (Drucille King); Vince M. Townsend, Jr., (Doorman).

CREDITS: Director, Irving Rapper; Producer, Pat Duggan; Scenarists, Julius J. Epstein, Philip G. Epstein. Based on the play *Rosalind* by James M. Barrie. Photographer, Harry Stradling; Art Directors, Hal Pereira, Joseph Macmillan Johnson; Editor Archie Marshek; Editorial Adviser, Doane Harrison; Sound Recorders, Harry Lindgren, John Cope; Musical Score, Victor Young; Costumer, Edith Head; Makeup Artist, Wally Westmore; Special Effects, Gordon Jennings; Process Photography, Farciot Edouart; Assistant Director, John Coonan.

SYNOPSIS: Aging actress Beatrice Page refuses to admit she is getting older, because she still yearns to play young parts until playwright Stanley Krown writes a new play expressly for a young actress to play.

With William Holden

214

REVIEWS

"The cast does well enough: Ginger Rogers as the reluctantly aging star, William Holden as the brash playwright and Paul Douglas as the producer. But by far the nicest thing about this *Forever Female* is the appearance of young Pat Crowley as the budding actress. Miss Crowley has an abundance of talent, charm, good looks, and youth, and does wonders with them. Irving Rapper directed."

Cue

"Miss Rogers, looking beautiful in attractive Edith Head-designed gowns, turns in a glittering performance as the amusingly penny-pinching star, one that rates with any of her top jobs. Douglas also clicks, particularly in a light, perfectly played drunk scene."

The Hollywood Reporter

"Performance of Misses Rogers and Crowley range from the too broad to the natural but, on the whole, they bring off the assignments excellently. Miss Rogers bears down on the stage queen character, but hits her peak in the sequence where she acknowledges her age."

Variety

NOTES: J.M. Barrie's short play *Rosalind* provided Ginger with a happy script which she deftly played. William Holden and Paul Douglas were perfect co-stars, and Pat Crowley, with the sheer impact of her freshness, almost stole the show from these veterans.

Irving Rapper's direction was serviceable, as was Harry Stradling's photography, but there were echoes throughout of *All About Eve*. Playing a young actress in the supporting cast was a girl named Kathryn Grandstaff, who later became Kathryn Grant, and, much later, Mrs. Bing Crosby.

With Paul Douglas and William Holden

Black Widow

A 20th Century-Fox Picture in CinemaScope Color by De Luxe, 1954

With Van Heflin, George Raft, and Reginald Gardiner

CAST: Ginger Rogers, (Lottie); Van Heflin, (Peter); Gene Tierney, (Iris); George Raft, (Detective Bruce); Peggy Ann Garner, (Nanny Ordway); Reginald Gardiner, (Brian); Virginia Leith, (Claire Amberly); Otto Kruger, (Ling); Cathleen Nesbitt, (Lucia); Skip Homeier, (John); Hilda Simms, (Anne); Harry Carter, (Welch); Geraldine Wall, (Miss Mills); Richard Cutting, (Sergeant Owens); Mabel Albertson, (Sylvia); Aaron Spelling, (Mr. Oliver); Wilson Wood, (Costume Designer); Tony de Mario, (Bartender); Virginia Maples, (Model); Frances Driver, (Maid); James F. Stone (Stage Doorman); Michael Vallon, (Coal Dealer); Bea Benaderet, (Party Guest).

CREDITS: Director, Nunnally Johnson; Producer, Nunnally Johnson; Scenarist, Nunnally Johnson. Based on a story by Patrick Quentin. Photographer, Charles G. Clarke; Art Directors, Lyle R. Wheeler, Maurice Ransford; Set Decorators, Walter M. Scott, Dorcy Howard; Editor, Dorothy Spencer; Sound Recorders, Eugene Grossman, Roger Heman; Musical Score, Leigh Harline; Musical Director, Lionel Newman; Orchestrator, Edward B. Powell; Costumer, Travilla; Wardrobe Director, Charles Le Maire; Makeup Artist, Ben Nye; Hair Stylist, Helen Turpin; Special Photographic Effects, Ray Kellogg; Assistant Director, A.F. Erickson; Color Consultant, Leonard Doss; Cinemascope Lenses by Bausch and Lomb.

SYNOPSIS: The death of Nanny Ordway, a young stage hopeful, throws suspicion on a number of theater notables with whom the actress had contact, including Lottie, an imperious actress, and Brian, her husband, who had a mild flirtation with the girl.

REVIEWS

"Ginger Rogers, Reginald Gardiner, and George Raft are visible along the way, and all of them seem to be tired. Miss Rogers is tired as a nasty actress, Mr. Gardiner is tired as a gentleman a lady is keeping, and Mr. Raft is tired as a detective. It's a fairly close race, but I's say the apathy sweepstakes must go to Mr. Raft."

John McCarten
The New Yorker

"Miss Rogers, beautifully garbed, gives an accurate portrait of a distasteful, phony, theatrical star."

Variety

"Featuring an outstanding performance by Ginger Rogers in the title role and a whole gallery of expertly handled character studies, this finely conceived suspense drama comes to a sock finish after a slow and halfhearted opening."

Hollywood Reporter

With Reginald Gardiner

NOTES: *Black Widow* was Ginger's first film in CinemaScope, as well as her first film for director Nunnally Johnson (he had produced and scripted *Roxie Hart*), and it was her return to melodrama. Johnson's script, from Patrick Quentin's story, provided a first-rate cast with a slick, melodramatic murder-mystery yarn. The production was given the usual Fox gloss, and Ginger was again gowned by Travilla. After repeated viewings, it still holds up and the finale still grips.

With Herbert Lom and Jacques Bergerac

CREDITS: Director, David Miller; Producers, Maxwell Setton, John R. Sloan; Scenarists, Robert Westerby, Carl Nystron. Based on an original story by Rip Van Ronkel, David Miller. Photographer, Ted Scaife; Camera Operator, Robert Day; Art Director, Geoff Drake; Production Designer, Don Ashton; Editor, Alan Osbiston; Sound Recorder, Buster Ambler; Production Manager, John Palmer; Musical Score, Malcolm Arnold; Wardrobe Mistress, Betty Adamson; Makeup Artist, Neville Smallwood; Hairdresser, Helen Penfold; Continuity, Constance Willis; Assistant Director, James Ware.

SONGS: *Love Is a Beautiful Stranger*, (sung by Lita Roza), by Jose Ferrer, Ketti Frings.

SYNOPSIS: Ex-actress, "Johnny" Victor now kept by Louis Galt becomes involved romantically with Pierre Clement, a handsome young potter on the Riviera. She then learns that Galt, her husband-to-be, is a dangerous criminal.

REVIEWS

"*Twist of Fate* twists several plots into a pretty frazzled rope of coincidence that finally throttles audience interest. It starts out as fashionable domestic drama. Then it becomes cops-and-robbers. After that it is a whodunit. And it winds up pure *Perils of Pauline*. The most you can say for it is that it is just another movie.

"This is too bad. The initial situation, involving Ginger Rogers as the glamorous mistress of a rich man (Stanley Baker) has interest."

Hollywood Reporter

"Ginger Rogers, as a lady who has a penchant for the finer things in life but has also kept herself admirably groomed for the true love that might come along, gives one of her best acting performances. Not too much depth is required of the characterization of a woman whom time and circumstances deal not too gently with, and Miss Rogers, consciously or otherwise, offers a polished performance."

Russ Burton
Los Angeles Daily News

Beautiful Stranger

A British Lion Film Corp. Ltd. Picture
Released in the U.S. Thru United Artists as *Twist of Fate*, 1954

CAST: Ginger Rogers, ("Johnny" Victor); Herbert Lom, (Emil Landosh); Stanley Baker, (Louis Galt); Jacques Bergerac, (Pierre Clement); Margaret Rawlings, (Marie Galt); Eddie Byrne, (Luigi); Coral Browne, (Helen).

NOTES: This was Ginger's only English film. David Miller's direction was conventional stuff, as was the script, but the cast rose well above the occasion and, at times, this melodrama seemed better than it actually was.

Ginger was lovely as an actress living on the Riviera who discovers her husband is a dangerous criminal. Herbert Lom and Stanley Baker gave her excellent support, while Ginger's husband young Jacques Bergerac, had little to do but look handsome, a task he accomplished with ease. The original British title—*Beautiful Stranger*—was called *Twist of Fate* in the United States. It was mildly received.

Tight Spot

A Columbia Picture, 1955

With Edward G. Robinson and Brian Keith

CAST: Ginger Rogers, (Sherry Conley); Edward G. Robinson, (Lloyd Hallett); Brian Keith, (Vince Striker); Lucy Marlowe, (Prison Girl); Lorne Greene, (Benjamin Costain); Katherine Anderson, (Mrs. Willoughby); Allen Nourse, (Marvin Rickles); Peter Leeds, (Fred Packer); Doye O'Dell, (Mississippi Mac); Eve McVeagh, (Clara Moran); Helen Wallace, (Warden); Frank Gerstle, (Jim Hornsby); Gloria Ann Simpson, (Miss Masters); Robert Shield, (Carlyle); Norman Keats, (Arny); Kathryn Grant, (Bit Girl Honeymooner); Ed "Skipper" McNally, (Harris); Erik Paige, (Bit Man); John Marshall, (Detective); Will J. White, (Plainclothesman); Tom de Graffenried, (Doctor); Kevin Enright, (Bit Man); Joseph Hamilton, (Judge); Alan Reynolds, (Bailiff); Tom Greenway, (Bit Man); Patrick Miller, (Plainclothesman); John Zaremba, (Second Cop); Dean Cromer, (Policeman); Robert Nichols, (Boy Honeymooner); John Larch, (First Detective); Alfred Linder, (Tonelli); Ed Hinton, (Second Detective); Kenneth N. Mayer, (Policeman); Bob Hopkins, (TV Salesman).

CREDITS: Director, Phil Karlson; Producer, Lewis J. Rachmil; Scenarist, William Bowers. Based on the play *Dead Pigeon* by Lenard Kantor. Photographer, Burnett Guffey; Art Director, Carl Anderson; Set Decorator, Louis Diage; Editor, Viola Lawrence; Sound Recorder, John Livadary, Lambert Day; Musical Score, George Duning. Conducted by Morris Stoloff. Costumer, Jean Louis; Assistant Director, Milton Feldman; Still Photographers, Lippman & Cronenweth.

SYNOPSIS: Hardened gangland moll Sherry Conley is released from prison—under tight security—to turn state's evidence on big-time gang leader Benjamin Costain. District Attorney A. Lloyd Hallett and detective Vince Striker are at her side throughout.

With Edward G. Robinson

With Brian Keith

REVIEWS

"Miss Rogers' self-sufficiency throughout hardly suggests anybody's former scapegoat, let alone a potential gone goose. But she tackles her role with obvious, professional relish. Mr. Keith and Mr. Robinson are altogether excellent. . . . If Academy Awards aren't in order, neither are apologies."

H.H.T.
The New York Times

"Miss Rogers has a pip of a character and romps home with it for a huge personal success . . ."

Variety

"If you've forgotten what a splended actress Ginger is, her performance in this one is a memory refueler. As a dame on temporary leave from a prison laundry, Ginger is superb."

Sara Hamilton
Los Angeles Examiner

"Ginger Rogers, slimmed down and looking delectable, is simply great in a leading role that has practically everything. Only an accomplished actress, capable of fine shadings and changes of pace could swing from comedy to pathos with the sureness that she does. Now fiery, now sniveling, she delivers a one-woman show that will fascinate all those who love the intricacies and fine points of the drama.

"Eddie Robinson, in the relatively quiet part of the district attorney, once more proves what a really expert trouper he is. He has a wonderful authority in the scenes requiring it, but it's even more exciting to watch the skill with which he supports and builds the effects of the actors he is working with. His listening helps the audience to listen and the subtle methods by which he directs spectator attention make him the all-important underscoring factor in many of Ginger's big scenes."

Jack Moffitt
Hollywood Reporter

"In short, *Tight Spot*, thanks to Ginger's emoting, and Edward G. Robinson's brilliant dramatics, is a first-rate film in its category."

Lowell E. Redelings
Hollywood Citizen-News

NOTES: *Tight Spot*, from Lenard Kantor's Broadway play *Dead Pigeon,* provided Ginger with one of the best working roles of her career, a challenge she met head-on with success. Her Sherry Conley was tough, sarcastic, human, and believable.

Co-star Edward G. Robinson handled his role with his usual polish and persuasion, while Brian Keith was effective as the cop assigned to guard Ginger from the underworld. Phil Karlson directed in a straightforward manner, getting the maximum effect from both script and cast. Burnett Guffey's photography added to the film's overall effect, as did Viola Lawrence's editing. Jean Louis designed Ginger's wardrobe, but her short hairstyle left much to be desired; it seemed unnecessary.

With Lucy Marlowe and Katherine Anderson

The First Traveling Saleslady

An RKO-Radio Picture in Technicolor, 1956

CAST: Ginger Rogers, (Rose Gilray); Barry Nelson, (Charles Masters); Carol Channing, (Molly Wade); Brian Keith, (James Carter); James Arness, (Joel Kingdon); Clint Eastwood, (Jack Rice); Robert Simon, (Cal); Frank Wilcox, (Marshall Duncan); Dan White, (Sheriff); Harry Cheshire, (Judge Benson); John Eldredge, (Greavy); Robert Hinkle, (Pete); Jack Rice, (Dowling); Kate Drain Lawson, (Annie Peachpit); Edward Cassidy, (Theodore Roosevelt); Fred Essler, (Schlessinger); Bill Hale, (Sheriff's Deputy); Lovyss Bradley, (Mrs. Bronson); Nora Bush, (Mrs. Pruett); Ann Kunde, (Mrs. Cobb); Hans Herbert, (Night Clerk); Lynn Noe, Joan Tyler, Janette Miller, Kathy Marlowe, (Bit Models); Robert Easton, (Young Cowboy); Belle Mitchell, (Emily); Ian Murray, (Prince of Wales); Roy Darmour, Peter Croyden, Al Cavens, Paul Bradley, Hal Taggart, (Bit Men); Gilmore Bush, (First Salesman); John Connors, (Second Salesman); Lester Dorr, Frank Scannel, Paul Keast, (Salesmen); Mauritz Hugo, Julius Evans, Stanley Farrar, Charles Tannen, (Bit Buyers); Hank Patterson, (First Cowhand); Britt Wood, (Second Cowhand); James Stone, Cactus Mack, Deacon Moor, Lane Chandler, (Ranchers); Chalky Williams, (Bit Spectator); George Barrows, (Meat Packer); George Baxter, (Headwaiter); George Brand, (Telegraph Operator); Tris Coffin, (Day Hotel Clerk); Theron Jackson, (Bellhop); Herbert Deans, (Secretary); William Fawcett, Casey Mac Gregor (Old-timers); William Forrest, (Supreme Court Justice); Jim Hayward, (Sam); Earl Hodgins, (Veterinarian); Johnny Lee, (Amos); Pierce Lyden, (Official); Tony Roux, (Mexican in Courtroom); Clarence Muse, (Amos).

CREDITS: Director, Arthur Lubin; Producer, Arthur Lubin; Scenarists, Stephen Longstreet, Devery Freeman; Photographer, William Snyder; Art Director, Albert S. D'Agostino; Set Decorator, Darrell Silvera; Editor, Otto Ludwig; Sound Recorder, Stanford Houghton; Musical Score, Irving Gertz; Assistant Director, Richard Mayberry.

SONG: *A Corset Can Do a Lot for a Lady*, by Irving Gertz, Hal Levy

SYNOPSIS: Rose Gilray, a corset saleslady who goes West at the turn of the century, is secretly selling barbed wire to the homesteaders.

With James Arness and Carol Channing

With Barry Nelson

REVIEWS

"Miss Rogers is pert and pretty and Miss Channing cavorts on the slapstick side, warbling *A Corset Can Do a Lot for a Lady* in okay fashion."

Variety

"Miss Rogers has three handsome leading men and she looks terrific. She has always been one of the screen's mistresses of comedy, but the lines are not here this time and neither she nor the talented Miss Channing can create humor where there is none. Barry Nelson is personable in an improbable part, while David Brian and James Arness do the best they can with roles for which practically no motivation is supplied and very little character delineation is offered. Clint Eastwood is very attractive as Miss Channing's beau."

Hollywood Reporter.

NOTES: By the mid-1950s, RKO-Radio was on its last legs as a production studio and, in a bold effort to keep going, tried to obtain the services of Mae West for *The First Traveling Saleslady*. Miss West must have read the script; it's a pity Ginger didn't.

Arthur Lubin's production sagged in the middle, and not even William Snyder's Technicolor photography could pick it up. Two of television's big Western stars were in support: James Arness and Clint Eastwood. Carol Channing was funny at times, but did not photograph particularly well. Ginger looked great in the period costumes, but really was wasted in this hodgepodge. Barry Nelson was his usual charming self.

In other words, this is a forgettable picture.

With Carol Channing

With Clint Eastwood and Carol Channing

Teenage Rebel A 20th Century-Fox Picture in CinemaScope, 1956

With Betty Lou Keim, Michael Rennie, Diane Jergens, Warren Berlinger, and Mildred Natwick

CAST: Ginger Rogers, (Nancy Fallon); Michael Rennie, (Jay Fallon); Mildred Natwick, (Grace Hewitt); Rusty Swope, (Larry Fallon); Lili Gentle, (Gloria—Teenager At Races); Louise Beavers, (Willamay); Irene Hervey, (Helen McGowan); John Stephenson, (Eric McGowan); Betty Lou Keim, (Dodie); Warren Berlinger, (Dick Hewitt); Diane Jergens, (Jane Hewitt); Suzanne Luckey, (Madeleine Johnson); James O'Rear, (Mr. Heffernan); Gary Gray, (Freddie); Pattee Chapman, (Erna); Wade Dumas, (Airport Porter); Richard Collier, (Cabdriver); James Stone, (Pappy Smith); Sheila James, (Teenager); Joan Freeman, (Teenager in Malt Shop); Gene Foley, (Soda Fountain Girl).

CREDITS: Director, Edmund Goulding; Producer, Charles Brackett; Scenarists, Walter Reisch, Edmund Goulding. Based on the play *A Roomful of Roses* by Edith Sommer. Photographer, Joe MacDonald; Art Directors, Lyle R. Wheeler, Jack Martin Smith; Set Decorators, Walter M. Scott, Stuart A. Reiss; Editor, William Mace; Sound Recorders, W.D. Flick, Harry M. Leonard; Musical Score, Leigh Harline; Musical Conductor, Lionel Newman; Costumers, Charles Le Maire, Mary Wills; Makeup Artist, Ben Nye; Hair Stylist, Helen Turpin; Assistant Director, Eli Dunn.

SONGS: *Cool It, Baby*, by Leigh Harline, Carroll Coates; *Dodie*, by Ralph Freed, Edmund Goulding.

SYNOPSIS: Nancy Fallon gets her daughter, Dodie, back from her ex-husband when he is about to remarry. Now also remarried, Nancy struggles to win her daughter's love.

REVIEWS

"Edith Sommer's story of an adolescent girl in search of love was a last-season Broadway flop as *A Roomful of Roses*, but the film version is a well made adaptation that should ring up tidy grosses from both younger patrons as well as their elders . . . . Miss Rogers adeptly portrays the temporarily rejected mother and shines in the frequent emotional conflicts that arise between herself and daughter.

With Irene Hervey and John Stephenson

With Betty Lou Keim

It's a fast 94 minutes under Edmund Goulding's deft direction.

Variety

"*Teenage Rebel* is a better picture than its title would seem to warrant .... Miss Rogers gives a fine performance as the mother, ably abetted by Rennie as her husband. Miss Keim, of course, is just as irritating in the film as in the play, which means she fulfills her acting assignment satisfactorily."

John L. Scott
Los Angeles Times

"The mother in the case is Ginger Rogers in all her chic, blonde, slimmed-down, tight-trousered glory. The clinch that ends the picture seems like the old-fashioned movie ending, despite the fact that the clinch is between mother and daughter."

Newsweek

"Rennie, to be sure, is somewhat wasted in that his part does not offer him very big opportunities. However, Ginger is marvelous. She looks like a million, and proves all over again that she is a dramatic actress who can deliver with the screen's very best."

Hazel Flynn
Beverly Hills Citizen

NOTES: Edmund Goulding took Edith Sommer's Broadway play *A Roomful of Roses* and skillfully created a warm, emotional story of family conflicts. The Charles Brackett production was well-mounted, but it was the splendid cast that especially deserves praise.

Ginger was understanding and sincere in a difficult role, and Michael Rennie was equally fine as her husband. The good supporting cast included Betty Lou Keim and Warren Berlinger, both of the original Broadway cast (Patricia Neal had the part of Nancy Fallon).

The art direction by Lyle R. Wheeler and Jack Martin Smith, the set decoration by Walter M. Scott and Stuart A. Reiss, and the costumes by Charles LeMaire and Mary Wills all won Academy Award nominations.

With Michael Rennie

Oh, Men! Oh, Women! A 20th Century-Fox Picture in CinemaScope Color by De Luxe, 1957

With Dan Dailey

CAST: Dan Dailey, (Arthur Turner); Ginger Rogers, (Mildred Turner); David Niven, (Dr. Alan Coles); Barbara Rush, (Myra Hagerman); Tony Randall, (Cobbler); Natalie Schafer, (Mrs. Day); Rachel Stephens, (Miss Tacher); John Wengraf, (Dr. Krauss); Cheryll Clarke, (Melba); Charles Davis, (Steward); Joel Fluellen, (Cabdriver); Clancy Cooper, (Mounted Policeman); Renny McEvoy, (Bartender); Franklin Pangborn, (Steamship Clerk); Franklyn Farnum, (Passenger); Hal Taggert, Alfred Tonkel, Monty O'Grady, Les Raymaster, Harry Denny, (Clergymen).

CREDITS: Director, Nunnally Johnson; Producer, Nunnally Johnson; Scenarist, Nunnally Johnson. Based on the play *Oh, Men! Oh, Women!* by Edward Chodorov. Photographer, Charles G. Clark; Art Directors, Lyle R. Wheeler, Maurice Ransford; Set Decorators, Walter M. Scott, Stuart A. Reiss; Editor, Marjorie Fowler; Sound Recorders, Alfred Bruzlin, Harold A. Root; Musical Score, Cyril J. Mockridge; Makeup Artist, Ben Nye; Hair Stylist, Helen Turpin; Assistant Director, Hal Herman.

SYNOPSIS: Mildred Turner, the bored wife of a home-loving movie star, seeks psychiatric help from Dr. Alan Coles. In helping Mildred and her husband find a proper path to happiness, Dr. Coles also solves his own emotional problems.

"Dan Dailey, who has chiefly 'drunk scenes' in the show, plays them with great energy; Ginger Rogers is almost as energetic when she is just lying there babbling on the analyst's couch. Barbara Rush is attractively feather-brained as the analyst's girlfriend. David Niven lends comic dignity with his expert playing of the imperiled analyst.

Summing Up: A fragile farce, on and off the analyst's couch."

Newsweek

"Ginger Rogers as the approaching-those-middle-years wife of Dan Dailey is chic, clever and skillful."

Sara Hamilton
Los Angeles Examiner

"Miss Rogers is excellent at suggesting that problem of about-to-be-middle-aged wives who want love, not chummy companionship. Niven is such a good actor that he is apt to be overlooked; it seems so easy the way he does it. Miss Rush displays a new vein of talent in her facility for light comedy."

Hollywood Reporter

"The thesps, all pros, turned in excellent performances. Miss Rogers is effective as the 'useless' wife determined to end her *Doll's House* existence. Dailey scores as the film star utterly confused by his wife's actions and Niven excels as the analyst who sees his own life crumbling. . . . The production values and the technical aspects of the film are all first-rate."

Variety

NOTES: Hollywood has often been guilty of over-blowing a simple story and, thus losing its effectiveness. *Oh, Men! Oh, Women!* was given "the treatment" at Fox in CinemaScope and color with lavish sets, but more attention should have been paid to the story itself.

Ginger was quite good as a wife who feels she is useless, while Dan Dailey tended to overact throughout (Nunnally Johnson directed). David Niven, as the psychiatrist, was well cast, as were Barbara Rush and Tony Randall. However, considering the first-string talent gathered, this consulting-room farce should have been much better.

With Dan Dailey and David Niven

Harlow A Magna Pictures Corp. Picture in Electronovision, 1965

CAST: Carol Lynley, (Jean Harlow); Efrem Zimbalist, Jr., (William Mansfield); Ginger Rogers, (Mama Jean); Barry Sullivan, (Marino Bello); Hurd Hatfield, (Paul Bern); Lloyd Bochner, (Marc Peters); Hermione Baddeley, (Marie Dressler); Audrey Totter, (Marilyn); John Williams, (Jonathan Martin); Audrey Christie, (Thelma); Michael Dante, (Ed); Jack Kruschen, (Louis B. Mayer); Celia Lovsky, (Maria Ouspenskaya); Robert Struss, (Hank); Sonny Liston, (First Fighter); James Dobson, (Counterman); Cliff Norton, (Billy); Paulie Clark, (Waitress); Jim Plunkett, (Stan Laurel); John "Red" Fox, (Oliver Hardy); Joel Marston, (Press Agent); Miss Christopher West, (Bern's Secretary); Fred Conte, (Photographer); Catherine Ross, (Wardrobe Woman); Buddy Lewis, (Al Jolson); Danny Francis, (Casino Manager); Frank Scannell, (Doctor); Maureene Gaffney, (Miss Larsen); Nick Demitri, (Second Fighter); Ron Kennedy, (Assistant Director); Harry Holcombe, (Minister); Lola Fisher, (Nurse); Fred Klein, (Himself).

With Carol Lynley

CREDITS: Director, Alex Segal; Producers, Bill Sargant, Lee Savin; Scenarist, Karl Tunberg; Executive Producer, Brandon Chase; Photographer, Jim Kilgore; Art Director, Duncan Cramer; Set Decorator, Harry Gordon; Dialogue Director, James Dobson; Sound Recorder, Dave Forrest; Musical Score, Al Ham, Nelson Riddle; Costumer, Nolan Miller; Assistant Directors, Greg Peters, Johnny Wilson, Dick Bennett.

SYNOPSIS: The life and times of Jean Harlow as she begins her climb up the Hollywood ladder of fame, with her ever-present Mama Jean and Mama's husband Marino Bello.

REVIEWS

"Carol Lynley, displaying as much of her anatomy as legally permissible, is, sadly, only a callow, sullen, pouting type, who generates about as much heat as a Girl Scout in a borrowed evening gown. Ginger Rogers and Barry Sullivan, as her clinging parents . . . . do little to probe deeply either into character or the period."

A.H. Weiler
The New York Times

"The script by Karl Tunberg is atrocious; it comes off like a poor 1930s movie, so bad you can see it for laughs. Efrem Zimbalist, Jr., Barry Sullivan, Ginger Rogers and others who should know better are the pawns. As for Miss Lynley, she is ridiculously inept in the role."

Cue

With James Dobson and Carol Lynley

"The grainy Electronovision process is distracting but does lend an aura of the 1930s. The performances, as one might expect from instant movie, lend an aura of the 1930s, with Barry Sullivan, Ginger Rogers and Efrem Zimbalist leading the melodramatic histrionics."

Al Cohn
Newsday

"The only wholly successful performance in the film is given by Ginger Rogers as the gluttonous self-created mother. Looking both marvelously ravaged and lushly attractive, Miss Rogers survives the idiotic requirements of the script and makes us wish that she were doing more in movies—other movies, that is."

Judith Crist
New York Herald Tribune

With Barry Sullivan and Carol Lynley

NOTES: Ginger further expanded her career when she agreed to appear in this Electronovision production, which was shot in just eight days. *Harlow* was the third film produced in this process. Richard Burton's *Hamlet* was first, and *The T.A.M.I Story* was second. However, this was the first time that controlled studio conditions existed. The production was further rushed along in order to beat the Carroll Baker *Harlow*, produced by Paramount, to the box office. Angela Lansbury appeared as Mama Jean in the other version. Neither version was very good.

As Mama Jean, Ginger gave a good account of herself, but at times she was moving in a script full of holes. Alex Segal's direction was sloppy and the casting was uneven. Carol Lynley, with proper guidance, might have been better, but some of her scenes were downright embarrassing. As performed by Jack Kruschen, Louis B. Mayer was played for comedy. Hermione Baddeley played Marie Dressler sans conviction, and Efrem Zimbalist, Jr. played a confused character that was a combination of William Powell and Clark Gable.

With Carol Lynley and Hurd Hatfield

Quick, Let's Get Married

With Ray Milland

A William Marshall Production
A Kay Lewis Enterprises Presentation
An Adrian Weiss Productions Release
in Eastman Color, 1964-1971
(Also known as *The Confession* and *Seven Different Ways*)

SYNOPSIS: Madame Rinaldi, proprietress of a bordello, helps big-time thief Mario Forni locate an ancient buried treasure. Finding it under a religious statue, Mario creates a "miracle" as seen through the eyes of a praying pregnant prostitute named Pia. In the ensuing chaos, Mario and Madame Rinaldi flee.

CAST: Ginger Rogers, (Madame Rinaldi); Ray Milland, (Mario Forni); Barbara Eden, (Pia); Walter Abel, (The Thief); Pippa Scott, (Gina); Elliott Gould, (The Mute); Carl Schell, (Beppo); Michael Ansara, (The Mayor); Cecil Kellaway, (The Bishop); David Hurst, (Gustave); Vinton Hayworth, (A Guest); with Leonardo Cimino, Carol Ann Daniels, Mara Lynn, Julian Upton, Michael Youngman and Charlotte.

CREDITS: Director, William Dieterle; Producer, William Marshall; Scenarist, Allan Scott; Script Supervisor, Charles Bryant; Production Supervisor, Lee Lukather; Photographer, Robert Bronner; Production Manager, Glen Cook; Art Directors, Jim Sullivan, Willis Connor; Camera Operator, Ted Saizis; Editor, Carl Lerner; Sound Recorder, Earl Snyder; Musical Score, Michael Colicchio. Titles by C.F.I. Title Design, Sal Mairnovie; Assistant Director, Phil Cook.

NOTES: *The Confession* was a co-production of William Marshall Productions and Kay Lewis Enterprises. The film was totally underwritten by Leo Lewis, a St. Louis financier. Victor Stoloff was originally hired as director, but was apparently fired and replaced by William Dieterle, who had previously directed Ginger in *I'll Be Seeing You*. Allan Scott, the scenarist, had scripted many of Ginger's pictures, notably *Primrose Path*. *The Confession*, filmed during April and May, 1964, was a total disaster and is best forgotten.

In 1965, there was threatened litigation, with Rogers and Marshall claiming that the film had been edited in New York without their approval. (Marshall insisted that the film be edited in Jamaica where it had been filmed). In June 1965, the title was changed to *Seven Different Ways*, but it was never released to the big circuits. In 1971, the title was again changed to *Quick, Let's Get Married*, and it has played in many secondary cities and towns throughout the United States, but has not been reviewed on a major level. The emphasis, during this release period, was placed on Elliott Gould and Barbara Eden, who had since come into their own.

With Michael Ansara, Pippa Scott, and Barbara Eden

"Manhattan Downbeat"

"I'll Be Hard to Handle"

"Isn't This a Lovely Day
(to Be Caught in the Rain)"

"The Castle Walk (Too Much Mustard)"

"I Used to Be Color Blind"

"They All Laughed"

"Let Yourself Go"

"The Tango"

"The Carioca"

"Waltz in Swing Time"

"The Fox Trot" and "The Polka"

"The Piccolino"

"The Swing Trot"

"Shall We Dance"

"They Can't Take That Away From Me"

"The Yam"

"Let's Call the Whole Thing Off"

"My One and Only Highland Fling"

"I'm Putting All My Eggs in One Basket"

"Cheek to Cheek"

"The Missouri Waltz"

"Let's Face the Music and Dance"

"The Maxixe"

"Lovely to Look At"

"The Continental"

"Change Partners"

"Night and Day"

"I Won't Dance"

A Theatrical Chronology

Dancing the Valencia in her vaudeville act

Vaudeville 1925-1929

After winning the Charleston contest in Dallas, Texas, Ginger appeared in various vaudeville acts during the next four years. These included "Ginger and Her Redheads," "Ginger and Pepper," and "The Original John Held, Jr., Girl."

Top Speed

A musical comedy in two acts by Guy Bolton, Bert Kalmar, and Harry Ruby; Staged by John Harwood; Dances by John Boyle; Settings by Raymond L. Sovey; Presented by Bolton, Kalmar and Ruby At Chanin's 46th St. Theatre; December 25, 1929; (102 performances)

CAST: Harland Dixon, (Tad Jordan); Sunny Dale, (Daisy Parker); Lloyd Pedrick, (Bellows); Paul Frawley, (Gerry Brooks); Lester Allen, (Elmer Peters); Laine Blaire, (Molly); Lon Hascall, (Pete Schoonmaker); Irene Delroy, (Virginia Rollins); Ginger Rogers, (Babs Green); Ken Williams, (Chauffeur); Shirley Richards, (Shirley); Theodore Babcock, (Mr. Rollins); Sam Critcherson, (Vincent Colgate); John T. Dwyer, (Spencer Colgate); George Del Drigo, (Waiter At Yacht Club); William Hale, (Souvenir Storekeeper).

Ginger's Song: *Hot and Bothered.*

Girl Crazy

A musical comedy in two acts by Guy Bolton and John McGowan; Music by George Gershwin; Lyrics by Ira Gershwin; Staged by Alexander Leftwich; Dances by George Hale; Produced by Aarons and Freedley at the Alvin Theatre; October 14, 1930; (272 performances).

CAST: Allen Kearns, (Danny Churchill); Ginger Rogers, (Molly Gray); Clyde Veaux, (Pete); Carlton Macy, (Lank Sanders); Willie Howard, (Gieber Goldfarb); Eunice Healy, (Flora James); Peggy O'Connor, (Patsy West); Ethel Merman, (Kate Fothergill); William Kent, (Slick Fothergill); Donald Foster, (Sam Mason); Olive Brady, (Tess Parker); Lew Parker, (Jake Howell); Chief Rivers, (Eagle Rock); Jack Classon, (Hotel Proprietor); Starr Jones, (Lariat Joe); Marshall Smith, Ray Johnson, Del Porter, Dwight Snyder, (The Foursome); and Antonio and Renee De Marco, "Red" Nichols & His Orchestra.

Ginger's Songs: *Embraceable You, But Not for Me, Cactus Time in Arizona.*

With Lester Allen in *Top Speed*

253

With Paul McGrath in *Love and Let Love*

Portrait of Ginger at 19—a Broadway star

Love and Let Love

A Comedy in two acts by Louis Verneuil; Produced by Anthony B. Farrell; Staged by Mr. Verneuil; Settings by Ralph Alswang; Costumes by Jean Louis; At the Plymouth Theatre October 19, 1951 (51 performances).

CAST: Tom Helmore, (Dr. Fred Stevens); Helen Marcy, (Shirley); David Perkins, (Harlan); Paul McGrath, (Charles Warren); Ginger Rogers, (Valerie King, Ruth Gage).

With Ray Hamilton in *The Pink Jungle*

The Pink Jungle

A Comedy-Musical in two acts by Leslie Stevens; Directed by Joseph Anthony; Music and Lyrics by Vernon Duke; Settings & Lighting by Donald Oenslager; Costumes by Jean Louis; Choral Arrangements by Jack Lattimer; Orchestral Arrangements by Albert Sendrey; Musical Director, Sherman Frank; Choreography by Matt Mattox. Opened October 14, 1959 at the Alcazar Theatre, San Francisco. Closed December 12, 1959 at the Shubert Theatre, Boston.

CAST: Agnes Moorehead, (The Shade of Eleanor West); Gavin Gordon, (Harvey West); Leif Erickson, (Brian West); Buck Class, (Simon West); Ray Hamilton, (David West); Maggie Hayes, (Chris Taylor); Marilyn Watson, (Suzy Harkness); Lisa Jonson, (Annette); Ginger Rogers, (Tess Jackson); Rene Paul, (Pierre Aubusson); Louis Nye, (Dr. Prescott Alcot); Judy Cassmore, Brad Craig, Janet Dey, Joan Fitzpatrick, Ginny Gan, Dick Hilleary, Ann Jennings, Sally Lee, Don Maloof, Edgar Mastin, Ruth Maynard, Bonnie Mead, Marion Miller, Norma Nilsson, Calvin Von Reinhold, Bruce Peter Yarnell, (Denizens of the Pink Jungle).

Musical Numbers: *Nobody But Tess, A Hundred Women in One, There Was I, Chic Talk, Persian Room-Ba, Free as the Air, Just Like Children, It's Tough to Be a Girl, It's Tough to Be a Man, Brian, Paris in New York, Where Do You Go When You Arrive?, Finale.*

Rehearsing *Hello, Dolly!* with director Gower Champion

Two 'Mames' with composer-lyricist Jerry Herman. New York's Angela Lansbury and London's Ginger Rogers

Applause from both sides of the footlights—Ginger's opening night in *Hello, Dolly!*

Hello, Dolly!

A Musical Comedy in two acts; Book by Michael Stewart; Music & Lyrics by Jerry Herman; Based on the play *The Matchmaker* by Thornton Wilder; Settings Designed by Oliver Smith; Costumes by Freddy Wittop; Lighting by Jean Rosenthal; Musical Direction & Incidental Music by Peter Howard; Orchestrations by Philip J. Lang; Vocal Arrangements by Shepard Coleman; Directed & Choreographed by Gower Champion; Produced by David Merrick & Champion-Five, Inc. At the St. James Theatre; August 9, 1965 (18½ months + national tour).

CAST: Ginger Rogers, (Mrs. Dolly Gallagher Levi); Mary Jo Catlett, (Ernestina); Charles Karel, (Ambrose Kemper); Patti Pappathatos, Beverly Baker, (Horse); David Burns, (Horace Vandergelder); Joan Kall, (Ermengarde); Will Mackenzie, (Cornelius Hackl); Jerry Dodge, (Barnaby Tucker); Patte Finley, (Irene Molloy); Sondra Lee, (Minnie Fay); Amelia Haas, (Mrs. Rose); David Hartman, (Rudolph); Gordon Connell, (Judge); Keith Kaldenberg, (Court Clerk); Nicole Barth, Monica Carter, Joyce Dahl, Joyce Devlin, Diane Findlay, Lee Hooper, Joan Buttons Leonard, Anne Nathan, Yolanda Poropat, Bonnie Schon, Mary Ann Snow, Pat Trott, (Townspeople, Waiters, Etc.); Ted Agress, Joel Craig, Dick Crowley, Hamp Dickens, David Evens, Gene Gebauer, Joe Helms, Richard Hermany, Woody Hurst, Neil Jones, Vernon Lusby, Jim Maher, John Mineo, Dan Merriman, Tony Falco, Paul Solen, George Tregre, Ronnie Young.

Miss Rogers's standby—Bibi Osterwald.

Ginger's Songs: *I Put My Hand In, Put on Your Sunday Clothes, Motherhood, Dancing, Before the Parade Passes By, Hello, Dolly!, So Long, Dearie.*

Mame

A Musical Comedy in two acts by Jerome Lawrence and Robert E. Lee. Music and Lyrics by Jerry Herman. Based on the novel *Auntie Mame* by Patrick Dennis and the play by Lawrence and Lee. Settings by William and Jean Eckart. Costumes by Robert Mackintosh. Lighting by Tharon Musser. Vocal Arrangements by Donald Pippin. Dance Music Arrangements by Roger Adams. Orchestrations by Philip J. Lang. Musical Direction by Ray Cook. Dances & Musical Numbers Staged by Onna White. Assistant Choreographer, Patrick Cummings; Choral Director, John McCarthy; Original New York Production Directed by Gene Saks. Restaged in London by Lawrence Kasha. Produced in London by Bernard Delfont and Harold Fielding in association with Fryer, Carr and Harris at the Theatre Royal Drury Lane, London, England; February 20, 1969

CAST: Gary Warren, (Patrick Dennis, Age 10); Ann Beach, (Agnes Gooch); Margaret Courtenay, (Vera Charles); Ginger Rogers, (Mame Dennis); David Wright, (Ralph Devine); Chris Dyson, (Bishop); Brian Jackson, (M. Lindsay Woolsey); Burt Kwouk, (Ito); Wallace Stephenson, (Doorman); George May, (Elevator Boy); Bruce Harris, (Messenger); Guy Spaull, (Dwight Babcock); Betty Winsett, (Art Model); Carolyn Gray, (Dance Teacher); David Wright, (Leading Man); Victor Woolf, (Stage Manager); Sheila Keith, (Madame Branislowski); John Raymon, (Gregor); Barry Kent, (Beauregard); Ted Gilbert, (Uncle Jeff); Eve Tunstall, (Cousin Fan); Betty Winsett, (Sally Cato); Sheila Keith, (Mother Burnside); Tony Adams, (Patrick Dennis, Age 19–29); Ken Walsh, (Junior Babcock); Sheila Keith, (Mrs. Upson); Norman MacLeod, (Mr. Upson); Wendy Lampard, (Gloria Upson); Jill Howard, (Pegeen Ryan); Christopher Reynalds, (Peter Dennis); Bernice Adams, Annie Bee, Sheila Coxhill, Carolyn Gray, Alison Ingram, Christine Artemis, (Mame's Friends); Honor Lewis, Mary Murphy, Eve Tunstall, Lindybeth Wiles, Roy Durbin, Chris Dyson, Ted Gilbert, Simon Gilbert, Eric Greenall, Bruce Harris, George May, Donald McLennan, Rhys Nelson, Alan Page, John Raymon, Wallace Stephenson, Ken Walsh, David Wright.

Ginger's Songs: *It's Today, Open a New Window, The Man in the Moon, My Best Girl, We Need a Little Christmas, Bosom Buddies, That's How Young I Feel, If He Walked into My Life*

Miss Rogers's Standby—India Adams

Ginger's London stage debut as Mame Dennis in the musical *Mame*

The Straw-Hat Circuit

Ginger Rogers began appearing in the straw-hat circuit, throughout the country, in 1958, with her husband William Marshall in John Van Druten's comedy, *Bell, Book and Candle* and repeated the tour in 1962. Since that time Ginger has appeared in theaters from Philadelphia to Phoenix in such musicals as Irving Berlin's *Annie Get Your Gun*, Meredith Wilson's *The Unsinkable Molly Brown*, Lee Pockriss's and Anne Croswell's *Tovarich*, and Alan Jay Lerner's and Andre Previn's *Coco*.